The

MUTUAL
FUND
INDUSTRY

The

MUTUAL
FUND
INDUSTRY

Competition and Investor Welfare

R. Glenn Hubbard, Michael F. Koehn, Stanley I. Ornstein,

Marc Van Audenrode, and Jimmy Royer

⧧ **Columbia Business School**
Publishing

Columbia University Press
Publishers Since 1893
New York   Chichester, West Sussex
Copyright © 2010 Columbia University Press
All rights reserved

Library of Congress Cataloging-in-Publication Data
The mutual fund industry : competition and investor welfare /
R. Glenn Hubbard . . . [et al.]
p. cm.
Includes bibliographical references and index.
ISBN 978-0-231-15182-5 (cloth : alk. paper)
1. Mutual funds—United States.   2. Investment advisors—United States.   3. Financial
services industry—United States.   I. Hubbard, R. Glenn.   II. Title.
HG4930.M852 2010
332.63′27—dc22
2009050351

Columbia University Press books are printed on permanent and durable acid-free paper.
This book is printed on paper with recycled content.
Printed in the United States of America

c 10 9 8 7 6 5 4 3 2 1

References to Internet Web sites (URLs) were accurate at the time of writing. Neither
the author nor Columbia University Press is responsible for URLs that may have expired
or changed since the manuscript was prepared.

Contents

Figures

Tables

Foreword

Mutual funds are the primary vehicle used by individuals to invest in the stock and bond markets, and they are the overwhelming choice in retirement plans. Thus, the effectiveness of 401(k), individual retirement account (IRA), and other savings plans depends upon the efficiency and the competitiveness of the mutual fund industry. If individuals are disadvantaged by anticompetitive practices in the industry and by excessive fees, the quality of life for millions of retirees will be compromised. Small wonder that the fees charged by the industry have come under close scrutiny, and the industry has attracted more than its share of critics.

Perhaps the most vocal critic has come from the industry itself—John C. Bogle, the founder and former Chief Executive Officer of the Vanguard Group of investment companies. Bogle has developed what he calls the "cost matters hypothesis." He believes that explicit and implicit costs from portfolio turnover are the prime determinants of fund returns. He is an evangelist for low costs, telling investors that with respect to mutual funds, "You get what you don't pay for."

We can certainly agree with critics such as Bogle that the fees charged by the providers of mutual fund services are a crucial determinant of the net returns earned by investors. Indeed, in my own research, I have found that total expenses, including both management expenses and the implicit costs of portfolio turnover, are the most important determinants of investor returns.

After accounting for differences in services across mutual fund providers, it is clear that investors are disadvantaged by high fees. But investors do have choices. In 2009, there were more individual mutual funds in the United

States than there were individual stocks traded on the New York Stock Exchange and NASDAQ. Consumers clearly have the ability to choose among competing fund offerings. Nevertheless, for competition to be effective, consumers must be sensitive to relative fees and services provided.

The Securities and Exchange Commission (SEC) concluded in the mid-1960s that mutual funds did not compete on price, and hence individual investors were put at a disadvantage. This conclusion, however, was based on studies of data from the 1950s and early 1960s, when there were barely more than 100 mutual funds from which investors could choose. The finding that competitive conditions did not exist a half century ago cannot be extrapolated to the far different industry that exists today. Similarly, the leading legal decision—the *Gartenberg* case[1]—which concluded that effective price competition did not exist, was based on a mutual fund industry environment that was very different from conditions today. Indeed, in 2008 the Seventh Circuit Court of Appeals came to a diametrically opposite conclusion. In *Jones v. Harris Associates*, the court concluded that competitive conditions did, in fact, exist in the mutual fund industry.[2] These competing decisions underscore the importance of careful modern analyses of the structure of competition at present in the industry.

This book provides that analysis. It presents an economic model of the mutual fund industry. The model examines the demand for equity mutual funds between fund companies and within fund complexes. The study allows for investor choices among funds, complexes, and channels of distribution. It presents precisely the empirical studies we need to understand the actual competitive conditions that exist in the industry today.

Estimates are provided of the price elasticity of demand for mutual funds (i.e., consumer sensitivity to the fees charged by different mutual funds). The careful empirical work presented shows that investors are very sensitive to the fees they face. Investors move their assets from fund to fund based on price differences, adjusted for product quality and fund performance. The very clear and robust conclusion is that effective competition among mutual funds does exist today.

The authors find that (1) price increases above competitive levels lead investors to switch to lower priced funds; (2) the vast majority of mutual fund assets are invested in the lowest priced funds; and (3) expense ratios (including the amortized value of sales loads) were declining at least through 2007. New products, such as exchange traded funds (ETFs), have also enhanced competition. Thus, the authors conclude that there is "no justification for . . . laws . . . to control monopoly pricing" in the mutual fund industry.

This is an important book. There has been considerable controversy, through the present time, about the competitiveness of the mutual fund industry and much recent criticism of what are called excessive fees. This careful study finds abundant evidence of price competition. The authors both enhance our understanding of the performance of the mutual fund industry and have produced useful findings for policy makers and for the legal profession. They present convincing evidence that there is no need to enact laws designed to prevent monopoly pricing in the mutual fund industry.

Burton G. Malkiel

Preface

The level of retail mutual fund fees has been a contentious issue among mutual fund investors, investment advisers, regulators, and members of Congress since the 1960s. There have been approximately three distinct waves of lawsuits against mutual fund investment advisers for overcharging mutual fund investors, the first in the late 1950s, the second in the late 1970s and early 1980s, and the third group of cases starting around 2004. During this last wave of lawsuits, counsel for various mutual funds invited us to examine price determination in the mutual fund industry. This book grew out of these initial research efforts.

U.S. courts have typically not sought to resolve claims of excessive fees by investigating the nature and extent of price competition between investment advisers. Instead, the courts have focused primarily on whether fees were disproportionately high relative to the costs of operating mutual funds. In addition, in the 1960s the Securities and Exchange Commission concluded that mutual fund fees were not set by price competition. The courts adopted this "no competition" position in the early 1980s. The courts' disinterest in examining price competition in the industry and their almost exclusive focus on a cost-based model of price determination provided motivation for this book.

Although there have been numerous government and academic studies on mutual fund fees, an economic model of demand and supply in the mutual fund industry has been largely missing in the controversy over fees, as well as a more economics-based study of the relevant empirical evidence. This book presents an economic model and analysis of advisory firm pricing.

We are especially grateful to those who provided support and research assistance, including Mark Egland, Eric Gravel, Lee Heavner, Susan Hoag, Herve Lohoues, Dominic Mitchell, Eric Nguyen, Lisa Pinheiro, Michael Quinn, and Kristen Willard. We also thank anonymous referees selected by the publisher for reviewing the book and offering insightful suggestions.

The

MUTUAL
FUND
INDUSTRY

Introduction

The benefits to consumers from competition are most apparent when competition is absent. As an example, there is a story told of men's shoe manufacturing during the 1950s in the Soviet Union.[1] Under the Soviet central planning authority, several plants manufactured identical style men's black shoes. Each plant was assigned a production quota, and each plant met its quota. There remained, however, a manufacturing problem that the central planners had not solved—the shoes tended to fall apart within a short time period. A young planner offered a bright idea—identify each pair of shoes by the plant of origin. Through this simple act, the plants were forced to compete on product quality. Each plant's reputation for shoe quality and its subsequent financial remuneration from the state were now at risk. Low-quality producers could easily be identified and their shoes shunned by consumers when making future purchases. Similarly, plants could be penalized for low quality by Soviet authorities. Introducing a way for consumers to choose between seemingly like products produced competition between shoe manufacturers, and shoe quality improved dramatically.

In countless other examples, the presence or absence of competition is of paramount importance to the well-being of consumers. Competition leads to lower prices, better product quality, more rapid technological improvements, lower firm costs, and greater consumer satisfaction.

In this book, we examine competition in the mutual fund industry.[2] For decades the mutual fund industry has been embroiled in controversy over the extent of price competition between fund investment advisers and the level of fees charged to fund investors. Critics contend that mutual fund investors are forced to pay excessive fees due to the absence of price competition between fund investment advisers.[3] A series of fund investor lawsuits have been filed asking for damages because of fee overcharges. In reaction to these claims, government and academic studies have examined the industry for the presence or absence of price competition since the 1960s, with conflicting empirical results.

Whether the mutual fund industry is price-competitive is of enormous importance to millions of Americans who depend on their mutual fund investments for retirement. It is no exaggeration to say that mutual funds are the bedrock foundation for retirement saving in the United States. Indeed, given the rapid historic growth of mutual funds in retirement investment accounts, this dependence on mutual funds will likely grow in coming years. If mutual fund advisers are free from the rigors of price competition and are able to set high fees with impunity, millions of investors will suffer relatively low returns and a poorer quality of life in retirement.

The Mutual Fund Industry and Its Critics

The mutual fund industry has received strong criticism for not sufficiently protecting the interests of fund investors from fund investment advisers intent on growing their profits by overcharging investors. According to John Bogle, founder of the Vanguard Group of mutual funds, over the 1983–2003 period, the stock market yielded an average return of 13.0 percent, but the average equity mutual fund investor earned only 7.9 percent, because of investment advisers' power to increase fund investors' fees.[4] A return differential of this magnitude, if valid, could have dire consequences for an investor's retirement years. Such a gap would suggest that fund investors suffered a substantial opportunity cost during this period. The main reason for excessive investor fees, according to fee critics, is a lack of price competition between equity mutual fund advisers.

The controversy over mutual funds and returns to fund investors has been ongoing since the 1930s. After a series of investor complaints in the 1930s, the U.S. Securities and Exchange Commission (SEC) collected evidence on fund investment managers exploiting shareholders, finding numerous incidences of fund managerial fraud. Government investigators found that investors were harmed, especially in closed-end funds, by managers engaging in such actions as embezzlement, granting low-interest loans to themselves and friends, and selling watered stock they owned to fund investors.[5] This record of investor abuses resulted in passing the Investment Company Act (ICA) of 1940 and the Investment Advisers Act (IAA) of 1940 to protect investors' assets from unlawful actions by investment advisers.

It is generally agreed that the ICA of 1940 achieved its goal of eliminating the gross abuses of investors taking place in the 1930s. However, the claim that price competition is absent has been leveled for over 50 years, with potentially long-term financial injury to fund shareholders. In the late 1950s, investors brought approximately 50 state-level lawsuits asserting that investment advisers charged excessive fees to mutual fund shareholders.[6] Twenty years after the ICA of 1940, studies commissioned by the SEC concluded that U.S. equity mutual fund advisers did not compete on price, leading to "excessive" fees and artificially reduced returns to mutual fund investors.[7] This finding, that the market for mutual funds was highly inefficient owing to the absence of price competition, informed the law from 1982 to the present, in litigation charging investment advisers with imposing excessive fees on mutual fund investors. A series of excessive investor fee cases were brought against money market fund advisers in the late 1970s and early 1980s. A similar wave of investor excessive fee lawsuits were filed following the market timing and investor favoritism scandals of 2003 and 2004.[8] Extending this line of attack, plaintiffs have brought a series of lawsuits against various administrators of employer-sponsored defined contribution retirement plans, asserting that they have charged excessive fees to administer 401(k) pension plans.

Mutual Funds and U.S. Retirement Assets

Open-end mutual funds were introduced in the United States in the mid-1920s, growing from one fund in 1924 to 19 funds in 1929, with approximately $140 million in assets.[9] Today the mutual fund industry is a colossus, with approximately $12 trillion in assets at the end of 2007.[10] Mutual funds have evolved into a crucially important investment product, owned by an estimated 55 million U.S. households and 96 million individuals.[11] The growth in mutual funds has been especially robust in tax-deferred retirement accounts since the 1970s introduction of Individual Retirement Accounts (IRAs) and employer-sponsored 401(k) defined contribution retirement plans. Mutual funds are the primary investment vehicle of choice in these types of retirement accounts, representing approximately 50 percent of total U.S. assets in self-directed retirement plans.[12]

Investing in mutual funds for retirement expanded greatly after the 1980s when traditional employer defined benefit plans started to be phased out in favor of defined contribution plans.[13] Defined benefit plans generally use investment advisers to actively manage portfolios of stocks, bonds, and other investments on behalf of a company-sponsor, while IRAs and defined contribution plans rely on self-directed investments by plan members. The rapid growth in mutual fund investing for retirement was likely accelerated by the baby boom generation's preparation for retirement and strong stock market performance in the 1980s and 1990s.

As the primary investment product in many retirement plans, the financial well-being of millions of retirees is dependent on the performance of mutual funds. The more competitive and therefore efficient the market for investing in mutual funds, the greater the benefits to investors. Inefficiencies and failures in the market for mutual funds can potentially cost retirees billions of dollars in foregone savings and diminish the quality of life in their retirement. Potential economic inefficiencies in mutual fund investing, such as relatively high costs to investors of switching between mutual funds, limited access to information on the costs of investing, or, more broadly, reduced price competition between mutual funds, raising investor costs above the competitive level, will decrease the value of retirement assets relative to the value in a more efficient, competitive market. Moreover, to the extent that inefficiencies in the mutual fund market disadvantage retirees, it will influence retirees' demands on government for future financial support, affecting society as a whole.

Mutual Fund Pricing

Studies on price competition in the mutual fund industry are often imprecise on how prices are determined, what constitutes price competition, how prices are changed, and what is meant by excessive prices. Some mutual fund studies address price competition in absolute terms: it is either present or absent, and when finding it absent, they conclude that prices must be excessive. Some studies accept that a degree of price competition exists, but argue that it is not sufficient to meaningfully affect mutual fund prices. Other mutual fund studies define price competition by the economic model of perfect competition, where competition results in a uniform price across all sellers. Any price above some competitive benchmark level is regarded as excessive and therefore illegitimate. Because of these disparate views and what constitutes a benchmark model of price competition, some background information on pricing in the mutual fund industry is useful.

As indicated, the nature of price competition, price setting, and what may constitute excessive prices in mutual funds is more complex than acknowledged in many studies. To illustrate, consider the creation and initial price setting by a new mutual fund. To create and market a new mutual fund, the organizing firm, typically an investment advisory firm, must fulfill all government-mandated legal requirements. Of more interest for our purposes, it must arrange to provide a multitude of services to the fund investors, including portfolio management, fund share transfers, share exchanges and redemptions, distribution networks, marketing, and legal and auditing services.

Adviser revenues are generated from fees, both as a percentage of total fund assets under management and from fixed periodic fees, in return for the adviser's services. As a new fund, the adviser announces a schedule of investor fees. The adviser's aim in selecting a fee schedule is to maximize the present value of its long-term profits. Establishing a schedule of investor fees requires consideration of a number of factors, including the amount of expected assets under management, operating costs, fund performance, rival funds' fee schedules, and the types and quality of services provided to the fund's investors.

Once marketing and distribution of the fund's shares begin, the investment adviser monitors the flow of investments to the fund. The fund's announced fee schedule may prove to be either too low or too high, depending on investor demand for the fund's product offering. If the announced fee schedule is too low, higher revenues have been foregone. If the announced price schedule is too high relative to the fund's attributes and investor demand, the adviser similarly incurs a loss in foregone revenues.

If the announced fee schedule is too low, given the fund's subsequent performance and quality of services provided to investors, the adviser's ability to raise prices is constrained. Raising announced fees in response to, for example, higher than expected demand is constrained by industry regulations. Mutual fund regulations require fee increases to be approved by the fund's shareholders, who are naturally loath to raise their own cost for fund ownership and thus lower their return on investment. Given the difficulty of gaining shareholder approval for higher fees, investment advisers must set their new fee schedules with care to obtain the highest possible present value of expected future profits.

An adviser operating under a performance contract provides a possible exception to the difficulty of raising fees. Under such a contract, fees can be adjusted up or down, within limits, depending on the fund's performance relative to the performance of some marketwide index of securities. If certain investor return targets are met, the investment adviser in some cases is allowed to raise fees a small amount in exchange for producing superior performance. Conversely, if performance targets are not met, the investment adviser must reduce investor fees a small, symmetrical amount.

In contrast to regulations hindering fee increases, if the announced fee schedule is too high, fees can be lowered without requiring shareholder approval. The principal methods of lowering fees are through fee waivers to investors, announcing a lower fee schedule, changes in product attributes, and in certain cases based on a fund's performance. Prices can be discounted from announced prices through fee waivers. Fee waivers are especially common in new, smaller size funds, to remain competitive with higher return funds, but large funds also lower fees at times through waivers. This results in a two-level pricing structure: the announced prices and actual or effective prices. It follows that announced and effective fund prices often differ, with higher announced than effective prices. As a consequence, examination of a fund's announced prices often does not reflect the influence of competition on mutual fund investor prices.

In contrast to more time-limited fee waivers, a reassessment of current and expected market conditions, fund costs, fund performance, and rivals' pricing may lead to a manager revising announced fees to a new, lower price schedule. However, this is a long-term commitment, given the difficulty of gaining shareholder approval to raise fund fees.

A further method for changing price is to change the attributes of the product purchased by fund investors. When purchasing a fund, investors purchase both the fund and the services of its investment adviser. For example, when investors purchase a Vanguard index fund, they are also selecting the Vanguard Group as the fund's investment adviser and administrator. Similarly in all other fund complexes,[14] investors purchase the fund jointly with the investment adviser. Continuing with Vanguard, the joint product of fund and investment adviser comes with a package of investor services (e.g., possibly 24-hour service, investment advice for an additional fee, and retirement planning), and attributes, such as Vanguard's experience and company reputation, past return performance, fee level, breadth of funds available from Vanguard, and available channels of distribution. Funds in each rival complex come with their own package of attributes. These attributes can be varied to change the effective price of owning the fund. For example, by increasing the number or quality of services to investors for a given price, investment advisers effectively reduce price by providing investors more value for the price. Similarly, by reducing services or the quality of services for a given price, price per unit of quality is increased. Thus, price per unit of quality can be changed by adding or subtracting product attributes for a given price. However, reducing product quality when rivals offer greater quality for the same price is a recipe for losses in sales and profits.

The "price competition" at issue in mutual funds is thus the effective price relative to the package of attributes provided by the fund's investment adviser.

Because different fund complexes provide different sets of product attributes, prices will vary across funds, both generally and within specific mutual fund investment style categories, such as growth, value, sector, and foreign stock funds. Higher prices may well reflect differences in demand and product differentiation across funds, rather than a fund adviser's ability to set excessive prices owing to an absence of price competition. However, for an equivalent set of product attributes (past performance, services to investors, fund and adviser reputations, etc.) within a specific investment style category—that is, for relatively substitutable funds—prices should be roughly comparable. Thus, claims of excessive investor prices in mutual funds due to a lack of price competition imply that a fund's investor fees, given the set of product attributes being purchased, are too high relative to the level they would be under competitive market conditions. Left unanswered is how an advisory firm is able to shield itself from price competition by other fund advisers and maintain excessive prices when investors are free to switch funds.

In summary, investment advisers negotiate a price schedule to maximize the present value of their profits, but that does not mean that advisers' prices are fixed and unresponsive to rivals' price levels. Price changes in the mutual fund industry can take various forms, such as waivers, cancelling waivers, lower fee schedules, performance-based price changes, and product attribute changes. Thus, the concepts of *price, price competition,* and *excessive fees* in the mutual fund industry are not as straightforward as some studies seem to imply. This ambiguity is important to keep in mind in succeeding chapters as we examine studies on mutual fund pricing, price trends, and price determination, as well as when we present our economic model of consumer choice and the demand for mutual funds and fund complexes.

Purpose of the Book

In this book we present a model of the supply and demand for mutual funds. Although various academic and government studies have examined the mutual fund industry for evidence of ineffective price competition, anticompetitive fees, and lower investor returns relative to competitive fee levels, models of the demand for and supply of mutual funds are largely missing. Instead, most empirical studies in this area, such as those estimating the demand for mutual funds, developed their statistical analyses without the benefit of an economic model, relying on intuitively plausible factors to explain the demand for mutual funds. Testable hypotheses based on an analytical model of mutual fund demand and supply have generally not been presented.[15] Our purpose is to provide more detailed and exacting tests for price competition between mutual fund investor advisers.

A further purpose is to use data from the contemporary mutual fund industry. Many previous studies are largely outdated. The pioneering studies on mutual fund fees of the 1960s, based on data from the 1950s and early 1960s (when there were about 100–150 mutual funds, and they were a minor segment of the securities investment industry) are clearly dated. The mutual fund industry is vastly different today from what it was in the 1950s and 1960s. Whatever the findings on price competition during that era, they cannot be credibly extrapolated to the present. To do so would make about as much sense as saying that competitive market conditions in the automobile industry today are little different from those in the 1950s. Competitive market conditions in the 1950s automobile or mutual fund industry have little relevance to each industry's present market conditions. Thus, given the critical role of mutual funds in retirement plans and individual retirement accounts in the United States, and the potential harm to fund shareholders from ineffective or an absence of price competition, mutual fund market efficiency deserves a new examination.

In addition, at the time of this writing, U.S. Appellate Courts that were addressing mutual fund excessive fee cases were in conflict over whether price competition prevailed between fund investment advisers. In the leading legal decision from 1982 onward, the *Gartenberg* case, the Second Circuit Court of Appeals concluded that effective price competition between investment advisers was absent in the mutual fund industry.[16] In 2008, the Seventh Circuit Court of Appeals concluded the opposite—that mutual fund pricing was guided by price competition.[17] Our analyses are intended to help resolve these contrary views of price competition in the mutual fund industry.

Organization of the Book

Chapter 1 describes growth in the mutual fund industry over the past 25 years or so, growth in investing for retirement, and the relative position of mutual fund assets among all retirement-directed assets. We show the increasing importance of mutual funds in investing for retirement and how the Pension Protection Act (PPA) of 2006 provides additional incentives for individuals to invest in mutual funds. Government pension plans, in which defined benefit plans continue to predominate, are shown to be increasingly subject to underfunding. If public defined benefit plans begin shifting to defined contribution plans to help solve the underfunding problem, it will lead to an additional large shift of retirement monies to mutual funds. The upshot is that returns on mutual funds and the competitive efficiency of the industry are vitally important to many types of retirement plans, and mutual funds will likely increase their presence in retirement plan investing.

Chapter 2 summarizes the debate and evidence on excessive fees and the absence of price competition among mutual funds. We place criticisms of investment adviser malfeasance in the mutual fund industry in historical perspective by describing the evolution of the mutual fund industry and federal regulations up to the ICA of 1940 and thereafter, especially in the 1950–1960s era, when the pioneering studies noted above concluded that fees were excessive owing to a lack of price competition. We conclude with a discussion of various regulatory proposals, starting in the 1960s, to restrain the setting of excessive fees.

Chapter 3 summarizes and discusses the *Gartenberg* decision, the historically major court case addressing excessive mutual fund fees. The district and appellate court decisions in this case provide a striking contrast in legal and economic analysis of excessive charges and help frame the debate over the extent of price competition in the mutual fund industry. The precedent-setting appellate decision concluded that there was no price competition in the industry, based on 1950s and 1960s studies and data, which begs the question of price competition in the industry both at the time of *Gartenberg* in the early 1980s and at present. Subsequent excessive fee cases deferred to *Gartenberg*, ruling out an inquiry on the extent of price competition, because the *Gartenberg* decision stated that investment advisers do not compete on price.[18] As mentioned, in 2008 the Seventh Circuit Court of Appeals rejected the reasoning in *Gartenberg*, concluding that price competition flourishes in the mutual fund industry.[19] Similarly, our analysis raises serious questions on the economic reasoning underlying the *Gartenberg* appellate court decision and how applicable that reasoning is to the present-day mutual fund industry.

Chapter 4 presents our economic model of the mutual fund industry. Technical details and results are presented in the Appendix to Chapter 4. We find that investors in U.S. equity mutual funds are highly sensitive to fee levels, with lower fees related to proportionately greater increases in the demand for mutual funds. And with investors sensitive to fees, investment advisers are compelled to compete on price and product attributes, resulting in competitive price levels.

Chapter 5 reviews mutual fund industry structure in terms of number of rivals, concentration levels, barriers to entry and firm expansion, and changes in market shares as indirect indicators of the presence or absence of price competition. All of the measures point to a highly competitive mutual fund industry. We also present direct evidence of competition, documenting the extent of annual price cutting by investment advisers and investor sensitivity to price based on the extent to which they concentrate their investments in the lowest priced funds.

Chapter 6 reviews and critiques fee critics' evidence in support of their claim of excessive pricing. These critics attempt to prove that mutual fund fees are excessive by arguing that (1) fees are substantially higher for retail compared to institutional investors, and competition exists in the market for institutional investors so the price difference represents the extent to which retail investors are overcharged; (2) mutual fund fees within an investment style vary widely, whereas in a competitive market, a large range in prices would not exist; and (3) there are large economies of scale in operating mutual funds, but cost savings are not passed on to investors in the form of lower fees, showing that competition is absent. We find serious errors in the fee critics' evidence and arguments.

Chapter 7 examines the governance structure of mutual funds and the extent to which this structure is associated with fund performance. Some critics argue that the unique governance structure of most mutual funds, with separation of ownership and control between a mutual fund and its investment adviser, allows advisers to dictate fees to funds' boards of directors, freeing investment advisers from having to compete on price. As examples of ideal mutual fund governance structures, free from the alleged tyranny of investment advisers, fee critics cite the organizational structures governing the Vanguard Group of mutual funds and the Teachers Insurance and Annuity Association — College Retirement Equities Fund (TIAA-CREF) complexes of mutual funds. They argue that the relatively low fees charged by each of these fund complexes are a result of their governance structures and nonprofit status. We test the fee critics' proposition that because these two complexes have relatively low investor fees, they provide higher investor returns than average, for-profit equity mutual funds charging higher fees. We find no evidence that these two complexes earn net returns persistently superior to complexes and funds with traditional mutual fund organizational structures.

Chapter 8 summarizes our findings and lessons learned. We find evidence of significant competition between mutual fund investment advisers. This finding is important. If competition is ineffective, allowing for shareholder fees above the competitive level, fund investors are harmed by lower returns, reducing their lifetime retirement savings. Alternatively, if effective price competition prevails, concerns over excessive investor fees artificially reducing returns are misguided, and regulations intended to control the level of investor fees cannot improve on competitive, market-determined fees.

CHAPTER ONE

Mutual Fund Industry Growth and Importance in Retirement Plans

Mutual Fund Growth

The mutual fund industry experienced slow, steady growth from approximately 1940 to 1980. Since then, the absolute amount of dollars invested in mutual funds has grown significantly. The number of households in the United States that owned mutual funds rose from approximately 4.5 million in 1980 to 50.4 million in 2007, or from 6 percent of total households in 1980 to approximately 44 percent in 2007.[1] Net new money flow into mutual funds totaled $5.0 trillion from 1990 to 2007. As shown in Table 1.1, total net assets under management grew via asset appreciation and new money investment from $1.1 trillion in 1990 to approximately $12 trillion in 2007.[2] The supply of mutual funds grew commensurately to meet this growth in demand, from 564 funds in 1980 to 8,029 in 2007.[3] These 8,000-plus funds were provided by more than 500 fund complexes and investment advisers, compared with less than 200 investment advisory firms in the mid-1980s.[4] By historic standards, growth in the number of funds and their asset value has been unprecedented since 1980, as the stock market offered the potential for relatively high returns during the 1980s and 1990s, and the aging baby boom population increased its savings for retirement.

Mutual Fund Growth in Retirement Plans

Mutual funds have become especially prominent in deferred tax retirement savings accounts, most directly in individual and employer-based individual

TABLE 1.1 Mutual Fund Assets, Number of Funds, and Fund Complexes, 1980–2007

Year	Assets	Number of Funds	Number of Fund Complexes
1980	134.76	564	
1981	241.37	665	
1982	296.68	857	
1983	292.99	1,026	
1984	370.68	1,243	
1985	495.39	1,528	229
1986	715.67	1,835	274
1987	769.17	2,312	317
1988	809.37	2,737	351
1989	980.67	2,935	382
1990	1,065.19	3,079	387
1991	1,393.19	3,403	408
1992	1,642.54	3,824	451
1993	2,069.96	4,534	484
1994	2,155.32	5,325	530
1995	2,811.29	5,725	550
1996	3,525.80	6,248	582
1997	4,468.20	6,684	616
1998	5,525.21	7,314	643
1999	6,846.34	7,791	679
2000	6,964.63	8,155	680
2001	6,974.91	8,305	656
2002	6,390.36	8,244	635
2003	7,414.40	8,126	624
2004	8,106.94	8,041	619
2005	8,904.82	7,975	626
2006	10,412.46	8,118	630
2007	12,021.03	8,029	636

Sources: Investment Company Institute, 2008 Investment Company Fact Book, p. 110. Strategic Insight, Simfund, Mutual Fund Database, 2008.

Note: Data excludes funds of funds. Numbers of fund complexes from Strategic Insight are available from 1985 onward.

retirement accounts (IRAs) and employer-based defined contribution plans, such as 401(k), 403(b), and 457 plans. Together, IRAs and defined contribution plans accounted for 52 percent of total retirement assets in 2007, compared with only 32 percent in 1985.[5] Mutual funds managed 55 percent of defined contribution plan assets in 2007, compared with 8 percent in 1990, and 47 percent of IRA assets in 2007, compared with 22 percent in 1990.[6]

The share of mutual funds in retirement accounts stems from a variety of factors, including government authorization of more attractive features for IRAs over time and the increasing conversion of defined benefit to self-directed defined contribution retirement plans. IRA investment expanded through new IRA plans that enhanced the incentive to invest, such as the Roth IRA, the employer-based saving incentive match plan for employees (SIMPLE IRA), the simplified employee pension (SEP IRA), and the salary reduction plan (SAP SEP IRA).[7] In 2007, IRAs represented 26.7 percent of United States retirement assets.[8]

Mutual funds share of retirement plan investments has also expanded because private sector employers have been freezing, terminating, and switching from traditional defined benefit to defined contribution retirement plans in increasing numbers since the 1980s. Participants in defined contribution plans and IRAs seeking the least costly way to gain the benefits of professional money management and asset diversification have increasingly turned to both passively and actively managed mutual funds.

The Shift from Defined Benefit to Defined Contribution Retirement Plans

The shift from traditional defined benefit to defined contribution retirement plans gained increasing momentum in the 1980s. Various hypotheses have been offered to explain this shift. Some claim the decline in U.S. manufacturing and mining jobs, where private sector defined benefit plans were most prevalent, and the accompanying decline in the power of labor unions explain the reduced use of defined benefit plans. Others point to increased competition from globalization and more pressure on U.S. companies to remain cost competitive. Still others claim that employees prefer defined contribution plans because of matching contributions from employers and the ability to direct their own savings and investments for retirement. Whatever the explanations offered, defined benefit plans, which are lifetime annuities to retiring workers, are more costly for employers than defined contribution plans, because with the benefit plans, employers must assume the risk of increases in life expectancy that come with advances in medical science as well as the risks of changes in interest rates and stock market portfolio values over time. As an example, the sharp decline in interest rates and stock market returns in 2000–2001 greatly increased the funding requirements of defined benefit retirement plans to meet future plan liabilities. Lower annual returns and interest rates reduced compounding effects on total plan assets, requiring larger future assets.

As employers abandoned defined benefit plans, they generally substituted cash balance and defined contribution retirement plans, sometimes offering both plans in place of a defined benefit plan. Like defined benefit plans, *cash balance* plans also provide a lifetime annuity but tend to reduce the retirement liability for employers, because such plans are generally based on an account balance developed from monthly contributions and some earned interest rate. However, this tends to reduce benefits for older workers compared to defined benefit plans. Defined contribution plans free employers from lifetime payments to retirees. They also shift the risks of stock and bond market changes and the retiree's longevity from the employer to the employee. Employers often increase their matching amounts in defined contribution plans when converting from defined benefit plans to compensate older workers, at least in part, for the lower benefits they will receive under a defined contribution plan relative to the replaced defined benefit plan.

Growth in IRA and Defined Contribution Retirement Plans

According to data compiled by the U.S. Department of Labor, defined benefit plan assets in 2005 accounted for 21 percent of private sector employer-sponsored plan assets, down from 32 percent in 1992–1993, while defined contribution plan assets rose over the same period from 35 to 42 percent of private sector retirement plan assets.[9]

The shift away from defined benefit plans has naturally resulted in IRAs and defined contribution plan assets growing at a much faster rate than assets in defined benefit plans.[10] Defined contribution plan assets exceeded private defined benefit plan assets for the first time in the early 1990s, and IRA assets exceeded defined benefit plan assets for the first time in 1998. At the end of 2006, defined benefit plans had grown to $2.3 trillion, but defined contribution plan assets and IRA assets totaled $4.1 and $4.2 trillion, respectively.[11] Together, self-directed plans were almost four times as large as defined benefit plans in 2006. As private sector defined benefit plans continue to be phased out in favor of defined contribution and cash balance accounts, mutual funds will continue to grow as a primary investment vehicle for defined contribution and IRA accounts.

Underlying the growth in mutual fund and retirement assets over the last two decades were favorable stock market conditions. The 15 percent or so market interest rates of the late 1970s combined with rate regulation on savings accounts in banks and savings and loan institutions led to substantial growth in the number and assets of money market funds. Money market assets jumped from $3.9 billion in 1977 to approximately $220 billion in 1982, and the number of money market funds during this period increased from 50 to 318.[12] This provided a first-time experience with mutual funds for many investors and, when the experience proved favorable, led to further investing in mutual funds. Recovery from the 1980–1981 and 1990–1991 recessions resulted in strong stock market appreciation and further investment in mutual funds. Demographic conditions were also highly favorable to mutual fund investing. When baby boomers began reaching middle age and increased planning for retirement, the demand for mutual funds grew through much of the 1990s.

Mutual Funds and the Pension Protection Act of 2006

The Pension Protection Act (PPA) of 2006 (Public Law 109-208), provides additional impetus for retirement investing via mutual funds. The PPA of 2006 includes somewhat inconsistent incentives for employers to continue or open new traditional defined benefit plans, but it provides unambiguous incentives for individuals to invest in IRAs and defined contribution plans. For defined benefit plans, the PPA of 2006 increases tax deductions for employers' contributions, encouraging employers to maintain their defined benefit plans. However, the Act requires that employers eliminate all underfunding in defined benefit plans by a specific date, which provides an incentive for employers with financially troubled, underfunded plans to convert to plans with less demanding future liabilities, such as cash balance and defined contribution plans. The PPA of 2006 also facilitates employers switching away from defined benefit plans. Conversions from defined benefit plans had faced legal uncertainty prior to 2006 because of numerous lawsuits against employers, charging them with age discrimination against older workers.[13] The lawsuits likely slowed the shift from defined benefit plans. The PPA of 2006 Act, however, protects employers from age discrimination lawsuits when switching to defined contribution plans, thus reducing the costs of switching.

The Act provided increased incentives for investing in IRAs and defined contribution plans. It raised the maximum amount of IRA contributions to

$4,000 in 2006 and $5,000 in 2008, and provided for inflation, adjusting maximum contribution limits thereafter, encouraging larger investment in IRAs. Similarly, the Act raised dollar limits to $44,000 for defined contribution plans and $10,000 for SIMPLE IRA plans in 2006. In addition, catch-up investing by older workers for IRAs, SIMPLE IRAs, and 401(k) plans authorized in 2001 but previously scheduled to end after December 31, 2010, were made permanent in the PPA Act of 2006. The Act also eased the burden on employees in completing rollovers into IRAs, and encouraged greater participation in defined contribution plans by automatically enrolling new employees in 401(k) plans, unless they specifically opt out. Over all, the PPA of 2006 provides greater incentives for investing in defined contribution and IRA plans, which has further contributed to the growing demand for mutual funds.

Government Pension Plans: Further Opportunity for Growth in Mutual Funds

Historically, defined benefit plans have dominated pension plans for public employees. In contrast to private sector retirement plans, the government's power to tax provided assurance to many that such plans would not be chronically underfunded. However, this has not always been the case. Government budget restraints, public employees' union demands, and voter hostility to higher taxes led some local and state governments to continue offering generous defined benefit plans while simultaneously underfunding employee pensions in favor of more immediate public expenditure priorities. A notable example was the city of San Diego, which expanded its unfunded pension liability from $96.3 million in 1995 to $1.4 billion in 2005 by increasing pension benefits but not providing for future funding. This ruined the city's credit rating and jeopardized its ability to issue bonds.[14]

Although San Diego may be an extreme example, local and state government pension plans are generally underfunded. A 2008 study by Wilshire Consulting on state-sponsored defined benefit plans found that for 56 state retirement systems reporting actuarial data in 2007, 75 percent were underfunded, with an average ratio of assets to liabilities of 82 percent.[15] This is an improvement from 2006, when 80 percent of the pension plans were underfunded, with an average ratio of 82 percent. The funding ratio for the 56 retirement systems declined from 112 percent in 2000 to 81 percent in 2003, then rebounded to 91 percent in 2007. The funding swung from a positive $55.3 billion in 2000 to a negative $154.7 billion at the end of 2007. For the 62 city and county retirement systems that provided actuarial data for 2006, 73 percent were underfunded, with an average ratio of assets to liabilities of 84 percent. In the aggregate, the ratio of assets to liabilities declined from 99 percent in 2001 to 90 percent in 2006.[16]

Underfunded government pension plans generally require increased tax revenues to meet future liabilities or other adjustments, such as raising the retirement age or requiring increased contributions from employees. As more and more private sector employees are offered defined contribution plans and view themselves as being disadvantaged on pension benefits relative to public sector employees on equity grounds, resentment against property tax and sales tax increases to fund government pensions will likely increase. Resistance to tax increases due to disparities between the relative generosity of public defined benefit plans and private defined contribution plans may lead to more use of defined contribution plans in the public sector and thus more retirement investment in mutual funds.[17]

Some public employees have the opportunity to invest in defined contribution plans, such as 403(b) plans for public education workers and 457 plans for state and local government employees. If a state or local government's defined benefit pension plan became dangerously underfunded, employees with an option would increase investments in IRAs or a defined contribution plan, further increasing investment in mutual funds.

Summary and Conclusions

In summary, mutual fund investments have grown substantially since 1980, as have investments in self-directed retirement plans. The long-term trend away from traditional defined benefit plans, changes in employers' and employees' retirement investment incentives under the PPA of 2006, and voter resistance to tax increases to fund government-defined benefit plans portend greater retirement plan investing in IRAs and defined contribution plans, which, in turn, means greater investment in mutual funds. The market for mutual funds will continue to be vitally important to the retirement savings plans of millions of people.

As noted, the extent to which the market for mutual funds provides its products in an efficient, cost-effective way has been debated in studies and the courts for over 50 years. Given the centrality of mutual funds in retirement accounts, whether the market for mutual funds provides products at an effectively competitive price is an important social welfare question, potentially affecting the lives of millions of U.S. retirees and taxpayers.

The next chapter reviews the basis for arguments about why mutual fund fees may be excessive and examines the historical origins of the debate.

CHAPTER TWO

Mutual Funds and Charges of Excessive Fees: The Historical Background

As noted, since the 1960s a number of mutual fund industry studies have concluded that investment advisers fail to compete on price, resulting in excessive fees and, importantly, artificially low returns to investors.[1] Many studies end with forceful conclusions of market failure in the mutual fund industry, accompanied by strong, critical views of investment advisers as well as the Securities and Exchange Commission (SEC) for not correcting the problem. No less than the chief investment officer of Yale University and the Yale Endowment concluded that mutual fund investors are abused by investment advisers in the form of "outrageous fees, excessive trading, bloated assets, unethical kickbacks, and indefensible distribution practices."[2] If all that is true, a pervasive pattern of excessive fees for at least 50 years would represent a huge transfer of wealth from mutual fund investors to fund advisory firms.

To see this, consider the examples in Table 2.1, showing the financial outcomes of investing in a tax-deferred account starting at ages 25, 30, and 40, and continuing to age 65, at different compound interest rates. A person investing $500 a month starting at age 25 and continuing until age 65 in a tax-deferred retirement account would amass about $1.8 million if earning an 8 percent long-term market rate of return. If excess fees lowered the return to 6 percent, the amount at age 65 would be reduced by about $800,000. Thus, for retirement savers as well as others, it is vitally important that mutual fund fees be set in competitive markets for the type and quality of services and fund attributes selected by each investor. The consequences are even more painful for those starting to save for retirement later in their working lives because of the shortened time for interest compounding to grow their retirement assets.

TABLE 2.1 Asset Values by Rates of Return and Years of Investing

Monthly Investment	Age 25 to 65			Age 30 to 65			Age 40 to 65		
	$100	$500	$1,000	$100	$500	$1,000	$100	$500	$1,000
r = 6%	$191,696	$958,482	$1,916,963	$147,549	$737,747	$1,475,494	$73,274	$366,371	$732,742
r = 6.5%	$233,526	$1,167,631	$2,335,262	$165,286	$826,428	$1,652,856	$79,125	$395,623	$791,245
r = 7%	$267,195	$1,335,976	$2,671,953	$185,402	$927,008	$1,854,017	$85,504	$427,521	$855,042
r = 7.5%	$312,118	$1,560,592	$3,121,184	$211,660	$1,058,299	$2,116,598	$93,486	$467,431	$934,862
r = 8%	$351,366	$1,756,831	$3,513,662	$234,138	$1,170,688	$2,341,375	$100,054	$500,270	$1,000,540

Asset values are determined by:

$$Value = \left(\frac{Monthly}{Payment}\right) \times \frac{(1+r_m)((1+r_m)^{Y \times 12} - 1)}{r_m}$$

$$r_m = \sqrt[12]{1+r} - 1$$

To better understand the concerns and arguments of those believing that fees are excessive due to an absence of price competition, we summarize their basic claims, look back to events prior to passage of the Investment Company Act (ICA) of 1940, and then to subsequent conditions and studies of the mutual fund industry.

Fees Are Excessive: The Critics' View

The view that mutual fund fees are excessive rests on several claims: (1) there is an inherent conflict of interest between a fund's external investment adviser and its shareholders that leads inevitably to the sacrifice of shareholders' interest by the investment adviser; (2) investment advisers create the fund, control the fund's board of directors, and are never fired, allowing them to price their services above the competitive level; (3) investors are either unaware of the fees they pay, or they are insensitive to fee differences between mutual funds because fees are so small they are not worth considering; and (4) investors are locked into their mutual fund investments because of load fees in either buying or selling funds, or capital gains tax consequences of selling fund shares so they are unable to switch to lower fee funds and thereby pressure advisers to reduce fees.

Fund Governance Structure and the Conflict of Interest

With few exceptions, investment advisers organize funds under separate ownership with separate boards of directors.[3] The SEC has championed the view that under this organizational structure, with an external investment adviser, there is an inherent conflict of interest between fund shareholders and their investment adviser.

As the SEC states the problem:

> Investment companies are unique in that they are organized and operated by people whose primary loyalty and pecuniary interest lie outside the enterprise. Consequently, conflicts of interest inhere in the structure of companies, creating great potential for abuse.[4]

> An investment adviser has an incentive to charge the highest possible fee for its services, while the fund and its shareholders wish to pay the lowest amount of fees possible because the fees directly reduce a fund's return to its investments.[5]

In other words, the claim is that mutual fund investment advisers maximize their profits by charging shareholders excessive fees, thereby reducing fund returns to shareholders. The market for mutual funds and investment advisers cannot correct this condition because investment advisers control the mutual fund's board and shareholders cannot shift to comparable, lower fee funds. Accordingly, income is transferred from fund shareholders to their investment advisory firm.

From the 1930s forward, the foundation of regulations and statutes directed at protecting mutual fund investors has been this conviction that an inherent conflict of interest exists between external investment advisers and mutual fund shareholders and their boards of directors. The ICA of 1940 and the Investment Advisors Act (IAA) of 1940 were directed at preventing the major abuses by advisers of fund investors that were taking place at the time. These acts were also intended to mitigate the adviser–investor conflict of interest by strengthening the bargaining position of fund shareholders relative to their investment advisers. This was done in part by requiring that 40 percent of a fund's board of directors be independent (unaffiliated) of the investment management firm and fund underwriters; that annual renewal of adviser contracts be approved by the majority of independent directors; and that adviser contracts be approved by the majority of outstanding shareholders.

The SEC has periodically reviewed the governance structure of mutual funds to reduce the alleged conflict of interest. At times it has called for new regulations to help protect investors, such as its 2004 proposal—made following the 2003 late trading and market timing scandals—for independent directors to constitute 75 percent of funds' boards of directors and that chairpersons be independent directors.[6] The idea that fund advisers' and shareholders' goals of maximizing their respective profits are mutually achievable through maximizing returns to shareholders, which would increase investments in the fund and adviser revenues as a percentage of assets, has not been a prominent part of the debate over whether fees are excessive. One study acknowledges that, in principle, by maximizing returns to fund shareholders, investment advisers maximize their own profits because high investor returns attract more assets, but dismisses the idea by arguing that advisers will deliberately grow funds beyond their optimum size to increase their own returns while reducing shareholder returns.[7] In a competitive market this reasoning is faulty. Sacrificing investors' returns increases fund redemptions, reducing advisers' profits. Indeed, mutual funds commonly close themselves to new investors when they reach a certain size, and they justify this action as a means to maintain strong performance for their existing investors.

The fact that sellers and buyers have different desires about price—one seeking a high price and one offering a lower price—is hardly surprising and, indeed, is the basis of all commercial trade and certainly not unique to mutual funds and their advisers. Such differences are resolved in a competitive market at the point at which the quantity demanded by buyers and the quantity supplied by sellers intersect, allowing buyers to purchase inputs at a competitive market price based on choosing between competing suppliers. In the case of mutual funds, this would lead to fund shareholders acquiring investment management, fund administration, and other investor services at a competitive price. The charge against mutual funds, however, is that a competitive price mechanism to reach the "fair" competitive price does not exist because mutual funds cannot replace their investment advisers without great cost, so buyers are forced to pay an "excessive" price, set by the investment adviser. Thus, the competitive price mechanism is argued to be broken as a result of the inability of funds to easily dismiss and replace their external investment advisers. Without this ability, funds' directors are said to lack the power to protect the interests of fund shareholders in negotiating with investment advisers over annual fees.[8] To support this view, fee critics point out that institutional investors, such as large public pension plans, change investment advisers routinely, and institutional investors' mutual fund fees are substantially lower than retail investors' fees, whereas retail funds rarely replace advisers. In short, they argue that investment advisers do not have to compete to manage retail mutual funds, so price competition for retail fund management simply does not exist.

Relationship Between a Fund's Board of Directors and Its Investment Adviser

Some studies have coupled the alleged conflict of interest created by mutual funds' governance structure with de facto control of funds' boards of directors by investment advisers as a prime cause of excessive fees. In this view, funds' boards of directors are seen as relatively powerless to discipline investment advisers for setting high fees, because boards cannot risk firing a poorly performing or high-fee investment adviser. Switching investment advisers entails costs and may leave the funds' portfolio management adrift during the transition period, resulting in large shareholder redemptions. The evidence shows that a retail fund's primary adviser is rarely replaced.[9] Fund advisory firms are changed at times, such as when one advisory firm acquires another. Nevertheless, a poorly performing fund is more likely to find a new portfolio manager within a given advisory firm than to replace the advisory firm. Accordingly, some studies view investment advisers as having de facto control over their funds' boards of directors, allowing advisers to set excessive fees with relative impunity. Funds' boards of directors are argued to be beholden to the investment adviser firm rather than the mutual fund shareholders (although directors have a fiduciary duty to fund shareholders just as investment advisers do). The arm's-length bargaining between buyers and sellers explicitly sought by the SEC and Congress is said to be nonexistent.

Investor Sensitivity to Annual Fees

Critics of fees argue that equity mutual fund investors do not pay much attention to annual fees either because the fees are too trivial to take into account or because the fees are so obfuscated by investment advisers that investors do not understand the true size of the fees they pay. Either way, investors are said to not consider the level of fees in comparing investments across equity mutual funds, allowing investment advisers to price above the competitive level.[10]

Investor Mobility

A purported lack of investor mobility is arguably the central factor alleged to give rise to excessive fees. Fee critics conclude that investors do not shop across funds, and thus investment advisers, because of high transaction costs. Investors purchase a package of goods, including fund shares, services to investors, and the fund's investment adviser. However, if investors can switch between funds for the best price, service, and performance, those arguing that fees are excessive must explain why investor mobility does not ensure price competition. If investors can easily "fire" the investment adviser by switching to a new fund and adviser at a lower fee, holding fund service and performance constant, then good substitutes are present and price competition must adapt to buyer mobility. Factors that could affect investor mobility include capital gains taxes, back-end loads, front-end loads, or very limited investment choices, such as in a 401(k) retirement plan with a highly restricted menu of investment options.[11] Alternatively, it may be that fees are so small relative to the transaction costs of moving assets that investors have little incentive to switch funds.

To summarize, the view that mutual fund fees are excessive is based on an inherent conflict of interest between fund shareholders and their investment advisers; no bargaining power by fund shareholders and their board of directors against the fund's investment advisers; investor insensitivity to relative annual fees; and lack of investor mobility between funds and alternative investments. If, however, investors can easily fire their investment adviser by switching to a comparable, lower-cost fund, questions are raised as to whether advisers can sustain fees above the competitive level.

This critical view of the mutual fund industry has evolved since the 1930s. As noted, the major abuses of fund shareholders in the 1920s and 1930s were addressed in the ICA of 1940, but the potential for excessive fees was not explicitly dealt with in the Act.[12] Regulations to help ensure competitive fees were introduced in the 1970 amendment to the Act, as will be discussed later.

Early Mutual Fund Management Malfeasance and U.S. Regulations, 1924–1940

Looking back, the view that mutual fund shareholders are at the mercy of investment advisers has been prominent in regulatory discussions since the early history of the industry. The modern day mutual fund industry in this country was born in 1924 with creation of the first open-end fund, the Massachusetts Investors Trust (MIT), and the first publicly traded closed-end company, the U.S. and Foreign Securities Corporation, formed by Dillon, Read and Company, a major investment banking firm at the time. MIT was managed by a board of trustees, who also managed its stock portfolio, unlike today's funds, which largely contract with separate investment advisory firms for portfolio management and other services. Closed-end investment companies dominated in the early years, vastly outnumbering open-end funds. In 1929, there were 162 closed-end companies, established mostly by investment banking firms and brokerage houses, and only 19 open-end fund companies.[13]

In response to poor performance by many closed-end companies following the 1929 stock market crash, investors began shifting from closed- to open-end investment companies in the 1930s. Many closed-end companies, which often invested in assets beyond the stock and bond markets, lost much of their asset value in the Great Depression, whereas open-end funds lost lesser amounts, approximately equal to the decline in the stock market. Closed-end companies accounted for 95 percent of investment company assets in 1929, but declined to 58 percent by 1940 as investors shifted to open-end funds.[14]

Closed-end companies also experienced relatively more managerial scandals in the 1930s related to defrauding investors, further damaging their reputation relative to open-end funds. The SEC's investigation in the 1930s revealed self-dealing behavior by various investment company founders through such actions as embezzling fund assets, granting low-interest loans to insiders at rates below market levels, failing to report financial statements, using misleading accounting practices to overstate earnings, purchasing low-value securities from insiders at inflated prices, and generating sales commissions by shifting investors from one investment company to another without benefiting the investor.[15] These and other alleged abuses were most common in closed-end companies because of the shares' relative illiquidity and the companies' relative lack of operating transparency, which accelerated the shift of investors to open-end mutual funds.[16]

Investment company managers in the 1930s were also accused of exploiting the slow reporting of net asset value (NAV) from one day to the next.[17] NAV was calculated at the close of trading each day but not reported until 10 o'clock the next morning. If the new NAV was above the old NAV, buyers could purchase at the old price before the new price was announced, gaining a built-in profit. However, this diluted the share value of incumbent shareholders.[18]

In reaction to the stock market crash of October 1929 and the Great Depression, New Deal–era legislation was enacted to safeguard stock and bond market investors. The Securities Act of 1933 and the Securities Exchange Act of 1934 mandated greater disclosure by publicly traded companies, and the 1934 Act created the SEC. The Public Utility Holding Company Act of 1935 curbed the use of holding companies and the investor abuses attributed to holding company structures, such as restricting shareholders' voting rights.

According to the SEC's 1930s investigation of investment companies, abuses of investors were not curtailed by these Acts. Investment companies existing prior to the 1933 Act did not have to register under the securities Acts, and the SEC was uncovering examples of adviser harm to investors well after the securities Acts were instituted.[19] Indeed, concerned that investor abuse under utility-holding companies, such as denying voting rights to public shareholders and purchasing assets from insiders at above market values, also existed in investment companies, the 1935 Public Utility Holding Company Act directed the SEC to study investment companies' actions and present the findings to Congress.[20]

The SEC's report to Congress on the investment company industry was submitted in five volumes over three years starting in 1939, with at least one volume devoted to abuses of investors by investment company managers.[21] Concerned with the level of managerial malfeasance at the expense of investors documented by the SEC, which was reported to have cost investors $1.1 billion in the 1920s and 1930s,[22] Congress passed the ICA of 1940 to protect investors from exploitation by investment companies. The ICA of 1940 focused on full disclosure of company policies and practices; use of independent accounting firms and regular reporting of financial performance and portfolio composition to the SEC and shareholders; capital structure requirements to eliminate fly-by-night operations and reduce financial risk from excessive leverage; creating arm's-length bargaining between a fund and its investment adviser by requiring 40 percent of a fund's board be composed of directors unaffiliated with the investment advisory firm; explicit prohibition of certain types of self-dealing by the investment adviser company; protecting shareholder voting rights; and preventing pyramiding of corporate structures by ownership control of other investment companies.[23] The Act also limited front-end load charges for investors using periodic payment plans and required that investment company shares be sold only at the price specified in the prospectus. The SEC was given broad oversight and the power to enforce various provisions of the ICA of 1940.

The historical basis for regulating mutual funds is clearly grounded in the abuses of investment company stockholders in the 1930s. Instead of managers maximizing investor long-run returns, the SEC found cases of investment managers finding ways to essentially steal investors' money. The ICA of 1940 is generally regarded as having stopped the gross abuses of investors practiced in the 1930s, though various industry critics believe it has not stopped investment managers from maximizing their own short-run profits by charging fund shareholders fees above the competitive level.

The 1950s and 1960s

Mutual fund investing and assets grew in the 1950s, with total assets under management increasing from $2.5 billion in 1950 to $17 billion in 1960.[24] The majority of this growth was due to new investment.[25] The SEC became concerned over the potential effects of large-scale mutual fund investing on the stock market. In 1958, the SEC commissioned the Wharton School of Finance and Commerce, Securities Research Unit, to conduct a comprehensive study of the mutual fund industry.[26] Initially, the study focused on the growth and size of the industry, and the effects of mutual fund size on fund investment policies, performance, and the securities markets. Subsequently, the study was expanded to cover investment adviser management practices toward fund shareholders. At approximately the same time, in the late 1950s, about 50 private action cases were filed against the largest externally managed funds and fund complexes, complaining of mutual fund shareholders being charged excessive adviser fees.[27]

The Wharton Report, based on a sample of 1950s mutual fund data, concluded that mutual fund fees were high relative to the services provided to investors and the costs of managing mutual funds. The study found that in the 1950s, mutual funds experienced large economies of scale (declining cost per unit of output, holding other factors constant) due to strong asset growth, but the cost savings were not passed on to investors in the form of lower annual fees because of the absence of price competition. Fees were found to be largely fixed at 0.5 percent of assets in the 1950s, regardless of the size of the fund, which the study concluded evidenced a lack of price competition.

As a consequence of finding that fees remained high despite declining costs, the Wharton Report concluded that mutual fund shareholders and boards of directors lacked bargaining power over the fee compensation of their investment advisers. The lack of price competition was also attributed to investment advisers not competing to manage mutual funds. The study also found that retail mutual fund fees were substantially higher than fees charged to other clients for portfolio management services, such as pension plans and banks, where advisers compete directly to be hired by institutional investors. The study further found that management costs were lower in companies that provided investment advisory services internally than in companies that contracted with external investment advisers.[28] The study attributed excessive fees in the mutual fund industry to the organizational structure of mutual funds and their management, based on funds relying on external investment advisers who controlled the funds' boards of directors and thus investor advisory fees.

The SEC conducted its own study following the Wharton Report and the failure of several private lawsuits to significantly lower the annual costs of investing in mutual funds.[29] The SEC's study largely agreed with the Wharton Report's findings and conclusions. According to both studies, the relationship between funds and their investment advisers, with advisers holding all the bargaining power, prevented arm's-length bargaining on advisory fees, resulting in excessive fees and the absence of price competition between mutual funds. Testifying before Congress, the then SEC chairman stated that

> by any objective standard the advisory fees paid by a member of the funds are excessive and that this is due, in the main, to the mechanical application of a formula related only to the assets of the fund—regardless of the extent to which the growth of these assets is caused by aggressive sales efforts without any proportional increase in the costs of advising the fund.[30]

In addition, the SEC found that after they purchased shares, shareholders were limited in their ability to search for lower cost funds because few such funds existed and because of the 8.5 percent load fee that many of them paid on first investing in a fund.[31] In the 1960s, load funds dominated sales relative to no-load funds. In June 1966, approximately 95 percent of mutual fund assets were in load funds.[32]

The SEC concluded that provisions in the ICA of 1940 intended to protect investors from excessive fees, such as 40 percent of directors being unaffiliated with the advisory firm and fees having to be approved by the directors annually, had failed to protect fund investors from excessive fees. Accordingly, the SEC proposed amending the ICA of 1940 to minimize investors' fees. First, it proposed imposing a "reasonableness" standard for determining whether fees were excessive; and second, it proposed granting shareholders the opportunity to sue investment advisers for damages with respect to the level of annual fees, a right not originally included in the ICA of 1940. The SEC proposed that reasonableness be established in part by comparing mutual fund adviser fees to the fees paid by financial institutions for like services and for assets of similar size and purpose, such as pension plans, insurance companies, and trust accounts, as well as other investment companies.[33]

In late 1970, based on the findings of the SEC and the Wharton Report and extensive Senate hearings, the 91st Congress amended the ICA of 1940 by adding section 36(b), devoted to advisory management fees, but changed the "reasonableness" standard on whether fees were excessive to a "fiduciary" standard. Under 36(b), advisers have a fiduciary duty with respect to their compensation for management services. Shareholders, acting on behalf of the fund, can bring an action against advisers for breach of fiduciary duty and damages with respect to adviser compensation.[34] As already indicated, prior to the 1970 amendment, only the SEC could bring legal action and the remedy was limited to injunctive relief. Though Congress did not define fiduciary duty, critics of mutual fund pricing tend to equate breach of fiduciary duty with excessive fees under a fairness or equity standard, or an arm's-length bargaining standard.[35]

Proposed Regulatory Solutions to Excessive Fees

According to both the SEC and the Wharton Report, the conflict of interest problem in mutual funds resides in the use of external advisers and their ability to prevent arm's-length bargaining. The 1969 Senate report on adviser fees agreed that arm's-length bargaining between investors as buyers and investment advisers as sellers did not work in the mutual fund industry, as it did in the rest of the economy.[36] However, Congress did not encourage vertical integration between mutual funds and investment advisers, a solution implicitly offered by the SEC and Wharton Report, arising from their findings of lower fees and expenses when funds managed their portfolios internally. Congress also explicitly rejected using traditional utility rate regulation and cost-plus pricing to set mutual fund fees. Congress recognized that investment advisers were free to earn profits commensurate with the risk they assumed in competing for mutual fund business. By not imposing price regulation, Congress endorsed using the market for investment management to determine the optimal organizational relationship between mutual funds and their investment advisers. Congress left it to the courts to set the standards for what constituted excessive fees relative to the services provided by advisory firms. The Congressional solution was to allow private lawsuits for damage penalties as an incentive to price competitively and for the courts to craft a framework for determining when fees were excessive.

Viewed over time, from 1940 to the present, the SEC's primary action for strengthening price competition in the retail sector of the mutual fund industry has been to call for improved disclosure of fees to investors and a higher proportion of independent directors on mutual funds' boards of directors. The SEC started with 40 percent of the board as independent directors, later moved to 50 percent, and, as discussed, called for 75 percent in 2004. The Government Accountability Office (GAO) joined with the SEC in calling for more fee disclosure as a means to stimulate greater price competition.[37] Interestingly, advocating greater transparency in fees necessarily implies a belief that investors are not locked into high-fee funds when provided with knowledge of lower-fee alternatives; that is, investors' mutual fund assets are easily mobile.

Still other commentators emphasize that because advisers desire to maximize their own profits at the expense of fund investors, investment management should be done internally, by the fund itself. These commentators also argue that mutual funds should be organized as nonprofit firms.[38] In this case, fund shareholders would own both the fund and its investment management services and also operate as a nonprofit firm. Some studies maintain that this removes the incentive for advisers to maximize their profits at the expense of fund shareholders and eliminates the conflict of interest between shareholders and their investment advisers. The Vanguard Group of funds and TIAA-CREF's fund family are frequently offered as examples of the ideal mutual fund organizational structure; both are known for having relatively low fees, a nonprofit ownership structure, and internal investment management. An empirical test of this view is presented in Chapter 7.

CHAPTER THREE

Mutual Fund Excessive Fees and the Courts

Outside the legislative process, the courts have grappled for decades with the question of whether mutual fund fees are excessive. In *Gartenberg*, the leading decision in this area from 1982 to the present, the District Court for the Southern District of New York found that the defendant, Merrill Lynch, did not charge excessive fees and that it faced effective price competition from rival money market funds.[1] On appeal, the Second Circuit Court of Appeals rejected the district court's opinion that price competition existed among money market mutual funds, but found in favor of Merrill Lynch due to shortcomings in the plaintiffs' evidence. As noted earlier, the appellate court determined that because advisers do not compete to manage rival mutual funds, advisers set their fees without regard to losing their funds' investors to rival funds.

This chapter reviews these two opposing opinions to better understand price competition, or the lack thereof, in the mutual fund industry and the economic issues addressed in mutual fund excessive fee lawsuits. More specifically, we analyze the economic reasoning used in the appellate court's decision. Our examination reveals shortcomings in the *Gartenberg* approach. Partly in response to these shortcomings, we developed the economic models and empirical tests presented in Chapter 4.

As investment in money market mutual funds grew from their inception in 1972 to the late 1970s and early 1980s, so did lawsuits brought by various money market fund investors against investment advisers for charging excessive fees. Total money market fund assets increased dramatically during this period, from $6.8 billion in mid-1978 to $185 billion at the end of 1981.[2] This growth in money market funds resulted from interest rates at the time on short-term paper being well above regulated savings account rates in banks and other financial institutions. Plaintiffs argued that as money market fund assets grew to historically high levels, investment advisers were earning unprecedented profits from fees calculated as a percentage of assets and from ancillary business activities, such as brokerage commissions. Although annual investor fees were typically reduced on a sliding scale as assets reached certain levels ("fee breakpoints"), plaintiffs claimed they remained "unfairly" high, out of proportion to the cost of services rendered, and in violation of Section 36(b) of the Investment Company Act (ICA) of 1940. Out of lawsuits during this period came the *Gartenberg* decision, in which the Second Circuit Court of Appeals gave its interpretation of Section 36(b) of the Act and what Congress intended when passing 36(b) in 1970.[3]

Gartenberg Case Background

Two investors in the Merrill Lynch Ready Assets Trust, a money market fund started in 1975, brought suit against the fund and the fund's investment adviser, Merrill Lynch Asset Management, and Merrill Lynch, Pierce, Fenner & Smith, the fund's broker for daily purchase and redemption orders.[4] For ease of discussion, we refer to the multiple defendants as "Merrill Lynch." The plaintiffs held that Merrill Lynch breached its fiduciary duty to the fund's shareholders under Section 36(b) because the fees were out of proportion to the services rendered and the costs of providing the services. The plaintiffs maintained that in passing Section 36(b), Congress intended mutual fund fees to be at a "fair" level, and not unreasonably high. In other words, Merrill Lynch's profits from the fund were too high relative to the services received by investors, Merrill Lynch's operating costs as the investment adviser and fund distributor, and fund investors' returns, so fees must be excessive.

In addition to annual fees, the plaintiffs argued that Merrill Lynch gained excess returns from the brokerage fees it earned from the fund's securities transactions, the interest rate float in processing redemption orders, the dealer spread when transacting in government securities, and further business from fund investors—so-called fall-out benefits—or indirect profits to a fund's investment adviser by virtue of the fund's existence. The plaintiffs argued that brokerage fees and other fall-out benefits should be used as offsets to reduce investors' annual fund fees, for without the fund, Merrill Lynch would not be generating the additional incremental income from these fall-out benefits.

As the fund's assets grew, Merrill Lynch added fee breakpoints, which reduced fees as a share of assets.[5] In 1976 and 1977, when the fund's assets were
below $500 million, it charged 0.50 percent on the first $500 million. In 1978,
the independent directors set fees at 0.425 percent of assets up to $500 million,
0.375 percent of assets up to $750 million, and 0.35 percent of assets when they
reached $1 billion and above. In 1979, with the fund's assets at $2 billion, two
additional breakpoints were added, with fees of 0.325 percent for assets over
$1.5 billion and 0.30 percent of assets for over $2 billion. At the time of trial in
1981, the fund's assets had reached $19 billion, and the effective fee rate was
0.288 percent, or $2.88 per $1,000 invested, which was reportedly one of the
lowest fee levels among then competing money market funds.[6] At the time,
Merrill Lynch's money market fund was the largest in the United States.

Both the district and appellate courts found that the plaintiffs did not offer
sufficient proof of their claims and granted dismissal of the lawsuit. However,
the courts reached their opinions from diametrically opposing perspectives
on competition among money market funds and in the mutual fund industry
more broadly. The appellate court's rejection of the district court's reasoning
helps clarify the appellate court's findings on what should and should not be
considered in determining whether mutual fund fee levels constitute a violation of the investment adviser's fiduciary duty, that is, what criteria should be
used in determining whether fees are excessive.

The District Court's Decision in *Gartenberg*

The district court concluded that in debates over alternative legislative bills
leading to the passage of Section 36(b), Congress explicitly rejected a "reasonableness" standard in favor of an investment adviser's "fiduciary duty" standard in judging a fund's annual investor fees.[7] Congress also rejected regulating investment advisers' profit rates. The district court stated, "The essence of
the [fiduciary] test is whether or not under all the circumstances the transaction carries the earmarks of an arm's length bargain."[8] Earmarks included
such factors as the fund's trustees or directors being fully informed on comparable mutual fund fees, the adviser's costs, and the fund's performance. The
district court reasoned that in order to rule for the plaintiffs, it had to find evidence demonstrating that Merrill Lynch received compensation that was unfair to the fund and its shareholders. The evidence showed that in March 1981,
only one fund out of well over 100 rival money market funds had a lower effective fee than the Merrill Lynch fund, implying in the judge's opinion that
Merrill Lynch's fee was fair, well in line with rival funds.[9]

The district court found that Congress intended investment advisers to take into account economies of scale from the growth of a fund in negotiating with a fund's directors over the level of annual fees and to share the cost savings of these economies of scale equitably with fund shareholders. After reviewing the fee breakpoints set by Merrill Lynch, the district court ruled that economies of scale had been taken into account. The court further concluded that economies of scale in mutual funds are exhausted at some point because the costs of processing orders and administering larger numbers of accounts eventually offset further economies in portfolio management and possibly other services. Based on this analysis, the district court concluded that Merrill Lynch's fees passed the test for meeting the adviser's fiduciary duty, that is, for fairness.

The district court further argued that other sources of income—from fallout benefits—were difficult if not impossible to measure because it was hard to attribute cause and effect between fund investors and nonfund transactions. For example, did the fund's investors engage in more separate brokerage business with Merrill Lynch because they invested in the fund, or did above-average brokerage business customers tend to invest in the fund? Plaintiffs offered no estimates of fall-out benefits or a conceptual approach to measuring such benefits. The district court ruled that plaintiffs had not shown that "meaningful estimates could be provided even with extreme difficulty and expense."[10] The court also ruled that Merrill Lynch had fulfilled its fiduciary duty by informing the fund's trustees that it was possible for the fund's existence to generate additional benefits without providing an estimate of such benefits. Finally, the district court ruled that fall-out benefits do not constitute an offset to annual fees because there is no logical reason why shareholders should be able to avoid paying for processing their fund orders just because they also pay a commission on separate orders for stocks or bonds.

The district court determined that the fund's board of trustees was adequately informed of the fees, the market price for comparable services, the scope of the services provided, the fund's performance, the costs of supplying the services, and the profitability of the fund's contract with the investment adviser. The court also found that the trustees had given careful consideration to this information before approving fee changes. Thus, the trustees had discharged their fiduciary duty to inform themselves properly before negotiating with the adviser and approving investor fees.

Importantly, the district court found that the market for money market funds was highly competitive, with large numbers of rivals, easy new entry, and investors able to cash out at any time and invest in a lower cost fund. It concluded that investors' fees were set in a competitive market. Advisers pricing above the competitive price level for the services offered would incur fund redemptions, reducing adviser revenues. Hence, with fees determined by competitive market forces, rivals' fees served as a benchmark for determining whether a given fund's fee was fair—in the sense of not violating Section 36(b) of the ICA of 1940.

This was a heretical position at the time, given that the Securities and Exchange Commission's (SEC) 1966 report found *no* price competition among mutual funds because advisers did not compete for advisory contracts. The SEC also found little price variation between mutual funds and concluded that investors paid little attention to fee differences between funds. In contrast, the district court's view was that investor mobility between alternative rival money market funds negated the SEC's concern that investment advisers had the power to set fees above the competitive level. The district court's view was that investors, or at least enough investors to ensure competitive pricing, were sensitive to fee differences between money market mutual funds and could easily move between competing funds. Funds might not be able to fire and replace their advisers, but fund shareholders could easily fire an investment adviser by cashing out and investing in a lower fee, higher return money market fund.

Altogether, the district court found no evidence of monopoly or restrictions on entry. Indeed, there were well over 100 substitutable money market funds in 1981 available for investors. The court found that adviser compensation from fees was set by market forces, not adviser leverage over fund directors when negotiating the level of fees. And as noted, the district court found that Merrill Lynch had properly shared its economies of scale with investors by lowering fees and expanding fee breakpoints over time as assets grew.

The Appellate Court's Decision in *Gartenberg*

While affirming the district court's decision to dismiss the complaint, the appellate court rejected major portions of the district court's analysis and reasoning. The appellate court rejected the district court's conclusions that (1) under the facts of the case, money market fund fees are set in a competitive market and competition provides a fairness standard for determining whether Merrill Lynch violated Section 36(b); (2) shareholders are protected from excessive fees in money market fund investments by their ability to shift at very low cost to any of a large number of substitutable money market funds; and (3) fall-out benefits do not represent offsets to fund fees and, in any event, are virtually impossible to measure with a reasonable degree of accuracy.

The appellate court's rejection of the lower court's opinion on price competition among money market funds was based in part on the 1970 Congressional view that price competition did not exist between equity mutual funds in the 1960s, which, in turn, was based on the SEC's 1966 study. In adopting the SEC's position, the appellate court assumed that the analysis of 1960s equity fund fees was applicable to money market funds 15 years later. This is highly questionable given that (1) money market funds did not exist in the 1960s; (2) money market funds have a decidedly different cost structure and generally fulfill a different purpose for investors than do long-term equity funds; and (3) the mutual fund industry, including money market funds, had undergone substantial changes in the number, entry, and types of mutual funds available by the early 1980s.

The appellate court defined the standard for excessive fees as "a fee that is so disproportionately large that it bears no reasonable relationship to the services rendered and could not have been the product of arm's-length bargaining."[11] One basis for determining what constituted disproportionately large, according to the court, was what the fee would have been under arm's-length bargaining. This is equivalent to saying what the fee would have been in a competitive market, because arm's-length bargaining presumes competition among alternative sellers. The SEC had concluded in 1966 that "an essential element of arm's-length bargaining [is] the freedom to terminate the negotiations and to bargain with other parties for the same services."[12] But this is unlikely for a mutual fund, just as it would be for most vertically integrated firms, because the costs of transitioning to a new adviser generally outweigh the benefits.[13] The appellate court characterized the relationship between the adviser and fund as "unseverable."[14] According to the appellate court, fund directors and investors were trapped because they lacked the ability to terminate and replace an adviser who was charging excessive fees, which left them without the leverage to bargain for a competitive market-determined lower fee.

Competition Among Money Market Funds

The appellate court dismissed in a two-prong attack the district court's finding that fees were competitively determined. The court held first that fees are not set in a competitive market so rivals' fees cannot be a benchmark for fair pricing, and second, that mutual fund investors do not have the ability to switch from high- to low-fee money market funds. The appellate court argued that the district court had based its analysis on the wrong market. Instead of viewing the market as money market mutual fund advisers competing for investors, which at the time likely included close substitutes in short-term bank and savings and loan savings accounts, the appellate court concluded that the district court should have focused on the market where investment advisers compete for contracts to manage money funds' assets. According to the court, that is where investors' fees should be determined. Using this definition of the product market, the appellate court concluded that the market was not competitive because advisers could not realistically be terminated and replaced. As such, the market lacked a necessary characteristic of competitive markets—good substitute products when engaging in arm's-length bargaining.

The appellate court determined that competition in the market for money market fund investors was irrelevant to the level of investor fees because it had no relationship to the market for advisers competing for contracts to manage fund investments. The appellate court stated that competition for investors may be vigorous, while competition to manage fund assets is virtually nonexistent, because "[e]ach [market] is governed by different forces" and "[r]eliance on prevailing industry advisory fees will not satisfy §36(b)."[15] Thus, the main factor in determining investor fees, according to the appellate court, was the lack of competition between advisers for money market fund management contracts.

The court's reasoning and conclusion seems attenuated. Markets form where the gains from trade between buyers and sellers outweigh the transaction costs of making an exchange. The SEC's 1966 report described various costs that fund shareholders face in replacing their adviser, such as expensive proxy contests, disruption to fund operations, and risks associated with switching portfolio managers and administrators.[16] Among the potential problems are that termination of an investment adviser may result in degrading a fund's liquidity and portfolio position if it is forced to sell securities to meet shareholder redemption demands. Also, a fund within a complex using the same adviser would lose the cost efficiencies, services, and marketing advantages of being part of a specific fund complex.

Thus, the appellate court repeated the SEC's 1966 report's finding that the market for fund advisory contracts was not competitive because it was uneconomic to replace an investment adviser. Based on this reasoning, the appellate court said in effect that the district court should have analyzed a market that for practical purposes did not exist at the time of the decision—the market for retail fund investment adviser contracts—and it did not exist because it was uneconomical to have such a market.[17] Therefore, the market for fund advisory contracts, which the appellate court stated determined investor fees, could not be competitive because it did not exist.

The appellate court's distinction between a market to manage a mutual fund's portfolio and a market for mutual fund investors is without basis if fund shareholders are free to shift to alternative funds. Assume a fund's shareholders agree to maintain their contract with the investment advisory firm that started the mutual fund, paying the negotiated price for management services plus a bonus for superior performance. However, to sell more shares to new and existing investors, the cost of managing the assets, as embodied in annual shareholders fees, must be competitive. Lacking a market for retail fund management contracts does not free adviser-managers from charging a competitive price for their services. Without a competitive annual fee for the services provided, new investors will not be attracted if comparable funds with lower fees are available. At least some if not the majority of existing investors would redeem their shares in favor of comparable, lower fee mutual funds.

An alternative way to understand the problem caused by ignoring the market for fund investors is as follows. Assume mutual funds are vertically integrated, with in-house portfolio management. External advisory services do not exist. Under these conditions, investors' fees are determined by competition among mutual funds for investors. In competition with comparable funds, low-fee funds will attract money and high-fee funds will lose investors. This is little different from the conditions in *Gartenberg*, although Merrill Lynch was an external adviser. Whether there is a market where advisers compete for management contracts or not, competition among fund advisers for investors determines the level of investor fees as long as some investors are sufficiently sensitive to fee levels to seek lower fee funds.

Investor Mobility

Perhaps realizing some flaws in its reasoning, that the market for fund investing and the hypothetical but nonexistent market for fund adviser contracts are not ruled entirely by separate market forces, the second prong of the appellate court's attack rejected the district court's claim that investors are sensitive to the level of fees and mobile in searching for lower fee funds. The appellate court stated, without providing supporting evidence, that fees paid for money market funds are so small that they are not worth an investor's time to monitor. It follows that the differences in fees between money market funds are even smaller, so in the court's view investors have no incentive to search for and switch to a lower fee fund. The appellate court regarded the difference in fees as "competitively insignificant."[18] This placed the appellate court in a curious position. If investor fees were too small and competitively insignificant for investors to consider when selecting a money market fund, how could the fees be so disproportionately large relative to the services provided and to fees determined under arm's-length bargaining as to constitute breach of an adviser's fiduciary duty?[19]

As discussed earlier, the appellate court's reliance on empirical evidence for equity market funds compiled 15 to 20 years earlier in judging whether money market fund fees in the late 1970s and early 1980s were excessive is strongly suspect. There is little reason to believe that the variation in equity fund fees found in the 1960s represented the range of fees across money market funds at the time of the *Gartenberg* case. It is well known that the level of fees is the main distinguishing difference between returns on short-term money market funds. There is a high, negative correlation between money market fund fees and returns to investors because the funds generally invest in the same types of short-term paper.[20] As such, differences in returns on money market funds are primarily a result of differences in fees (and differences in fees can reflect differences in services to investors). This suggests that the appellate court's claim that money market fund shareholders pay little if any attention to annual fees is doubtful. In choosing a money market fund, fees are a prime consideration for investors because net returns vary essentially because of differences in fees. Out of the main categories of mutual funds—equity, bond, hybrid, and money market—investors are likely to be most attentive to fees in short-term money market funds, because the lower the fees, the higher the return.

Competition and the Replacement of Investment Advisers

The appellate court's view that the inability to terminate and replace investment advisers economically prevented fees equivalent to those that would result from arm's-length bargaining is similarly questionable. If investors are sensitive to fee levels and incur only modest costs in switching between funds, then a money market fund must price competitively for the services delivered or the fund will suffer large redemptions, thereby reducing the adviser's income and possibly jeopardizing the fund's existence.

Another way to view negotiations over pricing between an adviser and its fund is as a transfer price between two divisions of a vertically integrated company. Because it is costly for a retail fund to terminate an adviser, the fund and adviser are in effect vertically integrated by contract. Assume an upstream division is selling an input to a downstream division in the same firm. The divisions do not negotiate as strangers in arm's-length bargaining, nor can they easily fire each other, but they can have a proxy price for arm's-length bargaining if there is a competitive market outside the firm for the input. The transfer price between the two divisions that most benefits the consolidated firm is the competitive market price. Similarly, the correct price between fund and adviser for adviser services—that is, the price that is most beneficial to both the fund and the adviser—is the competitive market price for adviser management and other services. If the adviser attempts to price above the competitive level for the services provided, reducing returns to fund shareholders, it will lose fund shareholders and revenue.

Gartenberg's *Framework for Determining Excessive Fees*

Having essentially rejected fees charged by comparable rival retail funds as a basis for determining whether a defendant's fees are disproportionately large, the appellate court attempted to provide guidance to lower courts on what evidence to consider in assessing the level of fees. The court said, "To make this determination all pertinent facts must be weighed,"[21] and it provided a list of factors that lower courts could use to determine whether fees were disproportionately large. Factors the court considered, as well as those it suggested should be investigated in determining whether a fee was "so excessive as to constitute a breach of duty," include (1) the adviser's cost in providing the service; (2) the nature and quality of the service provided; (3) the extent of economies of scale as the fund grows; (4) the volume of investor orders processed; (5) the extent to which fall-out benefits are passed on to fund shareholders; (6) the profitability of the fund to the adviser; and (7) the trustees' expertise, knowledge, and care in fulfilling their duties.

The appellate court made clear that while it ruled to dismiss the charges, its action should not be viewed to imply that it found Merrill Lynch's fees fair and reasonable. In fact, if potential fall-out benefits to Merrill Lynch had not been passed on to the shareholders, an area where the plaintiffs offered no evidence, the appellate court concluded that the fee could have violated the fiduciary duty of Merrill Lynch as the fund's adviser. The court encouraged the defendant fund's board of directors to undertake an investigation of the alleged fall-out benefits. The court implied by focusing on a single factor, fall-out benefits, that failure in any one of the seven factors was sufficient to constitute a breach of fiduciary duty. In support of its conclusion that funds do not compete on price, and if they do, it is largely irrelevant because price competition is taking place in the wrong market, the *Gartenberg* list of factors does not include fees charged by rival, comparable money market funds as relevant to determining whether a mutual fund's fees are excessive.[22]

Gartenberg's *Rejection of Competition for Investors to Ensure Competitive Pricing*

The denial of market forces affecting fees continued a long tradition in the history of mutual fund regulation. As noted in Chapter 2, the ICA of 1940 was in part a response to the perceived failures of market forces to protect closed- and open-end investment funds shareholders from abuses by the funds' sponsors. The larger backdrop at the end of the 1930s was the widespread view that open market economies were a failure, given 10 years of the Great Depression and the many unsuccessful attempts by the Roosevelt administration to renew economic growth and reduce unemployment. Numerous laws were passed to protect small businesses and consumers at both the state and federal levels from the perceived failures of capitalism. The ICA of 1940 sought to protect investors by greater regulation of mutual funds, mandating a greater role to trustees or boards of directors in protecting shareholders from exploitation by investment advisers and requiring greater information disclosure to directors and shareholders.

The mutual fund studies in the 1960s by Wharton and the SEC repeated the themes that competition could not be relied upon to protect shareholders from excessive fees and that investment advisers and mutual fund shareholders were inherently in conflict over the level of fees, requiring close regulation of the industry. The SEC's 1966 study concluded that investors were best protected from advisers by enlarging the power of independent directors to monitor fees, making it explicit that the investment adviser's fiduciary duty was to its level of compensation, and providing shareholders with the right to sue advisers for charging excessive fees.[23] The appellate court's *Gartenberg* opinion in 1982 preserved this understanding—that competition between investment advisers is nonexistent because it is uneconomical to replace an adviser, so advisers do not compete directly for mutual fund contracts.

After rejecting the potential influence of competitive market forces on fees, the appellate court set out its legal framework, based on the factors already listed, to determine when high fees are legally justified. As a consequence, judges in some subsequent cases dismissed testimony by economic experts on the role of competition in setting fees, based on the appellate court's having ruled that investment advisers seldom if ever compete with one another. As an example, the judge in *Schuyt* rejected testimony from both defendant and plaintiff economic experts on the grounds that the experts relied on a competitive market model, whereas the *Gartenberg* appellate court had already determined that investor fees were never set by price competition.[24]

Fall-out Benefits

A third dispute between the two courts occurred over the existence of fall-out benefits, whether they could be measured, and whether they were legitimate offsets to excessive fees. Rejecting the district court's view that such gains were not logically related to the fees shareholders are charged to cover the cost of running a fund, and that such benefits were virtually impossible to measure correctly, the appellate court found that fall-out benefits should be included and that they likely can be measured with sufficient accuracy given computers and modern statistical techniques. The appellate court held that the legislative history of Section 36(b) clearly established that Congress

> intended that the court look at all the facts in connection with the determination and receipt of such compensation, including all services rendered to the fund or its shareholders and all compensation and payments received, in order to reach a decision as to whether the adviser has properly acted as a fiduciary in relation to such compensation.[25]

The court concluded that fall-out benefits, "to the extent quantifiable, should be taken into account in determining whether the Manager's fee meets the standard of 36(b)."[26] In other words, is the adviser's compensation, including fall-out benefits, within the range consistent with arm's length bargaining?[27]

The appellate court's reasoning on fall-out benefits is suspect. One question is who owns this hard-to-measure stream of incremental income? The appellate court concluded without explanation that it was owned by the fund investors and could be used as an offset to investor fees. Assume that a landlord rents commercial space to a business at a fixed rate for a specific period of time. Assume that the business becomes wildly successful. Should the landlord be able to extract ex post part of the tenant's newfound income, arguing that but for the rental property location, the business would not have been as successful? Or, assume that a widely admired celebrity hires a personal trainer at a competitive price, consistent with the trainer's ability and reputation for assisting clients. Assume further that knowledge that the trainer is working with the celebrity enhances the trainer's reputation and increases demand for the trainer's services. Is the famous person entitled to extract part of the trainer's additional income by paying lower fees than originally contracted for? The district court in *Gartenberg* said no, whereas the appellate court said yes. This is fundamentally a contract issue, as are the fall-out benefits claimed by fund shareholders. If fall-out benefits are potentially significant, they will become part of the independent directors' annual fee negotiations with the investment adviser. However, in a competitive market, an adviser can only charge a competitive price for services to the fund, and shareholders can only obtain services by paying the full, competitive price. In such a setting, fall-out benefits are not a source of incremental income extracted from investors beyond an adviser's competitive rate of return.

Further Economic Issues Raised by Gartenberg

Based on the preceding discussion, whatever the legal standards underlying *Gartenberg* as precedent, such as following Congressional intent and being grounded in common law, the applicability of the court's economic reasoning on determining when fees are excessive deserves further review. As discussed, the court found that shareholder fees should be determined in a market in which investment advisory firms compete to manage retail funds' assets, a market that for practical purposes at the time was very limited, except possibly for subadvisory portfolio management services. The court claimed that the market for mutual fund investors has nothing to do with whether fees are set competitively or not, when, in fact, under competitive market conditions that is precisely where investor fees are determined—that is, in the demand and supply for mutual fund investing. The court further concluded that investors in money market mutual funds are not mobile because fees are so small to each shareholder that fees are not worth monitoring, and differences in fees are competitively insignificant, yet the court simultaneously assumed that fees may be excessive or disproportionately large.[28]

Theologians and philosophers, at least from the time of Aristotle, have debated when prices can be considered unfair, largely on moral and subjective grounds.[29] Economics, however, offers more objective guidance. Prices are excessive when they are set by an illegal monopolist or firms colluding to act as a monopolist.[30] In contrast, in the absence of monopoly, market prices are determined in a competitive market through the intersection of noncolluding rivals and reasonably well-informed consumers. Exchanges between buyers and sellers are mutually beneficial at the competitive price. At that point, sellers are able to cover their costs of supplying a product, including a competitive rate of return. A higher price, everything else equal, penalizes buyers by transferring wealth from buyers to sellers and restricts the quantity demanded relative to the competitive price, thereby misallocating resources. A lower than competitive price level penalizes sellers by forcing them to sell at a loss, and thus the low price similarly misallocates resources.

To determine if prices are unfairly high, price competition and investor sensitivity to price differences across mutual funds should be examined. Moreover, if the test on investment adviser compensation is whether the transaction produces a price equivalent to what would have occurred under arm's-length bargaining, then the test again is whether prices are set under competitive market conditions, because, as discussed, arm's-length bargaining presumes competition among sellers for buyers. The *Gartenberg* court's statement that an analysis of competition for investors between mutual funds does not satisfy whether Section 36(b) has been violated leaves lower courts to struggle with *Gartenberg's* list of factors that arguably have little bearing on whether prices are competitive or not.

The seven factors identified in *Gartenberg* as important determinants of whether fees are excessive provide little insight into the question of whether fees are at the competitive level. Most of the seven factors focus on the costs of managing a fund and thus are weighted toward a cost theory of value or pricing. The list includes the investment adviser's cost of supplying services, plus proxies for various components of that cost, including the nature and quality of investor services, the extent of economies of scale, the volume of orders processed, and any cost savings generated from fall-out benefits. The *Gartenberg* court implicitly assumed that price is determined solely by cost, ignoring demand-side factors. This led to the court's proportionality test for whether fees are excessive. This cost-based theory of value is analogous to the nineteenth century's labor theory of value, which argued that a product's value or price is determined by the cost of labor going into the production process. A cost-based pricing theory, be it labor or the extent and quality of services provided, economies of scale, processing costs, and so forth, is no more valid when applied to mutual funds than when it was used by Karl Marx to attack open market competition. Moreover, the legislative debate in the late 1960s makes clear that Congress rejected the use of Section 36(b) to impose a cost-plus standard on mutual funds,[31] yet that is precisely the framework adopted by *Gartenberg* in seeking to determine whether fees were disproportionately high relative to the cost of managing the fund. From an economics perspective, the appellate court's *Gartenberg* decision is highly selective in following Congressional intent in regard to Section 36(b).

Costs can vary across mutual funds, depending on differences in efficiency across investment advisers, but fees must be competitive to attract investments regardless of cost levels. As we discuss later, in Chapter 5, small funds waive fees more frequently and in larger percentage terms than large funds in order to remain competitive. If a start-up small fund priced according to costs, it would likely be priced out of the market. Funds price according to both costs and demand conditions based on market forces, not based on a proportionately appropriate cost-based formula as implied by the *Gartenberg* framework.

Gartenberg recommended two additional factors as determinative of whether fees are fair or disproportionately high: the profits earned by an investment adviser for managing the fund and the fund directors' expertise, knowledge, and care in performing their duties. From an economics perspective, both are largely irrelevant to assessing whether fees are excessive. Having relatively high- or low-profit rates, assuming the profit rate for a single fund among many could be measured with any semblance of accuracy, which is highly doubtful, says little about whether fees are fair, disproportionately high, or inconsistent with fees resulting from arm's-length bargaining. A monopolist can incur short-run losses, yet it remains optimal for the firm to set price above the competitive level, so above-competitive pricing is perfectly consistent with low- or negative-profit rates. More importantly for the *Gartenberg* decision, high-profit rates are perfectly consistent with fair or competitive prices. Firms in a price-competitive industry with differentiated products can earn above-competitive rates of return because of cost or demand superiority, so relatively high profit rates imply little about whether price is above the competitive level.

In addition, the expertise, information, and care used by independent trustees in performing their duties may be of the highest order, and they may unambiguously fulfill their fiduciary duties, but this exercise of duty does not necessarily ensure that price is not disproportionately high relative to the services provided, as the standard set forth in *Gartenberg* requires. For example, the appellate court held to the position that fund trustees have no, or very limited, bargaining power, so no matter how much expertise, information, and care was used, the board would be unable to influence the level of fees used to compensate the investment adviser or to prevent disproportionately high fees. Thorough effort in carrying out duties is central to fulfilling fiduciary responsibilities, but in the absence of price competition, as the appellate court concluded is the case in the mutual fund industry, prices can be above the competitive level with or without experienced, dutiful, and conscientious trustees.

Subsequent Court Decisions

From 1982 to 2008 excessive fee cases under Section 36(b) of the ICA of 1940 were largely decided based on *Gartenberg's* disproportionately high, arm's-length bargaining fee standard, in conjunction with at least some of the seven factors identified in *Gartenberg*. Interestingly, this has not proven to be an advantage for plaintiffs. In a series of cases going to trial after 1982, plaintiffs were unable to meet the excessive fee standard of proof for violation of Section 36(b) as set forth in *Gartenberg* and thus lost their claim of excessive fees.[32]

Following the mutual fund market timing and after-hours trading scandal of 2003, scores of new cases were brought against mutual funds, including renewed attempts to gain damages based on claims of excessive fees.[33] Some cases granted defendant motions for dismissal because plaintiffs did not adequately allege facts consistent with *Gartenberg's* disproportionately high fee standard,[34] but in other cases plaintiffs alleged sufficient facts to avoid a dismissal.[35]

In a significant break with the past, in 2008 the Seventh Circuit Court of Appeals rejected *Gartenberg's* interpretation of advisers' fiduciary duty under Section 36(b) to include earning only "reasonable" compensation.[36] According to the seventh circuit, based on the law of trusts, an adviser's fiduciary duty under 36(b) is to provide full disclosure and not deceive investors. It does not include determining whether advisers' fees and compensation are disproportionately high relative to some standard of reasonableness. In the seventh circuit's view, fund advisers are free to negotiate compensation with a fund's trustees without being subject to a court-imposed limit on what constitutes reasonable compensation, just as corporate executives with fiduciary duties are free to negotiate their compensation. As long as the fee negotiations are honest, with full disclosure, fee levels do not require judicial review.

In opposition to *Gartenberg*, the seventh circuit found that fund investors, not judges, are the best arbiters of whether investors are receiving sufficient value for the fees charged. If investors find their fees unjustified based on the net returns and services received, they can easily move to lower fee, close substitute mutual funds. The seventh circuit did not view Section 36(b) as a mandate from Congress for courts to regulate fees and adviser compensation by cost-plus pricing based on a judge's standard of "fair" compensation. Thus, the seventh circuit decision found that investment advisers' fees are constrained by market forces, and market forces necessitate that fees be set at competitive levels to retain existing investors and attract new investors.

Following the seventh circuit's *Jones* decision, the eighth circuit in *Gallus* disagreed with the decision to abandon *Gartenberg*, determining that both the *Jones* and *Gartenberg* decisions on assessing advisers' fiduciary duty were applicable.[37] On appeal to the U.S. Supreme Court, the Court agreed to hear the *Jones* case during its 2009–10 term to resolve the differences between deciding excessive fee cases under the *Gartenberg* and *Jones* standards.[38]

Summary and Conclusions

Without a sound economic model for determining whether fees are excessive, for courts following the *Gartenberg* precedent, a meaningful assessment of fees under Section 36(b) is doubtful. The *Gartenberg* decision does not provide an economically valid framework within which to assess whether fees are consistent with competitive market condition. *Gartenberg* rejected an analysis of competition between money market funds in determining whether fees are excessive, contrary to the approach used by the district court, on the grounds that fees can be set competitively only if funds can easily replace their investment advisers. However, if investors can switch at low cost to comparable, lower fee mutual funds, holding other factors constant, then fees are set under competitive market conditions. Given that net returns to investors on money market funds are distinguished primarily by differences in investor fees, entry into money market funds was easy, and there were at least 100 rival money market funds, and moving between money market funds entailed low transaction costs, it is difficult to understand why the *Gartenberg* court concluded that fees in money market funds are not set by competition.

Determining that investors pay no attention to mutual fund fees, *Gartenberg* listed seven factors to consider. None of the seven factors, however, has a foundation in economics for determining whether prices are excessive. Four of the seven factors are based on a fund's operating costs. The court relied on a cost-based theory of pricing, which has little basis in economics outside of certain types of regulatory rate setting or pricing contracts. In open markets, prices are determined by the interaction of supply and demand, not just the level of cost. It is also puzzling as to why the court advocated using a cost-plus basis for judging whether pricing is excessive, when the U.S. Senate in debates during 1968–1970 on amending the ICA of 1940 specifically rejected using a cost-plus approach to regulating mutual fund fees. *Gartenberg's* reliance on adviser profit rates and fund trustees' conscientiousness as indicators of excessive fees are similarly questionable because fees can be relatively high or low independent of the level of advisers' profit rates or the conscientiousness of fund trustees. Finally, *Gartenberg* relied on fee evidence from equity funds, gathered by the SEC in the 1960s, to conclude that competition between money market funds in 1981–1982 had no bearing on fees to money market fund shareholders. The use of inappropriate data further challenges the appellate court's economic reasoning and recommended framework for determining whether fees are excessive.

The seventh circuit's rejection of *Gartenberg's* view of advisers' fiduciary duty under Section 36(b) leaves open the direction to be followed in future excessive fee cases until possibly the Supreme Court's review of *Jones*. Pivotal to outcomes is whether courts follow *Gartenberg's* claim that advisers do not compete on price or follow the seventh circuit's view that investor fees and adviser compensation are best determined by market competition rather than judges' regulating adviser compensation.[39]

Given the seventh, eighth, and second circuits' conflicting views on the extent of price competition between mutual funds and the role price competition plays in determining shareholders' fees and advisers' compensation, a more rigorous economic and empirical analysis of price competition in the industry is called for. An economic foundation for such analysis along with associated empirical tests of price competition are presented in the next chapter.

CHAPTER FOUR

Price Competition and the Demand
for Mutual Funds

U
p to this point we have recounted the growth of mutual funds in the United States, the development of laws and regulations established over the last several decades that were designed to prevent the imposition of excessive fees on investors, discussed opposing district and appellate court opinions on how to judge fees and whether fees are set by competition, and presented the arguments advanced by fee critics for why current laws and regulations have failed to adequately protect investors from excessive fees. We now address directly the question of price competition and excessive fees by testing for the extent of investor sensitivity to price.

The fundamental pillars of price competition are twofold—consumer sensitivity to price and consumer choice, the ability to substitute between similar products. For example, in a pure monopoly—a firm whose products have no close substitutes—consumers are prevented from choosing between competing products. It follows that to have price competition there must be two or more noncolluding sellers. Consumers must also be sensitive to price differences between the products. If fund investors are insensitive to fund fees, as *Gartenberg* and some studies have concluded, investors are more susceptible to higher fees. However, given consumer mobility between substitute products and sensitivity to price, noncolluding rivals have no choice but to engage in price competition.[1]

Given investors' ability to switch among funds and the large number of mutual funds and fund complexes, almost all funds and complexes face multiple close substitutes. Thus, one pillar of competition, the opportunity of investors to choose among rival funds, is well established. The remaining question is whether investors are sufficiently sensitive to price that they will respond to excessive fees by substituting into a reasonably close substitute fund with a lower price. In this chapter we estimate the degree of price sensitivity of demand for United States equity mutual funds. Using these results, we simulate the dynamics of relative price, fund reputation, and market share in a simple two-complex mutual fund industry to analyze the competitive implications of our estimates of mutual fund demand price sensitivity.

Because of the technical nature of the model, statistical estimates, and simulations, the formal analytical model and estimation methodologies are available in the appendix to this chapter. This chapter presents a descriptive form of the model, along with the main empirical findings.

Prior Studies

Many mutual fund industry studies have relied on indirect tests to infer the presence or absence of price competition.[2] These tests include assessing whether (1) the trend in mutual fund expense ratios is rising even though average costs are assumed to have declined due to economies of scale in fund operations; (2) the range of investor fees as a percentage of assets is wide or narrow, under the assumption that price competition reduces the range of prices across competitors' products; and (3) retail investor mutual fund fee rates are greater than institutional investor fund rates, assuming that the products offered are comparable and that institutional rates represent a competitive benchmark (because institutional investors can fire and replace their advisers while retail funds rarely change investment advisers). Chapters 5 and 6 examine the evidence and arguments in support of these indirect tests of price competition in the mutual fund industry. Here we present our direct tests of price competition.

Studies estimating the demand for mutual funds have identified a number of factors that are associated with changes in industry demand, including the role of stock brokers,[3] past mutual fund returns,[4] mutual fund advertising,[5] and various measures of mutual fund fees and investor sales load charges. Although the areas of emphasis and variables tested differ, each study includes some measure of the price of funds or fund complexes as a key determinant of investor demand, thereby either explicitly or implicitly providing an estimate of investors' price sensitivity or "price elasticity."[6]

For the most part, prior studies estimating price sensitivity of demand measure demand either in terms of market share of assets under management for a fund or fund complex, or in terms of new money growth flowing into funds

TABLE 4.1 Implied Price Elasticity from Mutual Fund Demand Studies

Study	Implied Fund Elasticity				Implied Complex Elasticity			
	Expense Ratio	Front-end Load	12b-1 Fees	Total Fees	Expense Ratio	Front-end Load	12b-1 Fees	Total Fees
Panel A. Market Share Demand Models								
Baumol et al. (1990)	–	–	–	–2.09	–	–	–	–
Coates and Hubbard (2007)	–2.59	–	–	–	–1.73	–	–	–
Khorana and Servaes (2005)	–	–	–	–	–	–4.14	–	–4.92
Zhang (2007)	–.9.00							
Panel B. New Money Growth Demand Models								
Barber, Odean, and Zheng (2005)	–0.01	–0.05	0.01	–0.05	–	–	–	–
Bergstresser, Chalmers, and Tufano (2006)	–0.01	0.13	0.44	–	–	–	–	–
Gallaher, Kaniel, and Starks (2006)	–	–	–	–	–0.38	–0.18	–	–
Nanda, Wang, and Zheng (2004)	–0.08	–0.04	–	–	–0.05	–0.11	–	–
Sirri and Tufano (1998)	–	–	–	–0.02	–	–	–	–
Walsh (2004)	–1.68	–0.02	0.02	–	–	–	–	–
Zhang (2007)	–.3.90							
Zhao (2005)	–0.13	0.05	–0.03	–	–	–	–	–

Notes: Baumol et al. (1990) estimate a log-log model of demand for money market mutual funds. The elasticity is obtained by multiplying the negative of the yield elasticity by the ratio of fees on yield. The elasticity is computed using an expense ratio of 83 basis points and a yield of 10.64 percent, the average for their sample period, which spans 1980 to 1986. Coates and Hubbard (2007) estimate a log-log model of demand for actively managed domestic equity funds. Their sample period spans 1998 to 2004 and end-of-year cross sections are used. The elasticity is the average for all cross sections. Khorana and Servaes (2005) estimate a log-linear model of demand for open-end mutual fund complexes for the period 1979 to 1998. The elasticities are computed with sample period average excess expenses. Price elasticities for 12b-1 fees cannot be computed because average excess 12b-1 fees are not reported in the article. All of the models used to estimate the elasticities in Panel B have the same general specification; that is, new money growth is regressed on fees and other controls. For comparison purposes, the implied elasticities for flow models are 12-month elasticities, to be consistent with annual data used in stock models. These elasticities are obtained as $\varepsilon \approx T(\beta - 1/T)f$ where T is the yearly estimation frequency (monthly, quarterly or yearly), f is the average fee, and β is the estimated fee coefficient. This formula is derived by assuming negligible total net asset growth at the frequency level used and accounts for the impact of fees on net returns. Our elasticity calculations for Sirri and Tufano (1998) use the global coefficient for the

TABLE 4.1 (*continued*)

level of fees, which is different from the coefficients relating to the fee increase and fee decrease variables mentioned in their Table 1. For the fund level elasticity in Nanda, Wang and Zheng (2004), the average fund level fees are approximated by their corresponding averages at the complex level. The price elasticities in Bergstresser, Chalmers, and Tufano (2006) are calculated using the regression coefficients for both the direct and broker sold funds weighted by the total asset under management in each of the two distribution channels. Price elasticities for 12b-1 fees cannot be calculated from the information available in Gallaher, Kaniel, and Starks (2006) because mean values and standard deviations are not reported for this variable. Walsh (2004) uses a new money growth demand model but defines the expense ratio variable as the natural log of the share classes' asset value-weighted average expense ratio from the prior year. This specification properly relates percentage changes in new money growth to percentage changes in expense ratios. This yields a statistically significant elasticity consistent with results obtained in studies using market shares. In contrast, the front-end load and 12b-1 fee variables in Walsh are not specified as percentage changes and yield elasticities consistent with results obtained in the new money growth demand models. For Zhang (2007) we use price elasticities generated by his single nested model with instrumental variables, based on dependent variables of changes in market share and changes in money inflows. Zhang looks only at growth funds and restricts his sample to only positive money inflows. For Zhao (2005) we use the results of the analysis on the full sample of mutual funds (including load and no-load funds) to calculate the elasticities. Average expenses for Zhao (2005) are estimated by combining data in his Table 1 and Figure 1. Figure 1 is used to assume that roughly 35 percent of the sample's funds charge front-end load fees and 25 percent charge back-end load fees.

over some time period. Estimates of fund and complex own-price elasticities in 11 prior mutual fund demand studies are presented in Table 4.1. The studies are divided into two panels. Studies in Panel A measure demand by market share, and studies in Panel B measure demand by new money flow. The two panels produce substantially different estimates of price elasticity. Panel A studies find that demand is price-elastic, or strongly sensitive to fee levels in both funds and fund complexes. Panel B studies generally find that demand is price-inelastic and, in most cases, highly insensitive to fund and complex fee levels.[7] The results in Table 4.1 show that prior estimates of mutual fund price elasticity appear to depend on how demand is measured, either by market share or new money flows. The market share studies imply strong price competition in the mutual fund industry, whereas the new money flow studies generally imply very weak price competition.

Which measure of mutual fund demand—market share or new money growth—provides the most reliable estimate of price elasticity? Our analysis, cited below, demonstrates that the money flow demand studies are seriously flawed, yielding estimates of price elasticity that are strongly biased toward zero, which accounts for their finding that demand is insensitive to mutual fund fees.[8] Studies that measure demand by money flows estimate the relationship between the *level* of prices and *changes* in fund assets. However, this type of demand specification biases the price elasticity estimates toward zero, and the longer the time period of the estimation, the closer the price elasticity estimates are to zero. As a consequence, the studies in Panel B provide flawed and unreliable estimates of price elasticity. In contrast, the demand studies using asset shares or total assets do not suffer this estimation bias toward a zero response of demand to changes in price. These studies show that fund investors are strongly sensitive to fee levels, consistent with effective price competition among mutual fund investment advisers.

The studies in Table 4.1 generally fail to test whether certain features of mutual funds might affect fund investors' choices, specifically, choices of funds within and between fund complexes and across channels of distribution, and whether these features might affect investor sensitivity to price. Estimates of cross-price elasticities,[9] or the degree of substitutability among funds within and between complexes and across channels of distribution, are thus missing from prior studies. Cross-price elasticity estimates between funds within a complex allow one to calculate the amount of sales or assets lost due to a single fund's price increase, as well as whether assets are more likely transferred to funds within a complex or to funds in rival complexes. If all asset transfers are made to funds within the same complex, then the complex as a whole suffers far less than if all of the transferred assets are lost to rival complexes. In addition, prior studies estimate demand independent of supply changes, that is, changes in cost as sales volume increases or declines.

An Alternative Approach to Examining Competition in the Mutual Fund Industry

The studies in Table 4.1 generally do not set out a structural model of demand and supply for the mutual fund industry, starting from the fundamental economic principles that producers maximize profits and investors maximize their utility or well-being. We set out such a model.

Market Segments

In markets in which products are differentiated and consumers vary in their tastes, goods with similar characteristics or product attributes can be grouped into clusters, wherein products are closer substitutes within a cluster than across clusters. Take as an example new automobile sales. Automobiles can be clustered into various market segments, such as subcompact, high miles per gallon, low price, low horsepower, and no standard luxury features versus, say, midsize, high price, high horsepower, standard luxury features, and low miles per gallon. Automobile features and performance define the basis for product similarity and thus can be used to group automobiles with like characteristics for marketing and customer choice purposes. Competition is generally more vigorous within a market segment, such as subcompact, compact, midsize, or luxury sedan, given greater product similarity within than across market segments.

Further market segmentation takes place at the brand or company level, based on such factors as company and brand reputation, product quality, and service to customers. Continuing with the automobile example, new vehicle sales in the United States associated with a strong brand name, such as Toyota/Lexus and Honda/Acura, likely face different customer price sensitivity relative to products from, say, Kia Motors, a relatively newer and therefore currently weaker brand name in the United States.

Discrete Choice Models

Discrete choice models are well established in the fields of economics and marketing and have been used to estimate the structure of consumer demand in a variety of industries with large numbers of brands and product attributes, such as airlines, automobiles, breakfast cereals, personal computers, and pharmaceuticals.[10] The models allow testing for influences on demand both within and between various product segments. Discrete choice models use aggregate market data to examine consumer choice at the brand level. In doing so, these models estimate the probability of consumers selecting a brand when brands and consumer preferences are changing over time.[11]

The Model

Our model examines the demand for equity mutual funds using two dimensions of differentiation: (1) funds distributed by large, well-known fund complexes (the top 20–25 complexes) relative to each other and to all remaining funds and complexes as a group; and (2) channels of distribution for buying and selling mutual funds, such as through brokers or directly from funds. We select the largest complexes to segment demand based on several factors. First, the largest complexes are better known than smaller complexes, and the complex name is generally better known than the names of individual funds within the complex. Complexes promote their historical experience and funds' long-term performance as a means to build investor trust in the complex as a whole, which facilitates marketing individual funds under the umbrella of the complex's brand name.

Second, the largest complexes differentiate their products by offering investors one-stop shopping—a broad range of funds and services so that investors can achieve risk diversification, reduced transaction costs, and expected portfolio return performance wholly within the complex's investment options. If successful, this strategy builds a long-term, loyal customer base, reducing expenses due to shareholder redemptions and turnover. Third, large complexes are more likely to offer a broader range of investor services than small complexes, such as 24-hour customer service, financial counseling, and more channels of distribution.

In addition to large complexes being a principal basis for market segmentation, grouping complexes by size has an added benefit. Approximately 70 to 75 percent of equity mutual fund assets are in the top 20 to 25 complexes.[12] It follows that if price competition is absent, for example, because of investor insensitivity to price, the largest complexes should account for most of the harm to investors. In contrast, if investors are responsive to fees in the largest complexes, then claims of aggregate harm to investors from long-run excessive pricing have little merit.

Channels of distribution are the model's second dimension of differentiation. Channels serve as a proxy for different groups of investors with different demands for services. Some customers, reasonably confident in their investment ability and financial knowledge, can easily purchase shares directly from a fund or through discount, limited service brokerage houses offering hundreds of alternative funds in a "fund supermarket." Other customers, less confident in their financial knowledge and financial decision making, or without the time to manage their assets, can seek investment counseling at, for example, a bank, full-service brokerage firm, independent financial adviser, or fund complexes offering such services. The empirical question is how price sensitive investors are within a specific channel of distribution. Are direct purchasers, for example, more price sensitive than, say, investors using full-service brokers?

We allow for investors' choices among complexes, channels of distribution, and funds. To illustrate, assume there are two complexes and two distribution channels. Investors can choose between complexes A and B, and having chosen, say, complex A, investors can choose either distribution channel 1 or 2. Within the set of each complex/distribution channel, assume that there are four funds: a, b, c, and d. The funds represent different investment styles, such as large-cap growth, large-cap income, equity index funds, and so forth. At each decision point, investors make choices based on the attributes of the complexes, channels of distribution, and funds. With differentiated products, investors do not consider the alternative choices as perfect substitutes. Product attributes at the complex level might include such factors as the complex's reputation, number and quality of funds offered, and services provided to investors. Product attributes at the channel level might include services offered and ease of transactions for investors. Attributes at the fund level might include historic and recent fund performance, a fund's Morningstar rating, and annual investor fees. Our model, however, imposes no particular order on how investors make choices. Investors can choose a distribution channel first and then a complex/fund, or a complex/fund first and then a distribution channel.

Examining demand under this framework, we can estimate own-price and cross-price elasticities at the fund and complex/distribution channel levels. We can determine complex own-price elasticity by assuming the price of all funds within a complex increases by 1 or 2 percent (or more). The cross-price elasticity for a fund within a complex indicates how that fund's price change causes a transfer of assets from that fund to other funds within the complex. Similarly, we can estimate equivalent price elasticities for distribution channels.

Investor and Supplier Behavior in the Demand and Supply of Mutual Funds

Investor Behavior

We assume that fund investors act in their own self-interest, choosing funds and complexes based on price and other product attributes that maximize their utility. Given investors' specific preferences and goals for investing in mutual funds, they seek the best package of product attributes provided by funds, complexes, and channels of distribution. We thus assume that investor behavior in making mutual fund investment decisions is generally consistent with rational buyer decision making.[13]

Among the attributes widely available for review by an investor to determine whether a fund meets the investor's criteria for investing or for remaining as a shareholder are current and historic fund returns net of fees, Morningstar's fund rating (based on a fund's investor returns and risk), shareholder fees and sales loads, fund and complex reputation, number and types of funds within a complex, services to shareholders, and channels of distribution. Reputation is based on such factors as past, current, and expected fund returns; a fund's years of experience; a fund's freedom from scandal; investor services provided; and responsiveness to investors' requests. If one supplier's fees are high relative to substitute products, investors can choose the lower fee alternative. Investors are free to select complexes and funds based on the attributes and fees offered and thus are capable of substituting between funds within a complex, substituting between complexes, investing new money in alternative funds, or not investing in mutual funds.[14] Hence, investors can own funds in multiple complexes and purchase through different distribution channels.

Investment Advisers' Behavior

We further assume that investment advisory firms act in their own best interest to maximize the present value of expected profits. The question is whether advisers' attempts to maximize the present value of expected profits necessarily increase investor fees above the competitive level, as fee critics contend.

Adviser revenues come largely from mutual fund fees, which are calculated as a percent of a fund's assets, plus in some cases a percentage share of assets based on a fund's annual performance. Other things equal, the larger the fund's asset value is, the larger will be the revenues earned by the adviser. Advisers' incentives are thus generally to make their funds as attractive as possible to current and future investors.[15]

Given investors' freedom to select between complexes and funds, complexes offer a package of product and service attributes for a given price in an attempt to differentiate themselves and increase demand for their products. Because of product differentiation, each advisory firm faces its own demand schedule (the quantity demanded at different price levels) at the complex, channel, and fund level, in competition for assets and investors with other complexes, channels, and funds.[16] As profit maximizers, advisers attempt to profitably increase their revenues by growing fund assets through enhancing investor demand while minimizing their costs of producing, managing, marketing, and administering their funds. Given their understanding of rivals' products and services, and consumer preferences, investment advisers choose the level of product differentiation, marketing, and distribution to maximize profits. As rivals respond with their own offerings in products, services, and fees, advisers adjust to match or beat rivals' attempts to gain superiority through product differentiation and price competition. Advisers thus attempt to attract investors using all aspects of product, reputation, and service attributes, including fees to investors. The pattern of actions and reactions by rival advisers is more or less continuous, forcing the price per unit of attributes offered to investors toward an equilibrium level, based on the extent of product differentiation and substitutability between funds and complexes. As indicated, the question is whether the demand and supply equilibrium produced is consistent with producers offering competitive prices.

Importantly, not all investors have to switch between mutual funds to lower fee, comparable funds to keep fees at the competitive level; only the marginal investors have to switch. Given the cost structure of mutual fund complexes, the marginal investor, the last to purchase shares in a fund, represents the most profitable investor to an advisory firm. As marginal investors leave in response to price increases above the competitive level for a given level of service and performance, the price increase becomes unprofitable, disciplining the investment advisory firm to lower attribute/quality-adjusted prices to the competitive level.

The model also recognizes that competitive actions today can affect current as well as future demand for a fund and complex. If high fees today reduce current returns and market share, fund and complex reputation and brand name are affected, reducing the fund's future demand, market share, and adviser revenues.

In summary, using this model, we expect greater mutual fund substitutability within a complex and within a distribution channel. If average investor utility from a fund increases, it will have a stronger effect on the demand for other funds within the same complex or distribution channel than on the demand for funds outside the complex and distribution channel. Funds within the same market segment are thus closer substitutes for one another than funds in other market segments. Changes in the demand for funds should therefore be clustered along these two segments: complex and channel of distribution.

Estimating the Demand for Mutual Funds and Corresponding Price Elasticities

The key test of price competition in the mutual fund industry centers on the price elasticity of demand for mutual funds. Are investors relatively sensitive to price changes and price differences between funds, or not? Fee critics contend that fund investors are not sensitive to fees, and even if they are, they cannot economically switch at low cost to comparable, lower-fee funds and complexes. However, if demand estimation shows that investors are sensitive to price changes and can readily switch between funds, then investment advisers are disciplined by price competition and thus are unable to set excessive fees.

To test for the extent of price competition, we use statistical regression analysis, applied to the model described here. This allows us to estimate the relationship between the demand for U.S. equity funds, the price or fees for owning the fund, and other determinants of demand.[17] From the results we calculate price and cross-price elasticities. As discussed earlier, when demand is price-elastic, fund investors are relatively sensitive to price levels in choosing funds, consistent with price competition across mutual funds. Cross-price elasticity estimates are used to measure the extent of substitutability between funds within a complex and distribution channel, and with funds in rival complexes and channels of distribution.

We use monthly data for U.S. domestic equity funds from 2001 through 2007. Following our discussion of the demand studies in Table 4.1, we measure demand as dollar-asset market shares for each fund in the sample. At the complex level, we include individual observations of all complexes in each year that account for at least 0.85 percent of total U.S. domestic equity fund assets.

Descriptive statistics for the yearly samples are shown in Table 4.2. The number of funds in the sample varies over time, starting with 762 funds in June 2001 and ending with 1,606 funds in June 2007. The samples are dominated by the largest 23 to 25 equity complexes. The "outside good" variable shows that the top complexes accounted for approximately 76 percent of total equity fund assets in 2001 and 75 percent in 2007. The data indicate that the largest complexes more than doubled the number of funds they offered during this period. The average fund fee and weighted average complex fee in our samples changed little during this seven-year period.

As discussed, our main interest is the relationship between fund asset share and price or fees. Fund total expense ratios are used as a measure of fees. To control for other influences on fund market shares, the demand equation includes measures of current monthly returns; Morningstar's five-point scale ranking; the turnover ratio of stocks in a fund's portfolio; fund age; whether a fund's capitalization is large-, mid-, or small-cap; whether a fund is passively or actively managed; whether a fund has a deferred load charge; and the type of distribution channel(s) associated with a fund.

We include current monthly returns to account for possible short-term responses of market share to performance. On a longer-term basis, the Morningstar rankings reflect historical levels of performance and risk relative to rival funds. The stock turnover ratio indicates how actively managed a fund is and whether more transaction activity is associated with changes in market share. Fund age reflects longevity, a component of a fund's reputation, and serves as a proxy for long-term survival or the likelihood that the fund will exist when an investor wants to withdraw assets for retirement, educational purposes, or other reasons. The fund capitalization classifications indicate the sensitivity of market share to whether the fund is mid- or small-cap relative to a large-cap fund. The statistical analysis also controls for whether a fund is actively or passively managed. A variable is also included to indicate whether a deferred load charge, that is, a sales charge when fund shares are sold, is related to market share.[18]

The distribution channels we identify include *proprietary*, or funds sold through a captive sales force; *nonproprietary*, or funds sold through brokers not

TABLE 4.2 Descriptive Statistics,
June 2001–June 2007

	2001	2002	2003	2004	2005	2006	2007
Number of Complexes	23	24	25	23	23	23	25
Number of Funds	762	903	1,046	1,161	1,325	1,409	1,606
Size of Outside Good	24.16%	25.46%	25.21%	27.69%	27.97%	27.46%	25.29%
Number of Funds in Outside Good	1,968	2,309	2,614	3,155	3,478	3,588	3,588
Average Fund Share	0.09%	0.08%	0.07%	0.06%	0.05%	0.05%	0.04%
Average Fund Fee	0.013	0.014	0.014	0.014	0.013	0.013	0.013
Average Within Complex Share	2.48%	2.19%	2.08%	1.73%	1.56%	1.48%	1.41%
Average Number of Funds per Complex	40	46	48	58	64	68	71
Weighted Average Complex Fee	0.011	0.012	0.011	0.011	0.010	0.010	0.009

Note: Data are as of June 30 in each year.

affiliated with the fund's adviser; *direct*, or shares purchased by investors directly from a fund; *bank proprietary*, or shares sold primarily or exclusively by a specific bank; and *institutional*, or funds sold to institutional investors, such as pension plans, or individuals of high net worth. However, because of difficulties in accounting for all distribution channels when estimating our model, we limit the channel variable to institutional versus noninstitutional channels.

Annual estimates of fund own-price elasticities, cross-price elasticities between funds within a complex and distribution channel, cross-price elasticity with funds in outside complexes and channels, and complex and distribution channel own-price elasticity are shown in Table 4.3. They are derived from the regression results reported in Table A4.4 in the Appendix to this chapter.

Fund own-price elasticities range from approximately −2.0 to somewhat below −6.0, with one exception. All are highly statistically significant, indicating that investors are quite sensitive to price differences between funds. As an example, for June 2004 the own-price elasticity estimate for an individual fund is approximately −2.4, indicating that a 1.0 percent price increase leads to a 2.4 percent decline in a fund's market share. To illustrate, a fund that had a 1.0 percent share among all equity funds and raised its price 1.0 percent would experience a share decline to approximately 0.976 percent, other factors held constant. For the same time period, our estimate of own-price elasticity for a complex/channel, or all equity funds within a complex/channel, is approximately −2.2 percent, as shown in the last row of Table 4.3. For a 1.0 percent market share in June 2004, a 1.0 percent price increase would have resulted in an approximately 2.2 percent market share decline for the segment as a whole, or a share decline from 1.0 to 0.978 percent.

The cross-price elasticity within a complex/channel in June 2004 indicates that a fund's 1.0 percent price rise would lead to a 0.015 percent increase in the share of all other funds in the complex/channel. Similarly, the cross-price elasticity within a complex with an outside distribution channel indicates that a 1.0 percent price rise would lead to an approximately 0.02 percent increase in the share of all funds in the outside distribution channels.

The main issue of interest is whether there is sufficient mutual fund substitutability between complexes to make a noncompetitive price increase unprofitable; that is, whether price increases lead to sufficient investor switching to outside complexes to defeat a price increase. If so, fees are determined by price competition. To examine this issue more closely, we calculate the profit implication of a 1 percent price increase using the own-price and cross-price elasticity estimates generated from our regression results.

Before examining the results, consider the optimal pricing policy of a profit-maximizing adviser surrounded by close, outside substitute complexes

TABLE 4.3 Two Nested Model Price Elasticities and Product Segment Results, June 2001–June 2007

	June 2001	June 2002	June 2003	June 2004	June 2005	June 2006	June 2007
ρ_c	0.287	0.185	0.268	0.258	0.103	0.050	0.050
ρ_d	0.950	0.950	0.829	0.744	0.507	0.357	0.281
Own-Price Elasticity	−3.294	−2.819	−1.665	−2.389	−2.150	−3.128	−5.780
Within Complex / Within Distribution Channel Cross-Price Elasticity	0.063	0.028	0.019	0.015	0.006	0.023	0.034
Outside Complex / Outside Distribution Channel Cross-Price Elasticity	0.001	0.000	0.000	0.000	0.000	0.000	0.000
Outside Complex / Within Distribution Channel Cross-Price Elasticity	0.002	0.005	0.001	0.002	0.002	0.004	0.004
Within Complex / Outside Distribution Channel Cross-Price Elasticity	0.043	0.028	0.025	0.022	0.001	0.007	0.006
Total Complex / Distribution Channel Own-Price Elasticity	−2.869	−2.589	−1.482	−2.220	−2.067	−2.822	−5.260

and funds. In principle, the price will be set so that an incremental increase in price above the optimal level will just push the marginal investor to a competing complex, reducing a fund's assets and the adviser's profits. Conversely, if the price is set below the optimum level, profits are not being maximized. If a fund's price rise leads the marginal investor to an alternative fund within the same complex, total complex assets are unchanged and the most profitable investor remains within the complex, although their contribution to the complex's profits may change depending on where the assets are reinvested.

Take June 2004 again as an example. Table 4.2 shows that the average complex market share for the top complexes in June 2004 equals approximately 4.0 percent.[19] Multiplying this share by the own-price elasticity of −2.39 and adding the market share of all other complexes (96.0 percent) times the cross-price elasticity within a complex and distribution channel gives the profit implication of a −0.08 percent decline in the fund's market share. In other words, when an average fund in June 2004 increases fees by 1.0 percent, the total assets of the funds within the complex and distribution channel decrease by an estimated 0.08 percent.

The profit implications by month over the sample period are shown in Table 4.4. The last column in Table 4.4 displays the total asset share implication of a 1 percent price increase in each month in our data set. For June 2004, the profit implication shows a share decline of −0.027.[20] Thus, the most profitable investors are lost to outside complexes for the given price increase, making the price increase unprofitable. As seen in the last column of the table, the total profit implication of a price rise is a decline in asset share each month over the sample period, indicating lower profits for advisers. These results support the view that mutual funds' advisers are pricing optimally, and from this competitive outcome, an incremental price increase will result in investors switching to rival complexes and therefore to a loss in adviser profits.

A distinct feature of our analysis is the ability to estimate directly the extent of product differentiation or substitutability within a demand segment. As products within a segment become more similar, competition becomes more segmented or localized within segments in response to changes in market conditions, such as price movements. Thus, the less products are differentiated within a segment, the greater the extent of substitutability and the higher the cross-price elasticity. As we show in the Appendix, Rho C and Rho D in Table 4.4 measure the similarity between funds within complexes and distribution channels. The trend in these two measures shows that complexes and distribution channels became more segmented over the sample period, with greater segmentation occurring within complexes.

TABLE 4.4 Profit Implications for a 1 Percent Price Rise, Using Estimated Own-Price and Cross-Price Elasticities

Month	Rho C (1-sigma)	Rho D	Average Fees	Own-Price Elasticity	Within Complex / Within Distribution Channel Cross Price Elasticity	Outside Complex / Outside Distribution Channel Cross Price Elasticity	Outside Complex / Within Distribution Channel Cross Price Elasticity	Within Complex / Outside Distribution Channel Cross Price Elasticity
April-01	0.2684	0.9500	0.0130	−3.0809	0.070834	0.000249	0.004268	0.039278
May-01	0.2142	0.9500	0.0129	−3.1702	0.058009	0.000241	0.006231	0.034476
June-01	0.2869	0.9500	0.0129	−3.2943	0.063046	0.000580	0.002304	0.043222
July-01	0.2244	0.9500	0.0131	−3.3033	0.078835	0.000221	0.006004	0.032726
Aug-01	0.2450	0.9500	0.0131	−3.2458	0.081591	0.000274	0.006366	0.028725
Sept-01	0.2738	0.9500	0.0130	−3.2057	0.064054	0.000445	0.003227	0.036617
Oct-01	0.2353	0.9500	0.0132	−2.8948	0.041672	0.000270	0.003030	0.026755
Nov-01	0.2194	0.9500	0.0131	−2.8974	0.044490	0.000361	0.002474	0.028092
Dec-01	0.2025	0.9500	0.0131	−2.8449	0.042536	0.000343	0.002025	0.026104
Jan-02	0.1633	0.9500	0.0133	−3.0605	0.044946	0.000297	0.002910	0.018419
Feb-02	0.1925	0.9500	0.0137	−2.8578	0.028125	0.000304	0.006258	0.019331
March-02	0.3346	0.6984	0.0135	−3.2170	0.051886	0.000532	0.007132	0.029293
April-02	0.2009	0.9500	0.0135	−2.8519	0.030169	0.000252	0.005536	0.028038
May-02	0.1978	0.9500	0.0135	−2.7391	0.029728	0.000218	0.005177	0.030782

(continued)

TABLE 4.4 (continued)

Month	Rho C (1-sigma)	Rho D	Average Fees	Own-Price Elasticity	Within Complex / Within Distribution Channel Cross Price Elasticity	Outside Complex / Outside Distribution Channel Cross Price Elasticity	Outside Complex / Within Distribution Channel Cross Price Elasticity	Within Complex / Outside Distribution Channel Cross Price Elasticity
June-02	0.1850	0.9500	0.0135	−2.8189	0.027878	0.000248	0.004903	0.028113
July-02	0.1763	0.9500	0.0135	−2.7282	0.032404	0.000195	0.007462	0.012257
Aug-02	0.1631	0.9500	0.0135	−2.6176	0.024613	0.000294	0.006236	0.010272
Sept-02	0.1605	0.9500	0.0136	−2.8366	0.031425	0.000221	0.005468	0.011581
Oct-02	0.2278	0.9500	0.0137	−2.5459	0.029062	0.000074	0.008852	0.012109
Nov-02	0.1931	0.9500	0.0137	−2.4183	0.029036	0.000083	0.005722	0.010871
Dec-02	0.1899	0.9500	0.0138	−2.4081	0.029564	0.000087	0.005805	0.010719
Jan-03	0.1756	0.9500	0.0137	−2.2511	0.024391	0.000069	0.004905	0.008834
Feb-03	0.1375	0.9500	0.0140	−1.8734	0.019191	0.000042	0.001501	0.025574
March-03	0.1363	0.9500	0.0140	−1.8153	0.021149	0.000052	0.000861	0.024695
April-03	0.1163	0.9500	0.0141	−2.0806	0.024898	0.000053	0.001193	0.028852
May-03	0.1675	0.9500	0.0141	−1.8777	0.020177	0.000041	0.000720	0.025451
June-03	0.2680	0.8292	0.0140	−1.6652	0.018840	0.000067	0.000953	0.025018
July-03	0.2161	0.8491	0.0141	−1.8384	0.010993	0.000060	0.001115	0.026092
Aug-03	0.1098	0.9500	0.0140	−2.3382	0.019058	0.000057	0.001650	0.033283

Sept-03	0.1146	0.9500	0.0140	−2.3119	0.019225	0.000057	0.001365	0.032760
Oct-03	0.1567	0.7937	0.0140	−1.8404	0.010055	0.000059	0.001241	0.029569
Nov-03	0.1411	0.8440	0.0140	−1.6560	0.010657	0.000047	0.001154	0.026091
Dec-03	0.0500	0.8647	0.0140	−1.6539	0.016567	0.000050	0.001524	0.027679
Jan-04	0.2896	0.7820	0.0139	−1.8252	0.011221	0.000079	0.001154	0.009546
Feb-04	0.2735	0.7742	0.0137	−2.0569	0.012486	0.000088	0.001230	0.011267
March-04	0.2529	0.7884	0.0137	−1.9401	0.010377	0.000080	0.001104	0.010507
April-04	0.2469	0.7594	0.0137	−2.4042	0.014581	0.000126	0.001575	0.021630
May-04	0.2300	0.7729	0.0137	−2.3209	0.013635	0.000117	0.001530	0.020812
June-04	0.2580	0.7436	0.0137	−2.3891	0.015380	0.000133	0.001604	0.021954
July-04	0.0500	0.6028	0.0138	−2.1599	0.011486	0.000047	0.001639	0.025867
Aug-04	0.0500	0.4859	0.0138	−1.8942	0.009399	0.000035	0.001835	0.025030
Sept-04	0.0500	0.4381	0.0138	−2.1880	0.008205	0.000033	0.002139	0.025395
Oct-04	0.2012	0.5064	0.0138	−2.5009	0.026893	0.000080	0.002050	0.026725
Nov-04	0.2140	0.5432	0.0138	−2.5322	0.026991	0.000094	0.002163	0.026388
Dec-04	0.1841	0.5125	0.0138	−2.6727	0.033219	0.000089	0.002033	0.027966
Jan-05	0.0948	0.5235	0.0137	−2.0434	0.013407	0.000033	0.001483	0.027104
Feb-05	0.1615	0.4119	0.0133	−3.2249	0.025169	0.000126	0.003099	0.032437
March-05	0.1667	0.4011	0.0133	−3.1418	0.025023	0.000113	0.002695	0.031845
April-05	0.1255	0.4702	0.0133	−2.2353	0.009051	0.000026	0.001510	0.003274
May-05	0.1232	0.4367	0.0133	−2.2072	0.010637	0.000020	0.001476	0.003323

(continued)

TABLE 4.4 *(continued)*

Month	Rho C (1-sigma)	Rho D	Average Fees	Own-Price Elasticity	Within Complex / Within Distribution Channel Cross Price Elasticity	Outside Complex / Outside Distribution Channel Cross Price Elasticity	Outside Complex / Within Distribution Channel Cross Price Elasticity	Within Complex / Outside Distribution Channel Cross Price Elasticity
June-05	0.1031	0.5073	0.0133	−2.1496	0.006490	0.000028	0.001609	0.001113
July-05	0.0741	0.4028	0.0133	−2.0502	0.015652	0.000040	0.001997	0.001253
Aug-05	0.0819	0.4242	0.0133	−2.2188	0.010644	0.000049	0.002105	0.001478
Sept-05	0.0789	0.4172	0.0133	−2.3266	0.012006	0.000054	0.002328	0.001505
Oct-05	0.0500	0.6989	0.0134	−2.8452	0.012244	0.000092	0.002703	0.000380
Nov-05	0.0500	0.6786	0.0134	−2.8586	0.015295	0.000092	0.002907	0.000364
Dec-05	0.0500	0.6353	0.0134	−2.6825	0.017783	0.000083	0.002895	0.000316
Jan-06	0.0500	0.4870	0.0133	−2.2363	0.011509	0.000027	0.003110	0.000694
Feb-06	0.0500	0.4504	0.0130	−2.6881	0.013902	0.000029	0.003091	0.007826
March-06	0.0500	0.3592	0.0130	−3.0934	0.017579	0.000021	0.003227	0.006628
April-06	0.0500	0.3628	0.0130	−2.8730	0.015274	0.000021	0.003062	0.006556
May-06	0.0500	0.3619	0.0130	−2.5742	0.014169	0.000019	0.002928	0.004717
June-06	0.0500	0.3572	0.0131	−3.1280	0.022674	0.000024	0.003502	0.006793
July-06	0.0500	0.3508	0.0131	−3.1986	0.020871	0.000021	0.003009	0.005904
Aug-06	0.0500	0.3643	0.0130	−2.7737	0.018264	0.000023	0.002991	0.006576

Sept-06	0.0500	0.3544	0.0130	−3.0077	0.010278	0.000021	0.002930	0.005159
Oct-06	0.0500	0.3613	0.0131	−2.9614	0.012963	0.000021	0.002600	0.005595
Nov-06	0.0500	0.3442	0.0131	−3.2318	0.011589	0.000021	0.002896	0.006752
Dec-06	0.0500	0.3039	0.0132	−4.3439	0.036634	0.000021	0.003110	0.003217
Jan-07	0.0500	0.2813	0.0131	−5.2381	0.077548	0.000019	0.002928	0.011387
Feb-07	0.0500	0.2854	0.0131	−5.5984	0.047855	0.000021	0.002694	0.006608
March-07	0.0500	0.2975	0.0130	−4.9141	0.033737	0.000034	0.003385	0.012208
April-07	0.0500	0.2963	0.0130	−4.9232	0.033568	0.000034	0.003357	0.013285
May-07	0.0500	0.2989	0.0130	−4.8594	0.034733	0.000033	0.003375	0.013138
June-07	0.0500	0.2810	0.0130	−5.7801	0.033548	0.000022	0.003566	0.005596
July-07	0.0500	0.2682	0.0130	−6.2360	0.041601	0.000022	0.003389	0.005562
Aug-07	0.0500	0.2801	0.0130	−5.8910	0.033637	0.000023	0.003408	0.005212
Sept-07	0.0500	0.2874	0.0129	−5.1963	0.030011	0.000021	0.002632	0.010138
Oct-07	0.0500	0.2796	0.0129	−5.5572	0.039344	0.000021	0.002637	0.011771
Nov-07	0.0500	0.2568	0.0129	−6.9026	0.030272	0.000018	0.002253	0.014386
Dec-07	0.0500	0.9500	0.0128	−2.8199	0.002337	0.000025	0.000300	0.000944
Average	0.1359	0.6514	0.0134	−2.9770	0.026670	0.000108	0.002998	0.016862
Median	0.1255	0.6984	0.0133	−2.7391	0.022674	0.000057	0.002703	0.013138

(continued)

TABLE 4.4 (*continued*)
Profit Implications for a 1 Percent Price Rise, Using Estimated Own-Price and Cross-Price Elasticities

Month	Total Complex / Distribution Channel Own-Price Elasticity	N	Distribution Channels	Complexes	Within Complex / Distribution Channel Average Market Share	Profit Implication for Within Complex, Within Distribution Channel	Profit Implication for Within Complex, Outside Distribution Channel	Total Profit Implication for the Complex
April-01	-2.58508	785	4	23	11.72%	-0.2985%	0.0393%	-0.0452%
May-01	-2.77865	765	4	23	12.03%	-0.3302%	0.0345%	-0.0567%
June-01	-2.86873	762	4	23	12.07%	-0.3423%	0.0432%	-0.0532%
July-01	-2.73174	810	4	23	11.36%	-0.3053%	0.0327%	-0.0518%
August-01	-2.65427	809	4	23	11.37%	-0.2968%	0.0287%	-0.0527%
September-01	-2.74126	801	4	23	11.49%	-0.3115%	0.0366%	-0.0504%
October-01	-2.56144	885	4	23	10.40%	-0.2636%	0.0268%	-0.0458%
November-01	-2.55258	860	4	23	10.70%	-0.2702%	0.0281%	-0.0465%
December-01	-2.51525	861	4	23	10.69%	-0.2660%	0.0261%	-0.0469%
January-02	-2.70091	883	4	24	10.87%	-0.2927%	0.0184%	-0.0594%
February-02	-2.61873	931	4	24	10.31%	-0.2695%	0.0193%	-0.0529%
March-02	-2.80191	870	4	24	11.03%	-0.3088%	0.0293%	-0.0552%
April-02	-2.60305	904	4	24	10.62%	-0.2759%	0.0280%	-0.0479%
May-02	-2.49382	901	4	24	10.65%	-0.2653%	0.0308%	-0.0432%
June-02	-2.58887	903	4	24	10.63%	-0.2748%	0.0281%	-0.0476%

July-02	-2.45273	4	931	24	10.31%	-0.2523%	0.0123%	-0.0539%
August-02	-2.40841	4	922	24	10.41%	-0.2505%	0.0103%	-0.0549%
September-02	-2.56945	4	933	24	10.29%	-0.2637%	0.0116%	-0.0572%
October-02	-2.26983	4	1009	24	9.51%	-0.2159%	0.0121%	-0.0449%
November-02	-2.14250	4	1009	24	9.51%	-0.2038%	0.0109%	-0.0428%
December-02	-2.13462	4	1005	24	9.55%	-0.2033%	0.0107%	-0.0428%
January-03	-2.02552	4	993	25	10.07%	-0.2048%	0.0088%	-0.0446%
February-03	-1.69107	4	1012	25	9.88%	-0.1678%	0.0256%	-0.0228%
March-03	-1.61443	4	1011	25	9.89%	-0.1605%	0.0247%	-0.0216%
April-03	-1.83780	4	1051	25	9.51%	-0.1754%	0.0289%	-0.0222%
May-03	-1.67591	4	1065	25	9.39%	-0.1580%	0.0255%	-0.0204%
June-03	-1.48150	4	1046	25	9.56%	-0.1422%	0.0250%	-0.0168%
July-03	-1.72849	4	1075	25	9.30%	-0.1610%	0.0261%	-0.0207%
August-03	-2.15241	4	1053	25	9.50%	-0.2048%	0.0333%	-0.0262%
September-03	-2.12448	4	1054	25	9.49%	-0.2019%	0.0328%	-0.0259%
October-03	-1.73485	4	1109	25	9.02%	-0.1568%	0.0296%	-0.0170%
November-03	-1.54411	4	1108	25	9.03%	-0.1398%	0.0261%	-0.0154%
December-03	-1.47993	4	1106	25	9.04%	-0.1345%	0.0277%	-0.0129%
January-04	-1.70739	4	1114	23	8.26%	-0.1404%	0.0095%	-0.0280%
February-04	-1.92584	4	1106	23	8.32%	-0.1597%	0.0113%	-0.0315%
March-04	-1.83118	4	1109	23	8.30%	-0.1514%	0.0105%	-0.0300%

(continued)

TABLE 4.4 (continued)

Month	Total Complex / Distribution Channel Own-Price Elasticity	N	Distribution Channels	Complexes	Within Complex / Distribution Channel Average Market Share	Profit Implication for Within Complex, Within Distribution Channel	Profit Implication for Within Complex, Outside Distribution Channel	Total Profit Implication for the Complex
April-04	−2.24380	1163	4	23	7.91%	−0.1768%	0.0216%	−0.0280%
May-04	−2.17093	1164	4	23	7.90%	−0.1709%	0.0208%	−0.0271%
June-04	−2.21995	1161	4	23	7.92%	−0.1752%	0.0220%	−0.0273%
July-04	−2.02785	1210	4	23	7.60%	−0.1536%	0.0259%	−0.0190%
August-04	−1.79083	1165	4	23	7.90%	−0.1409%	0.0250%	−0.0165%
September-04	−2.09773	1169	4	23	7.87%	−0.1646%	0.0254%	−0.0221%
October-04	−2.19835	1195	4	23	7.70%	−0.1677%	0.0267%	−0.0219%
November-04	−2.22858	1195	4	23	7.70%	−0.1700%	0.0264%	−0.0227%
December-04	−2.29900	1197	4	23	7.69%	−0.1748%	0.0280%	−0.0227%
January-05	−1.88587	1240	4	23	7.42%	−0.1392%	0.0271%	−0.0145%
February-05	−2.92288	1261	4	23	7.30%	−0.2119%	0.0324%	−0.0287%
March-05	−2.84149	1263	4	23	7.28%	−0.2057%	0.0318%	−0.0275%
April-05	−2.11986	1322	4	23	6.96%	−0.1471%	0.0033%	−0.0343%
May-05	−2.07156	1326	4	23	6.94%	−0.1432%	0.0033%	−0.0333%

June-05	−2.06690	1325	4	23	6.94%	−0.1432%	0.0011%	−0.0350%
July-05	−1.84277	1381	4	23	6.66%	−0.1220%	0.0013%	−0.0296%
August-05	−2.07782	1381	4	23	6.66%	−0.1379%	0.0015%	−0.0334%
September-05	−2.16748	1375	4	23	6.69%	−0.1445%	0.0015%	−0.0350%
October-05	−2.67379	1443	4	23	6.38%	−0.1699%	0.0004%	−0.0422%
November-05	−2.64452	1445	4	23	6.37%	−0.1677%	0.0004%	−0.0416%
December-05	−2.43358	1446	4	23	6.36%	−0.1540%	0.0003%	−0.0383%
January-06	−2.08950	1330	4	23	6.92%	−0.1440%	0.0007%	−0.0355%
February-06	−2.51081	1337	5	23	8.60%	−0.2185%	0.0078%	−0.0374%
March-06	−2.86483	1367	5	23	8.41%	−0.2441%	0.0066%	−0.0435%
April-06	−2.67063	1370	5	23	8.39%	−0.2272%	0.0066%	−0.0402%
May-06	−2.38644	1378	5	23	8.35%	−0.2018%	0.0047%	−0.0366%
June-06	−2.82189	1409	5	23	8.16%	−0.2345%	0.0068%	−0.0415%
July-06	−2.91680	1410	5	23	8.16%	−0.2417%	0.0059%	−0.0436%
August-06	−2.52712	1407	5	23	8.17%	−0.2099%	0.0066%	−0.0367%
September-06	−2.86635	1430	5	23	8.04%	−0.2324%	0.0052%	−0.0424%
October-06	−2.77347	1491	5	24	8.05%	−0.2264%	0.0056%	−0.0408%
November-06	−3.06373	1489	5	24	8.06%	−0.2498%	0.0068%	−0.0446%
December-06	−3.80352	1528	5	24	7.85%	−0.3074%	0.0032%	−0.0589%
January-07	−4.07490	1549	5	25	8.07%	−0.3514%	0.0114%	−0.0612%

(continued)

TABLE 4.4 (continued)

Month	Total Complex / Distribution Channel Own-Price Elasticity	N	Distribution Channels	Complexes	Within Complex / Distribution Channel Average Market Share	Profit Implication for Within Complex, Within Distribution Channel	Profit Implication for Within Complex, Outside Distribution Channel	Total Profit Implication for the Complex
February-07	−4.88053	1541	4	25	6.49%	−0.3185%	0.0066%	−0.0747%
March-07	−4.39959	1575	4	25	6.35%	−0.2804%	0.0122%	−0.0609%
April-07	−4.41132	1579	4	25	6.33%	−0.2804%	0.0133%	−0.0601%
May-07	−4.32976	1577	4	25	6.34%	−0.2756%	0.0131%	−0.0590%
June-07	−5.26010	1606	4	25	6.23%	−0.3284%	0.0056%	−0.0779%
July-07	−5.58080	1616	4	25	6.19%	−0.3469%	0.0056%	−0.0825%
August-07	−5.36121	1614	4	25	6.20%	−0.3334%	0.0052%	−0.0795%
September-07	−4.71615	1644	4	25	6.08%	−0.2879%	0.0101%	−0.0644%
October-07	−4.92774	1648	4	25	6.07%	−0.3003%	0.0118%	−0.0662%
November-07	−6.41825	1651	4	25	6.06%	−0.3896%	0.0144%	−0.0866%
December-07	−2.78542	1515	4	23	6.07%	−0.1690%	0.0009%	−0.0416%
Average	−2.688829	1203	4	24	8.52%	−0.2222%	0.0169%	−0.0410%
Median	−2.510814	1169	4	23	8.17%	−0.2099%	0.0131%	−0.0416%

Our remaining statistical results indicate that mutual fund market shares tend to be greater when a fund has the maximum Morningstar rating of 5 (or 4 in some years); the longer the fund has been in business; and for the 2004–2007 period, when a fund has a deferred load charge. Current monthly return, the turnover ratio, capitalization size, and whether a fund is passively managed are not statistically significantly related to market share. The channel variable results indicate that funds in institutional channels tend to have smaller market shares. Not surprisingly, the best performing funds, with the greatest experience, tend to grow relative to rivals and have higher market shares.

Simulations of the Model

To analyze price competition in the mutual fund industry in more detail, we use our price elasticity estimates and simulate a simple model of the industry. This allows for a closer examination of how price changes might take place over time within the mutual fund industry. The simulation generates a time path of rival mutual funds' relative prices, reputations, and market shares. The results are generated under different scenarios: (1) no expected economies of scale, (2) expected economies of scale, (3) expected equal investor returns across complexes, (4) expected unequal investor returns, and (4) with and without product differentiation.

Among the questions we address are the following:

1. Will advisers expecting higher relative returns for investors set higher relative prices because of expected greater demand for their funds?
2. Will higher investor prices tend to negate superior returns to investors?
3. When expected high investor returns decline to the market average, does a fund's price remain above the industry average price due to a lack of price competition and investor inertia?
4. Do advisers' price schedules reflect cost reductions generated by economies of scale?

To construct a workable model for simulation purposes, we make some simplifying assumptions. First, we set aside the choice of distribution channel and limit investors to choices based on complex and fund. Second, we focus on advisers' schedules of fees, holding other product attributes constant, such as services to investors. Third, rather than attempt to simulate day-to-day competitive outcomes, we examine market outcomes over a long time period, assuming zero salvage value at the end of the period. As noted, choices in one period are assumed to affect choices in future periods.[21]

In a world of uncertain market outcomes, assuming mutual fund advisers' price choices are interconnected is not unrealistic. As discussed in the Introduction, mutual fund fees are not perfectly free to move up as demand and cost conditions change. Federal regulations constrain upward price movements by requiring that a proposed price increase above the level stated in a fund's prospectus be approved by the fund's shareholders. As such, advisers must establish a fee schedule applicable over some time horizon that is expected to maximize the present value of their profits. If they set initial fees too high, constraining sales, they can easily be reduced. However, if they set initial fees too low, they forego future income.

To illustrate, consider a world with no mutual funds. A pioneering investment adviser comes along and creates the first open-end mutual fund. Assume the first entrant expects to be a monopolist (for whatever reasons), facing no close substitute products. Assume further that existing U.S. mutual fund price regulations are in place, requiring the approval of the fund shareholders to increase price. Given that future price increases above the initially set level are unlikely, the monopolist selects a price schedule based on expected demand that will maximize the present value of expected profits over the life of the fund.

In our model, instead of one advisory firm entering as a monopolist, we consider two advisers entering simultaneously. The industry consists of two fund complexes, A and B, each with two funds 1 and 2. The funds and complexes are differentiated to some degree, with, for example, different fund investment styles, such as a growth fund and an income fund, so the complexes and funds are not perfect substitutes. The sales strategy of a fund complex is multidimensional, including such components as product positioning, prices charged, product innovation, breadth of funds offered, and choice of targeted investors. Complexes invest in achieving higher returns to enhance their reputation and satisfy customers. Reputation is based on historical and current returns to investors, and all other attributes valued by investors. As noted, if high fees in one year reduce returns in that year, those fees affect a fund's reputation for earning high returns in the future and thus reduce future demand for the fund's shares. Advisers set a price to maximize profits given their expected costs and their rivals' fees and product offerings. Investors can substitute between funds, both within and across complexes, as they seek to maximize their utility through asset diversification and higher returns for a given level of risk.

We examine three scenarios: (1) there is no product differentiation, the complexes have identical reputations, and the complexes' advisers expect to earn equal returns for investors; (2) one complex expects to achieve higher gross returns and greater initial size than its rival, and thus differentiates its product based on a reputation for higher returns, but there are no expected economies of scale; and (3) this is the same as scenario 2, but with expected economies of scale for the higher-return, larger-size complex. We compare the empirical results with respect to price, performance reputation, and asset size over the expected time horizon.

The first scenario represents the textbook perfectly competitive outcome, with identical results across all firms. A fourth scenario would represent the monopoly case, as discussed earlier, in the same spirit as studies arguing that each mutual fund investment adviser charges excessive fees. Relative to the competitive outcome, investors in the monopoly adviser's funds pay "excessive" fees.

Given the monopoly case, under what conditions will price and nonprice competition emerge, driving fees for a given set of product attributes toward the competitive level? One prerequisite is a second (noncolluding) investment adviser offering a rival set of mutual funds. If we have two investment advisers seeking to offer a set of fund and complex attributes (including fee levels) that best match the preferences of fund investors, then the framework for competition exists. As stated, in our model, the investment advisers set a fee schedule expected to maximize their long-term profits given their products' attributes and the attributes and fee schedule of their rival.

Simulation Results

In the first scenario, with homogeneous products, equal returns and therefore equal reputations for returns, the complexes have equal costs, face equal investor demand, and charge equal fees to investors, splitting the market with 50 percent market shares. Without one complex and fund having a performance and product differentiation advantage, funds charge the same price and have no competitive advantage over rival funds, leading to equality in fees. Price is driven to the competitive level.

In the second scenario, which examines how rivals react when one fund expects superior returns, we assume complex A expects superior performance relative to complex B over a six-year time period. The time horizon for superior returns is limited because complex A believes it cannot exceed its benchmark target return indefinitely. Assuming no expected economies of scale, fund 1 in complex A generates higher gross returns than fund 1 in complex B, with complex A's fund 1 returns first rising relative to complex B's fund 1 and then declining to equal those of complex B's fund 1 over a six-year time period. As shown below, complex A's fund 1 market share is initially approximately six times larger than that of fund 1 in complex B, but declines as its return performance advantage over complex B declines until the total market is split

50-50. Complex A initially expects to gain a substantial reputation or goodwill advantage over complex B, based on superior performance. Under these conditions, the profit-maximizing outcome shows that the higher return fund can charge higher fees than its rival based on greater expected investor demand for higher return funds.

The simulation results for the second scenario are graphically displayed in Figure 4.1A. The upper line depicts complex A's goodwill superiority relative to complex B, based on expected superior performance. The next lower line shows complex A's fee schedule relative to complex B's fee schedule. With no expected economies of scale, the complexes have equal marginal costs, the third line down. Complex A's fund 1 sets higher prices than complex B's fund 1, with the price differential persisting over the six-year period of expected unequal returns, but narrowing sharply after the funds' returns equalize in year 6. Complex A's fund 1 maintains a price schedule advantage over complex B for a few years after returns are equalized based on its past reputation for superior performance, and its goodwill advantage lingers long after returns are equalized in year 6. Thus, while expected performance superiority declines over time, adjustments in investor demand for the fund lag behind changes in actual returns to investors, based on the fund and complex's past reputation for superior performance.

The market share advantage of complex A, based on A's expected higher returns, as seen in Figure 4.1B, declines rapidly as the expected performance differential narrows, so that by approximately year 7 the two complexes' shares are approximately equal.

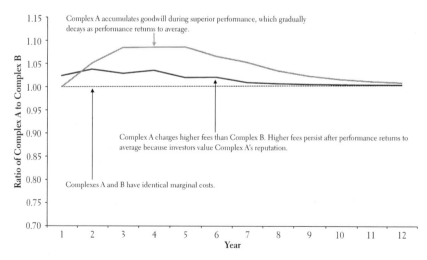

FIGURE 4.1A Simulation Results: Changes in Relative Costs, Fees, and Goodwill

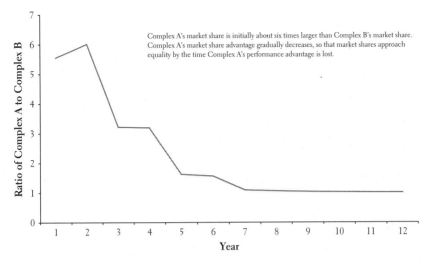

FIGURE 4.1B Simulation Results: Changes in Relative Market Shares

To summarize the second scenario simulation results, fund investors have a higher demand and are willing to pay more for funds with expected above-average returns and for funds with a reputation for above-average returns. Thus, variation in relative fees across mutual funds reflects in part differences in demand according to the product attributes offered by rival funds.

If reputational superiority outlasts superiority in actual returns because of investor expectations, funds with a reputation for strong performance might sustain a somewhat higher than industry average price for a time based on past performance, even after performance reverts to the average level, as investors expect funds to regain their past return superiority. In time, however, with equal returns across funds, outdated reputation advantages disappear. The results are consistent with investor sensitivity to differences in funds' performance. With product differentiation through differences in returns to investors, a price advantage remains for a time, but then disappears as returns equalize at the competitive level.

In the third scenario, complex A expects to gain lower costs through economies of scale. With economies of scale, the marginal cost of complex A is initially substantially lower than that of complex B. Again, complex A's fund 1 earns above average returns over a six-year period and starts with a market share approximately six times larger than that of complex B. The results are depicted in Figure 4.2A, which again show that complex A's fund 1 has a relative reputation advantage during the period of expected superior performance.

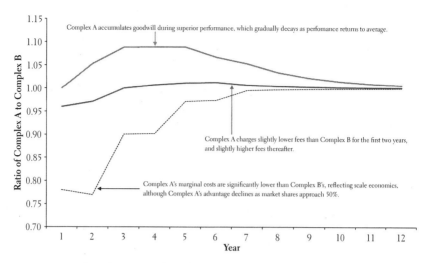

FIGURE 4.2A Simulation Results: Changes in Relative Costs, Fees, and Goodwill

However, in this case, the results show that complex A sets its profit-maximizing fees somewhat lower than its rival in the first two years of competition, followed by slightly higher fees until the two funds' fees are equalized. Fees relative to the lower return fund never rise as high as they did when there were no economies of scale, indicating that as advisers compete on price in the presence of economies of scale, fees decline with cost decreases. Complex A's fund 1 fees are lower than those of complex B's fund 1 in the first two years of economies of scale, as complex A builds its investor and asset base through low fees and relatively high investor returns, creating a reputation for high returns. Figure 4.2A shows that the higher return fund's fees are never more than slightly above its rival's fees, indicating that the ability of a higher return fund and complex to raise price is limited by product substitution and price competition. Figure 4.2B shows, as did Figure 4.1B, that complex A's market share advantage declines sharply as it loses its returns performance advantage.

The results in the third scenario show that with economies of scale, complexes with expected above-average performance have an incentive to reduce fees to attract investors and increase growth and market share. With lower fees, a complex earns higher profits by attracting more assets at lower incremental costs. Price differences between the funds, however, are constrained by investor demand and the ability to substitute between funds. Importantly, these results are inconsistent with the claims of fee critics that economies of scale are captured solely by a fund's investment adviser and that mutual fund fees are never reduced due to the lack of price competition. As in the second

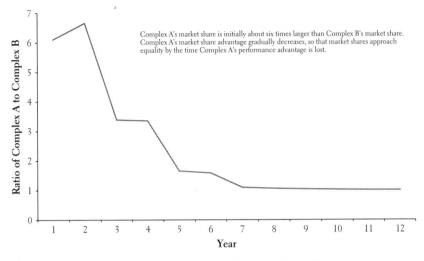

The chart contains the following annotation:

Complex A's market share is initially about six times larger than Complex B's market share. Complex A's market share advantage gradually decreases, so that market shares approach equality by the time Complex A's performance advantage is lost.

FIGURE 4.2B Simulation Results: Changes in Relative Market Shares

scenario, when returns are equalized, prices move toward the competitive benchmark level.

In summary, our results show that with investors' sensitivity to fees and their ability to substitute across complexes and funds, investment advisers must offer products with a desirable set of product attributes and fees to compete effectively. Prices and reputations differ based on performance and product attributes. Nevertheless, prices are always close to the competitive level.

Summary and Conclusions

If fund investors paid little attention to fees, the price elasticity of investor demand for mutual funds would be highly inelastic. We find that investor demand is significantly price-elastic, indicating that investors are sensitive to the fees they face and move their assets to minimize price for a given level of product and service quality and fund performance, consistent with effective price competition between mutual funds.

A more detailed test of price competition examines price changes through both own-price and cross-price elasticity effects. This more extensive analysis explores substitution effects between rival products when price increases and whether substitution ensures the existence of price competition. We examine whether the average U.S. equity fund in the top 20 to 25 complexes can profitably raise price given price-elastic demand for mutual funds and the extent of cross-price elasticity between funds within and between fund complexes. If a price increase results in sufficient lost sales to rival complexes, the price increase is not profitable. The most profitable investors for advisers shift to rival complexes. Using own-price and cross-price elasticity estimates derived from our demand model for the period 2001 to 2007, we find sufficient substitutability between complexes to make a fund's noncompetitive price rise unprofitable. Contrary to fee critics, equity mutual funds in the largest U.S. complexes are not free to raise price independently of rivals: Any such attempt will soon be disciplined by a loss of market share and profits to rival fund complexes.[22]

Our results using a simulation methodology are consistent with the view that firms in the mutual fund industry compete on price for investor assets and grow market share by building goodwill through superior performance. These actions are the result of competitive pressures from rivals' pricing and performance, which in turn result from investors' sensitivity to price and their ability to move assets among mutual funds and fund complexes. Investor demand varies according to funds' performance, as do investor fees, consistent with price competition between funds.

CHAPTER FIVE

Mutual Fund Industry Structure and Indicators of Price Competition

Industry Structure

As discussed in Chapter 3, the 1982 *Gartenberg* decision relied on the 1966 conclusion of the Securities and Exchange Commission (SEC) that equity mutual funds do not compete on price. Similarly, Congressional debates from 1968 to 1970 concerning proposed legislation to guard against excessive mutual fund investor fees, leading to the addition of Section 36(b) to the ICA of 1940, relied on the same SEC conclusion of no price competition. The 1982 *Gartenberg* guidelines for investigating excessive fee cases are still applied, over 40 years after the SEC concluded that mutual funds do not compete on price.[1]

Just as the mutual fund industry at the time of *Gartenberg* was much different from the industry in the 1960s, with hundreds of new funds and fund complexes, new distribution channels, and new products, such as money market and index funds, the mutual fund industry today is much different from the industry at the time of the *Gartenberg* decision. This chapter presents an overview of changes in the mutual fund industry since *Gartenberg*, including changes in industry structure, products, and distribution channels, along with a review of direct evidence on price competition beyond the price elasticities presented in Chapter 4.

Number of Funds and Fund Complexes

Using conventional economic indices of competition—number of rivals, entry conditions, information available to consumers, consumer product choice, and industry concentration—the mutual fund industry appears to be highly competitive. With thousands of funds and hundreds of fund complexes competing for individual and institutional investors, as shown in Table 5.1, the probability of investment advisers colluding to fix prices is virtually zero. Moreover, even if investment advisers attempted to collude on price, each advisory firm would have a strong incentive to cheat on any price agreement so an attempted cartel would be highly unstable and thus inconsistent with the position that price competition has been absent for decades.

In 1965, the year before release of the SEC's report on mutual funds, there were 170 mutual funds, mostly equity funds, with a few bond funds and no money market or index funds.[2] As seen in Table 5.1, at the time of *Gartenberg*, there were about 850 mutual funds, with equity and money market funds accounting for about 75 percent of the total. The number of mutual funds grew rapidly after 1980. By 2006 and 2007, there were over 8,000 mutual funds, with the majority being equity funds. In contrast to the early 1980s, money market funds in 2007 were a much smaller share of the total number of funds. From 1985 to 2007, the number of competing fund complexes grew from 193 to a high of 615 in 2000, declining to 564 in 2007.[3] The likelihood that 500 to 600 fund complexes could choose not to compete on the basis of price, when such competition can provide significant gains to investment advisers from growth in assets, is highly unlikely.

Industry Concentration

Whether assets are concentrated within a few firms controlling a high percentage of market share or are more equally distributed across rival firms is a long-standing initial screen in antitrust cases for possible anticompetitive behavior, as exemplified by horizontal merger and collusion cases.[4] The share of assets accounted for by the largest 5, 10, and 25 fund complexes is presented in Table 5.2. There is no discernible increase in concentration over the approximately 20-year period from 1985 to 2007 among the 5 largest complexes. There were, however, declines in the share of assets controlled by the top 10 and top 25 largest complexes, indicating a loss of market share by large complexes to smaller, apparently more successful mutual fund complexes. Although the majority of assets are held by the largest 25 complexes, there are over 500 additional fund complexes competing for investors. In addition, having 25 direct rivals in an industry would generally be considered more than sufficient to produce competitive prices.

Table 5.3 presents equity fund concentration measures from 1985 to 2007, and Table 5.4 provides comparable data at the complex level. The data in Table 5.3

TABLE 5.1 Number of Mutual Funds by Investment Categories, 1980–2007

Year	Equity Funds	Hybrid Funds	Bond Funds	Money Market Funds
1980	288		170	106
1981	306		180	179
1982	340		199	318
1983	396		257	373
1984	459	89	270	425
1985	562	103	403	460
1986	678	121	549	487
1987	824	164	781	543
1988	1006	179	942	610
1989	1069	189	1004	673
1990	1099	193	1046	741
1991	1191	212	1180	820
1992	1325	235	1400	864
1993	1586	282	1746	920
1994	1886	361	2115	963
1995	2139	412	2177	997
1996	2570	466	2224	988
1997	2951	501	2219	1013
1998	3512	526	2250	1026
1999	3952	532	2262	1045
2000	4385	523	2208	1039
2001	4716	483	2091	1015
2002	4747	473	2035	989
2003	4599	508	2045	974
2004	4547	510	2041	943
2005	4586	505	2013	871
2006	4769	508	1993	848
2007	4767	488	1967	807

Source: Investment Company Institute, 2008 Investment Company Fact Book, p. 114, and 2007 Investment Company Fact Book, p. 97.

Note: Bond funds include bond and income funds from 1980 to 1983 and bond funds only from 1984 to 2007.

TABLE 5.2 Share of Industry Assets in Largest Mutual Fund Complexes, 1985–2007

Fund Complexes	1985	1990	1995	2000	2005	2006	2007
Top 5	37%	34%	34%	32%	37%	38%	38%
Top 10	54%	53%	47%	46%	48%	49%	50%
Top 25	78%	75%	70%	74%	71%	71%	71%

Source: Investment Company Institute, 2008 Investment Company Fact Book, p. 21.

show declining concentration in each of five major investment categories listed over the time period, reflecting growth in the number of fund competitors and a shift in market share to smaller funds. Concentration also fell at the complex level, except in the large-cap growth investment category.

We measure concentration by the Herfindahl-Hirschman Index (HHI), the sum of the squared values of each firm's (fund or complex in this case) market share in a given year, which ranges from 10,000 for a single, monopoly supplier to well below 100 for a very large number of small firms. In analyzing the antitrust implications of horizontal mergers, the U.S. antitrust agencies regard industries with an HHI below 1,000 as competitive.[5] In 2007, each investment category in Table 5.2 had a concentration level well below 1,000. At the complex level, HHI was below 1,000 in the mid- and small-cap growth sectors and close to 1,000 in large-cap value and international funds. Only in large-cap growth portfolios has concentration increased within the last few years to above 1,000. Based solely on the U.S. government's concentration standards for investigating horizontal mergers, mutual funds in each sector other than possibly large-cap growth funds since 2004 would be regarded as highly competitive.

Entry of New Funds and Complexes

The total number of funds at the end of each year represents a combination of new and existing funds in that year. Terminated funds are frequently merged into a better performing fund within a complex. From 1965 to the peak in 2001 (when there were 8,305 funds), the number of new fund entrants far exceeded the number of fund exits, as the total number of funds increased in each major mutual fund investment category. This record of new

TABLE 5.3 Equity Fund Concentration by Investment Category, 1985–2007

Year	Large Growth	Large Value	Mid-Cap Growth	Small-Cap Growth	International	All Funds
1985	785.83	1,018.69	498.39	980.77	1,195.17	79.30
1986	781.96	866.93	382.93	817.40	793.13	78.81
1987	715.97	770.88	356.43	735.23	724.24	71.13
1988	707.37	804.74	367.09	794.05	745.51	75.12
1989	674.61	822.22	361.24	821.16	647.71	78.91
1990	626.39	786.79	349.62	769.31	416.77	73.47
1991	569.63	736.51	302.06	806.76	381.38	72.07
1992	543.99	647.68	266.31	570.12	306.89	66.01
1993	575.01	558.46	262.54	520.75	179.02	57.79
1994	611.78	508.02	282.73	521.10	159.42	55.20
1995	612.81	497.37	323.62	453.49	175.76	57.09
1996	586.75	473.91	350.44	423.75	169.98	50.52
1997	512.49	382.80	477.07	447.17	184.54	49.88
1998	377.12	353.99	449.25	371.05	180.79	53.54
1999	275.51	363.47	332.98	354.85	203.05	50.44
2000	233.11	330.63	233.25	351.05	213.62	45.69
2001	238.66	344.03	201.03	260.79	227.32	45.99
2002	242.13	448.93	202.68	252.67	220.17	46.73
2003	299.51	461.98	231.55	285.89	213.09	46.66
2004	390.84	415.83	279.73	338.75	222.87	48.35
2005	525.18	409.57	294.09	424.03	222.00	49.22
2006	598.56	424.92	303.46	274.91	216.32	51.03
2007	574.55	417.57	278.22	272.34	221.04	53.99

Source: Strategic Insight, Simfund Mutual Fund Database, 2008.

Notes: Excludes closed-end funds, ETFs, funds of funds, exchange funds, and variable annuities. "International" is an aggregation of all funds in the following Morningstar categories: Diversified Emerging Markets, Diversified Pac/Asia, Europe Stock, Foreign Large Blend, Foreign Large Growth, Foreign Large Value, Foreign Small/Mid Growth, Foreign Small/Mid Value, Foreign Stock, Japan Stock, Latin America Stock, Pac/Asia Excluding Japan Stock, World Allocation, and World Stock. Fund and complex concentrations are measured by the Herfindahl-Hirschman Index (HHI), where HHI is defined by:

$$HHI = \sum_{i=0}^{n} (Market\ Share)^2$$

TABLE 5.4 Complex Equity Fund Concentration by Investment Category, 1985–2007

Year	Large Growth	Large Value	Mid-Cap Growth	Small-Cap Growth	International	All Complexes
1985	1,076.53	1,295.38	758.71	1,329.74	2,439.91	367.42
1986	1,027.57	1,251.28	596.42	1,172.13	1,343.01	411.25
1987	956.22	1,209.05	549.80	1,035.82	1,320.36	400.04
1988	955.85	1,274.11	550.13	1,102.20	1,605.57	422.20
1989	971.18	1,368.01	535.77	1,064.39	1,519.62	446.50
1990	939.09	1,406.46	517.49	921.06	1,093.12	451.08
1991	958.52	1,395.83	473.64	926.02	1,050.30	473.15
1992	925.04	1,336.17	436.80	685.40	870.83	487.38
1993	952.30	1,263.92	446.10	620.96	616.98	537.02
1994	994.29	1,247.61	511.71	597.99	558.45	569.89
1995	965.06	1,262.39	622.84	520.51	589.20	595.34
1996	902.46	1,191.92	771.67	488.05	589.17	559.94
1997	783.00	854.57	1,090.64	508.11	644.29	549.54
1998	694.87	833.93	832.62	443.11	588.15	575.04
1999	830.48	995.31	534.15	403.22	596.14	558.60
2000	831.75	825.59	483.35	455.61	648.75	542.01
2001	687.00	899.33	396.11	349.73	730.00	555.01
2002	662.47	1,174.08	387.03	374.21	771.01	582.43
2003	713.61	1,193.38	485.29	419.64	813.46	598.08
2004	943.20	1,057.31	419.24	454.65	876.86	627.88
2005	1,115.41	1,043.81	442.96	531.25	890.90	646.49
2006	1,443.52	909.88	471.04	405.42	937.84	665.05
2007	1,355.75	895.09	463.80	429.17	959.11	696.56

Source: Strategic Insight, Simfund Mutual Fund Database, 2008.

Note: Excludes closed-end funds, ETFs, funds of funds, exchange funds, and variable annuities. "International" is an aggregation of all funds in the following Morningstar categories: Diversified Emerging Markets, Diversified Pac/Asia, Europe Stock, Foreign Large Blend, Foreign Large Growth, Foreign Large Value, Foreign Small/Mid Growth, Foreign Small/Mid Value, Foreign Stock, Japan Stock, Latin America Stock, Pac/Asia Excluding Japan Stock, World Allocation, and World Stock.

Fund and complex concentrations are measured by the Herfindahl-Hirschman Index (HHI), where HHI is defined by:

$$HHI = \sum_{i=0}^{n} (Market\ Share)^2$$

entries indicates that attempts by advisers to price above the competitive level are constantly threatened by the ability of new funds and fund complexes to enter and compete on price.

Hundreds of new complexes and thousands of new funds have entered since the 1970s, indicating the relative ease of entering the mutual fund industry. New entrants further pressure existing funds and complexes to face the challenges of potentially more efficient rivals. New fund complexes are credible threats to the status quo because rapid growth and financial success can come quickly in the mutual fund industry. Table 5.5 presents the top equity fund entrants since 1997 and the assets and shares they amassed by the end of 2007. Table 5.6 presents similar data for the top equity fund complexes. Recent entrants amassed billions of dollars in assets in approximately 10 years, and some reached billions in assets in fewer years, demonstrating how quickly new mutual funds, if successful, can gain market acceptance, challenging incumbent funds and complexes for existing and new fund investors. Here are two examples from Table 5.5: The Dodge & Cox International Stock fund entered in 2001, growing to almost $53.5 billion at the end of 2007, making it larger than 99.6 percent of all then existing funds. Toward the bottom of the largest 20 equity funds that did not exist in 1997, Allianz NFJ Dividend Value fund entered in 2000 and grew to $8.6 billion by the end of 2007, making it larger than close to 97 percent of all then equity funds. At the fund complex level, in Table 5.6, Vantage Point Advisors entered in 1999 and grew to $10.9 billion by the end of 2007, making it larger than approximately 88 percent of all then existing complexes. Toward the bottom of the top 20 new complexes, New Covenant Trust entered in 1999 and was larger in 2007 than 65 percent of then existing complexes.

To summarize, although the distribution of assets across equity funds and complexes is skewed toward the largest sellers, with the top 25 funds and complexes accounting for the majority of assets, hundreds of smaller funds and complexes are able to enter and compete, and some have grown their assets in a relatively short period to outrank the majority of existing rivals at both the fund and complex level. The data indicate that there are no significant barriers to entry or expansion in the mutual fund industry, which is consistent with strong competition.

Changes in Fund and Complex Shares

Changes in product and firm shares reflect the effects of competition: the gainers, the losers, and those maintaining their share. Table 5.7 presents the

TABLE 5.5 Twenty Largest Equity Mutual Funds in 2007
Not Existing in 1997

Fund	Fund Inception Year	Equity AUM (millions)	Asset Size Percentile
Dodge & Cox International Stock	2001	$53,479	99.6%
Vanguard Mid Cap Index	1998	$19,669	98.8%
New World	1999	$18,584	98.7%
Thornburg International Value	1998	$17,975	98.7%
Fidelity Advisor Diversified International	1998	$15,092	98.4%
AllianceBernstein International Value	2001	$13,154	98.1%
PIMCO Commodity Real Return	2002	$12,129	97.9%
Vanguard IL Tot Stock Market Index	2001	$9,870	97.4%
Julius Baer International Equity II	2005	$9,783	97.3%
Fidelity Advisor New Insights	2003	$9,480	97.2%
Columbia Marsico 21st Century	2000	$8,930	97.0%
SEI SIIT Large Cap Discipline Equity	2003*	$8,633	96.9%
Allianz NFJ Dividend Value	2000	$8,591	96.8%
Janus Contrarian Fund	2000	$8,212	96.7%
GMO U.S. Quality Equity	2004	$8,069	96.6%
DFA Emerging Markets Value	1998	$7,788	96.4%
Fidelity Leveraged Company Stock	2000	$7,694	96.4%
Legg Mason Opportunity	1999	$7,331	96.2%
JPMorgan Mid Cap Value	1997	$7,282	96.1%
Fairholme Fund	1999	$6,690	95.8%

Source: Strategic Insight, Simfund Mutual Fund Database, 2008.

Notes: AUM = assets under management. Excludes closed-end funds, ETFs, funds of funds, exchange funds, and variable annuities. A mutual fund in the xth percentile has more assets than x percent of all equity mutual funds.

* Simfund does not provide an inception date for SEI SIIT Large Cap Discipline Equity. The first year in which total assets are greater than zero was used as the inception year.

TABLE 5.6 Twenty Largest Mutual Fund Complexes in 2007
Not Existing in 1997

Complex	Complex Inception Year	Equity AUM (millions)	Asset Size Percentile
Vantage Point Advisors	1999	$10,938	87.4%
Fairholme Capital Management	1999	$6,690	83.3%
Henderson Global Investors	2001	$6,340	83.2%
SBC Financial Services	2001	$6,277	82.8%
Causeway Capital Management	2001	$4,283	80.0%
LSV Asset Management	1999	$3,029	77.0%
Hussman Econometrics Advisors	2000	$2,957	76.6%
AssetMark Investment Services	2001	$2,695	75.7%
Cambiar Investors	1998	$2,208	74.5%
Wintergreen Advisers	2005	$1,558	70.9%
Kensington Investment Group	1999	$1,270	68.3%
Epoch Investment Partners	2005	$1,041	66.5%
PRIMECAP Management	2004	$1,037	66.3%
Westport Advisors	1998*	$994	65.8%
New Covenant Trust Co	1999	$969	65.4%
Brown Investment Advisory	1998	$956	64.9%
EII Realty Securities	1998	$904	63.8%
E*TRADE Asset Management	1998	$856	63.3%
Absolute Investment Advisers	2005	$790	62.8%
Pacific Life	2001	$789	62.6%

Source: Strategic Insight, Simfund Mutual Fund Database, 2008.

Notes: AUM = assets under management. Excludes closed-end funds, ETFs, funds of funds, exchange funds, and variable annuities. A mutual fund complex in the xth percentile has more equity mutual fund assets than x percent of all mutual fund complexes.

* Simfund does not provide an inception year for Westport Advisors. The first year in which total assets are greater than zero was used as the inception year.

asset shares of the top 20 equity mutual fund complexes from 1985 to 2007. Shares of complexes not in the top 20 in a given year are shown in italics. As seen, many complexes moved in and out of the top 20 as they gained or lost assets and investors. The largest complexes, American Funds, Fidelity, and Vanguard, were in the top 20 over the whole period examined, but others

TABLE 5.7 Twenty Largest Fund Complexes Equity Fund Asset Shares, 1985–2007

Complex	1985	1990	1995	2000	2007
AllianceBernstein	1.35%	0.86%	*0.72%*	1.42%	1.00%
American Century	2.11%	2.34%	2.43%	2.19%	1.05%
American Funds	7.75%	9.72%	9.49%	8.51%	17.24%
BlackRock	1.51%	2.43%	2.90%	1.90%	1.31%
Columbia Funds	0.99%	0.96%	1.53%	1.37%	1.77%
Davis-Selected Advisors	*0.27%*	*0.35%*	*0.28%*	0.86%	1.10%
DFA	*0.00%*	*0.40%*	*0.30%*	*0.34%*	1.50%
Dodge & Cox	*0.05%*	*0.09%*	*0.24%*	*0.29%*	2.30%
Dreyfus	3.23%	1.90%	0.96%	1.14%	0.65%
DWS Scudder	2.49%	2.51%	2.12%	1.65%	0.66%
Evergreen	1.86%	1.57%	0.97%	0.73%	0.35%
Fidelity	10.27%	13.39%	18.56%	15.39%	12.82%
Franklin Templeton	4.84%	5.51%	4.21%	2.78%	3.90%
Grantham Mayo	*0.02%*	0.89%	0.74%	*0.23%*	0.96%
Invesco Aim	1.17%	2.11%	3.50%	3.75%	0.93%
Janus	*0.36%*	*0.62%*	1.74%	4.55%	1.54%
JPMorgan Funds	*0.04%*	*0.16%*	0.75%	0.93%	0.79%
Legg Mason Partners	2.04%	2.42%	1.34%	1.08%	0.60%
Lord Abbett	2.41%	1.32%	*0.47%*	*0.46%*	0.72%
MFS	2.80%	1.78%	1.14%	2.30%	1.05%
Morgan Stanley	1.25%	2.32%	2.10%	1.63%	0.30%
OppenheimerFunds	2.41%	1.69%	1.35%	1.68%	1.63%
Pioneer	3.41%	2.30%	1.01%	0.62%	0.40%
Prudential Financial	*0.85%*	1.88%	1.15%	0.98%	0.47%
Putnam	4.27%	2.76%	3.44%	5.43%	1.07%
RiverSource	3.57%	2.52%	2.06%	1.74%	0.68%
T Rowe Price	3.17%	2.29%	2.54%	2.33%	3.22%
Van Kampen	3.35%	1.60%	0.73%	1.12%	1.07%
Vanguard	6.36%	7.32%	7.71%	10.60%	13.08%
Waddell & Reed	1.95%	1.66%	0.86%	0.72%	0.70%

Source: Strategic Insight, Simfund Mutual Fund Database, 2008.

Notes: Excludes closed-end funds, ETF funds, funds of funds, exchange funds, and variable annuities. Shares of equity assets under management are measured as of year-end. Complexes with italicized/bold values for a given year are not in the top 20 in that year. Strategic Insight data on assets begin in 1985.

gained sufficient share to join the top 20, such as Dodge & Cox and DFA. Conversely, others lost share to rivals over this period, such as American Century, Dreyfus, Pioneer, and Waddell & Reed. Over a longer period, going back to the 1960s, Dreyfus was one of the largest funds, Vanguard did not exist, and no Fidelity fund ranked in the top 10 funds.[6] At present, Vanguard and Fidelity are among the largest fund complexes, and Dreyfus's share has fallen so far from its earlier position that it is no longer in the top 20 funds.

Fund complexes' shares of assets are thus anything but stable over time, reflecting competition between funds and between complexes.[7] The shifts in mutual fund complexes' shares indicate that investors are mobile, willing to move assets or invest new money with rival fund advisers or outside the mutual fund industry to gain higher returns for a given level of risk. Similar large shifts in shares take place at the individual equity fund level. Table 5.8 presents equity fund shares in the top 20 mutual fund complexes for large-cap growth funds. In an open market system, money moves to its highest valued use, and mutual funds are no exception, indicating competition between investment advisers.

Investors' Willingness to Switch Mutual Funds

Mutual fund investor mobility is reflected in the extent of annual fund redemptions. Substantial annual redemptions indicate that investors incur low transaction costs in redeeming and reinvesting their fund shares. Table 5.9 presents redemption rates for total mutual funds, as well as separately for equity, hybrid, and bond funds. As seen, redemption rates vary widely over time. Annual redemption rates for equity funds range from 73 percent in 1987 to 23 percent in 2004–2005. Redemption rates in the 20 percent range are common for hybrid funds and in the 30 percent range for long-term bond funds. These results are consistent with a base of highly mobile investors, able to switch between funds and fund complexes to enhance their returns, or to shift between funds and nonfund uses of their money. Adviser profits depend on the switching decisions of investors. To retain their shareholders, and especially their most profitable shareholders, mutual funds must remain competitive on annual fees and performance.

Fund Distribution Channels

The more distribution channels that are available for mutual fund sales, the greater will be the fund's availability and contacts with investors. A single channel—the full-service brokerage firm—accounted for most buying and

TABLE 5.8 Top Twenty Large-Cap Growth Equity Mutual Fund
Complexes, 1985–2007

Complex	1985	1990	1995	2000	2007
AllianceBernstein	0.00%	0.00%	0.00%	2.41%	0.38%
American Century	12.04%	12.57%	21.94%	6.55%	1.81%
American Funds	18.71%	20.97%	12.92%	5.93%	24.02%
BlackRock	0.00%	1.61%	0.97%	1.21%	0.67%
Calamos Advisors	0.00%	0.00%	0.00%	0.00%	1.68%
Columbia Funds	4.49%	2.63%	1.43%	1.24%	2.51%
Consulting Group	0.00%	0.00%	1.07%	0.24%	0.27%
Dreyfus	1.77%	1.27%	1.00%	0.71%	0.38%
DWS Scudder	3.77%	3.63%	3.29%	0.49%	0.23%
Fidelity	1.70%	3.35%	10.44%	20.27%	25.67%
Franklin Templeton	0.00%	0.00%	0.00%	0.29%	0.85%
Gabelli	0.00%	1.08%	0.60%	0.00%	0.10%
Harbor Capital	0.00%	0.33%	1.12%	1.02%	0.98%
Invesco Aim Advs	0.00%	0.19%	0.08%	2.27%	1.40%
Janus	0.06%	1.29%	4.17%	12.14%	4.57%
John Hancock	0.68%	0.54%	0.30%	0.14%	0.80%
Legg Mason Ptnrs	0.00%	5.06%	3.13%	1.27%	1.51%
Marsico Capital	0.00%	0.00%	0.00%	0.42%	1.11%
MFS	8.57%	4.14%	1.29%	5.02%	1.12%
Morgan Stanley Adv	0.41%	0.47%	2.69%	1.85%	0.38%
Nations Funds	0.00%	0.00%	1.00%	0.09%	0.00%
Oak Assoc	0.00%	0.00%	0.01%	0.72%	0.05%
OppenheimerFunds	1.12%	0.28%	0.87%	1.20%	1.38%
Phoenix Investment	1.28%	4.37%	3.43%	0.62%	0.08%
PIMCO/Allianz Glbl	0.91%	1.82%	1.68%	0.34%	0.31%
Prudential Finl	0.00%	0.00%	0.41%	1.32%	0.59%
Putnam	0.00%	0.00%	0.00%	10.61%	1.12%
RiverSource	11.21%	8.31%	10.04%	1.35%	0.35%
Seligman	5.93%	2.53%	0.68%	0.15%	0.05%
Shay Asset Mgmt	1.38%	0.45%	0.06%	0.02%	0.00%
T Rowe Price	0.00%	0.00%	0.00%	0.01%	4.30%

TABLE 5.8 *(continued)*

Complex	1985	1990	1995	2000	2007
The Hartford	0.76%	0.76%	0.32%	0.08%	0.53%
Van Kampen	16.62%	11.42%	2.81%	2.67%	0.75%
Vanguard	1.41%	1.89%	4.79%	4.28%	6.96%
Waddell & Reed	4.04%	3.85%	1.42%	0.38%	1.07%
Wells Fargo	2.21%	3.43%	1.54%	1.21%	0.82%

Source: Strategic Insight, Simfund Mutual Fund Database 2008.

Notes: All close-ended funds, ETF funds, and funds of funds are excluded from this analysis. Shares of equity assets under management are measured as of year-end. Complexes with italicized/bold values for a given year are not in the top 20 in that year.

selling of mutual funds in the 1960s, as sales load funds dominated sales. Investors can now purchase through a host of channels besides full-service brokerage houses, including discount brokers, independent financial advisers, fund supermarkets offered by discount brokers, employer-based retirement plans, and directly from funds.[8]

Competition for investors exists both across and within distribution channels. For example, as defined contribution retirement and individual retirement account (IRA) plans continue to attract investors and serve as a prime channel for mutual fund investing, competition between investment advisers to be part of a retirement plan's investment offerings intensifies. In 2007, approximately 50 percent of mutual fund investors used a defined contribution retirement plan as their primary purchase channel for mutual funds.[9]

The cost of access to mutual funds has declined over time as investors have shifted from load to no-load funds. In 2007, net new cash flow to long-term funds totaled $223 billion. No-load funds accounted for $177 billion, and load funds only $21 billion.[10] These figures can be compared with those of 2000, when no-load funds accounted for $108 billion of the total $229 billion in net new cash flow and load funds accounted for $70 billion.[11] The shift to no-load funds has been ongoing since the 1960s, when load funds accounted for approximately 90 percent of sales.[12]

This competition between different distribution channels—load and no-load fund channels—has resulted in lower load fees over time. The average maximum equity fund load fee declined from 8.0 percent in 1980 to 5.6 percent in 2007, and the actual fees paid fell over the same period from 5.6 to 1.2 percent.[13] The proportion of funds invested in front-end load funds declined

TABLE 5.9 Long-Term Mutual Fund Annual Redemption Rates,
1985–2007

Year	Equity Funds	Hybrid Funds	Bond Funds	Total
1985	35.6%	26.3%	24.0%	29.8%
1986	50.9%	30.2%	30.7%	38.6%
1987	73.0%	40.7%	47.5%	56.7%
1988	45.9%	35.8%	30.4%	36.9%
1989	38.0%	25.7%	27.7%	31.9%
1990	37.7%	23.0%	26.2%	31.0%
1991	33.1%	22.2%	24.1%	28.1%
1992	26.7%	17.1%	32.7%	28.8%
1993	28.7%	16.3%	33.8%	29.9%
1994	31.6%	24.2%	43.2%	35.2%
1995	29.4%	21.3%	30.5%	28.9%
1996	30.7%	19.8%	32.0%	30.0%
1997	31.9%	18.9%	31.0%	30.5%
1998	34.0%	21.7%	30.6%	32.2%
1999	34.9%	26.0%	36.8%	34.5%
2000	41.6%	28.3%	36.4%	39.9%
2001	35.2%	22.6%	34.7%	34.2%
2002	41.0%	25.8%	35.8%	38.7%
2003	29.4%	20.5%	40.7%	31.5%
2004	23.0%	18.9%	32.1%	24.7%
2005	23.0%	17.9%	28.4%	23.7%
2006	23.6%	19.1%	27.2%	23.9%
2007	26.8%	23.3%	30.2%	27.2%

Source: Investment Company Institute, 2008 *Investment Company Fact Book,* p. 134.

Note: The redemption rates are calculated by summing regular redemptions and redemption exchanges for each year as a percentage of average net assets at the beginning and end of the year.

from 90 percent in the early 1960s, when load fees were about 8.5 percent, to 35 percent in 1999, when maximum load fees averaged approximately 5.0 percent.[14] The decline in load fees has been partially offset by increases in 12b-1 fees, which are used primarily to pay for management services to investors and to compensate investors' financial advisers.[15]

Product Innovations and Price Competition

Various new fund products have been introduced since the 1960s that affect the potential for price competition. Among the post-1960s products are money market mutual funds, introduced in the mid-1970s, and exchange traded funds (ETFs), introduced in 1993. Annual fees for money market funds are substantially lower than for equity and bond funds.[16] Lower fees in money market funds can enhance their relative returns, as they did in the late 1970s and early 1980s, 1990–1991, 2000–2001, and 2007, adding pressure on equity and long-term bond funds to maintain competitive fees.[17]

ETFs grew from one ETF in 1993 to 629 in 2007.[18] ETF assets grew over the period from zero to $608 billion.[19] ETFs generally mirror a market index, such as the S&P 500 or Russell 2,000, and are traded like conventional stocks.[20] ETF shares are valued by the underlying company shares in the ETF. ETFs are often sector-specific, such as international, industry-specific, or oriented toward commodities. Instead of purchasing mutual funds, investors can diversify by purchasing ETFs. As such, ETFs can be used as either a substitute for or complement to mutual funds for some investors, providing diversification and liquidity at a relatively low price, comparable in some cases to fees for broad-based index funds, and adding further pressure on investment advisers to maintain competitive fees.[21]

Further Direct Evidence of Price Competition

Common observation contradicts the belief that price competition does not exist among mutual funds. Vanguard and other complexes, such as TIAA-CREF, are well known for promoting their fees as the lowest in the industry. Vanguard has competed as a low-cost leader in index funds since it shifted from a load to a no-load fund complex in about 1977. Fidelity and Vanguard engaged in a widely reported price war on their index funds throughout 2005 and 2006 for both small and large investors.[22] Vanguard executives have long attributed its rapid growth from the 1970s onward, becoming one of the three largest U.S. mutual fund complexes, to engaging in aggressive price competition.[23] Beyond Vanguard and TIAA-CREF, firms undercutting their rivals' prices in ETF stocks are commonplace.[24]

Further evidence of systematic, industry-wide price competition is reflected in price discounts to investors. Investment managers' announced prices are often discounted to investors through fee waivers. As discussed earlier, small funds tend to offer fee waivers more commonly than do large funds in order to be more competitive with larger funds. As shown in Table 5.10, over 75 percent of funds with assets below $25 million generally provided fee waivers to their shareholders. Even among larger funds with assets above $1 billion, more than 45 percent provided fee waivers to their shareholders in 2005–2007.[25] The data show that waivers from announced fees are commonplace and provide direct evidence that advisers compete by reducing price.

A remaining question concerns the extent to which fund investors are sensitive to fee levels. The estimated price elasticities presented in Chapter 4 indicate that investors are strongly price sensitive. However, as discussed in Chapter 3, the *Gartenberg* decision concluded that investors are highly insensitive to price because mutual fund fees are too trivial for investors to consider and thus are competitively insignificant (but according to the court, may still be judged excessive under the Investment Company Act [ICA] of 1940). Hence, *Gartenberg* concluded that investors do not respond to differences in fee levels between rivals' funds. Evidence on the distribution of mutual fund investments by fee levels indicates otherwise; investors do respond to lower prices in the purchase of mutual funds, just as consumers do with most economic goods.

Studies show that mutual fund shareholders concentrate their investments in lower priced funds. The simple average equity fund expense ratio in 2007 was 1.46 percent, while the asset-weighted average expense ratio was 0.86 percent, indicating that the majority of assets were invested in lower cost funds.[26] The Investment Company Institute (ICI) found that approximately 90 percent of new fund assets from 1998 to 2007 were invested in funds with below-average expense ratios.[27] Similarly, in the case of index funds, such as widely available S&P 500 index funds, most of the assets are invested in the lowest fee funds, indicating that investors have knowledge of fund fees and act on that knowledge. The ICI found that 82 percent of assets in S&P 500 index mutual funds in 2007 had expense ratios of 20 basis points or less, 12 percent had expense ratios of 21 to 40 basis points, and only 6 percent had expense ratios higher than 40 basis points.[28] These data, along with the evidence on fee waivers and longtime price competition by Vanguard, TIAA-CREF, and other complexes show that investors are aware of and respond to lower fee mutual funds.

Summary and Conclusions

The SEC's 1966 conclusion that mutual funds do not compete on price has informed the law on excessive fees from 1982 to the present. However, claims that price competition is absent today because it was found to be absent in the

TABLE 5.10 Fraction of Actively Managed Equity Mutual Fund Share Classes That Engaged in Fee Waivers, 1998–2007

Mutual Fund AUM (millions)	1998	1999	2000	2001	2002	2003	2004	2005	2006	2007
<$25	73.9%	76.2%	75.5%	69.5%	76.3%	78.0%	76.8%	74.1%	77.8%	74.3%
$25–50	63.8%	63.6%	66.1%	70.0%	66.4%	68.1%	63.8%	62.9%	72.3%	67.7%
$50–100	52.9%	57.6%	53.3%	58.9%	62.2%	56.0%	53.5%	56.4%	59.4%	58.5%
$100–250	40.5%	43.2%	36.9%	44.1%	43.0%	44.8%	47.5%	46.6%	46.8%	51.6%
$250–500	24.8%	38.8%	30.2%	33.4%	40.1%	38.4%	42.5%	46.4%	45.5%	41.9%
$500–1,000	19.1%	23.7%	24.5%	29.2%	26.7%	26.9%	31.9%	37.1%	42.8%	48.1%
$1,000+	19.0%	25.2%	18.0%	19.3%	21.5%	20.8%	39.1%	47.6%	45.2%	48.5%
All Sizes	41.0%	46.2%	40.2%	44.5%	48.3%	47.5%	48.6%	50.7%	51.5%	52.6%

Source: Strategic Insight, Simfund Mutual Fund Database, 2008.

Notes: AUM = assets under management. Excludes closed-end funds, ETFs, funds of funds, exchange funds, index-enhanced funds, and variable annuities. A fund manager is identified as having waived a portion of its fee if the fund's gross expense ratio exceeds its actual expense ratio in a year.

1950s and 1960s make no economic sense. Mutual fund market conditions 40 to 50 years ago have little relationship to market conditions today and thus provide no credible basis for judging the extent of recent and current price competition.

Mutual fund industry structure, along with investor mobility, rule out successful attempts to price above the competitive level. There are hundreds of fund complexes and thousands of funds competing for individual investors using multiple sales channels. There has been extensive entry and expansion of existing funds over the past 25 years, and assets are not concentrated in the hands of a few advisory firms—two factors that eliminate any threat from industry-wide collusion.

Simple observation demonstrates vigorous price competition among investment advisers. Price discounting from mutual funds' announced prices has been commonplace for years, especially for newer entrants and smaller funds, as they seek to attract and retain shareholders. Investor redemption rates indicate that a substantial share of investors are highly mobile and can switch easily from higher to lower fee mutual funds. New products and distribution channels, such as index funds, ETFs, and fund supermarkets, have enhanced investor choice, increasing competition. At the same time, there has been a massive shift from load to no-load funds since the 1960s, accompanied by large decreases in sales load charges, demonstrating price competition and investor sensitivity to fees. The distribution of investor assets by fee levels shows that investors concentrate their investments in the lowest fee funds, further demonstrating investor sensitivity to lower fees, which pressures investment advisers to remain price competitive for the package of services and performance they offer to investors.

CHAPTER SIX

Mutual Fund Pricing, Excessive Fees, and Empirical Evidence

Introduction

Studies concluding that retail mutual fund investors pay excessive fees generally base their claim on one or some combination of three observations: (1) Retail fund investors pay substantially higher management fees than institutional investors; (2) retail investor fees vary widely across competing mutual funds; and (3) economies of scale, which produce declining unit costs in mutual fund operations, are not closely related to trends in average fund expense ratios. Fee critics contend that management fees are lower in the institutional sector because investment advisers compete vigorously on price to gain institutional clients, whereas retail investors incur higher fees because retail fund advisers do not compete on price. Fee critics further argue that institutional prices provide a competitive price benchmark for retail mutual fund management, indicating the amount by which retail prices are artificially elevated above the competitive level. This view rests, of course, on the assumption that the same product is being sold to both retail and institutional investors.

It follows, according to fee critics, that were there price competition in both the retail and institutional sectors, investors' fees would be close to identical; that is, the "law of one price" would hold. The law of one price states in effect that under competitive pricing, nearly identical goods will sell for nearly identical prices. From this perspective, the greater the dispersion of prices across retail mutual funds in the same investment category (assuming the funds are nearly identical in size, services to investors, performance, etc.), the less price competition.

Finally, critics' studies contend that mutual fund operations are characterized by large economies of scale due to, for example, fixed costs in portfolio management (no matter the amount of assets being managed, costs allegedly do not change), but reductions in cost per unit of output from scale economies are not passed through to fund investors in the form of lower fees because price competition is absent, thereby leading to excess profits for investment advisers. As evidence, various studies argue that if cost reductions generated by economies of scale were passed to investors, expense ratios would decline over time, whereas such ratios have arguably increased over time. We address each of these arguments and the accompanying empirical evidence.[1]

Mutual Fund Market Segments and Fee Disparities

Beginning with the reports of the Wharton School and the Securities and Exchange Commission (SEC) in the 1960s, various studies have reported that large institutional investors, such as public and private defined benefit pension funds, college and university endowments, commingled investment pools,[2] foundations, banks, and insurance companies, pay substantially lower fees than retail mutual fund investors.[3] As discussed, critics maintain that retail fund investors are exploited relative to institutional investors because competitive, arm's-length bargaining underlies institutional fees, whereas retail fund fees are set by investment advisers with sufficient monopoly power to ignore rivals' prices.[4] More specifically, pension funds and other institutional investors choose investment advisers among competing candidates and can generally fire advisers with short notice, approximately 30 to 60 days, or simply not renew their contract, and investment advisers are commonly replaced when they generate poor returns.[5] In contrast, retail mutual fund advisers are rarely fired, although, as discussed in Chapter 2, retail fund investors can easily fire their investment adviser by switching funds. To maintain or increase their funds' assets, retail fund advisers must compete to replace redeemed assets. Nevertheless, fee critics argue in effect that if arm's-length bargaining and price competition existed at the retail fund level, as it does for institutional investors, and retail fund advisers could be easily replaced, the price differences paid by retail and institutional investors would vanish, with retail fees declining until they matched institutional fees.

The fee critics' observation raises the question of what factors explain price differences between different buyer segments in an economic market? The fee critics' explanation, lack of price competition, is one possibility, but certainly not a universal explanation. Other explanations can account for such price differences. Different products, implying different costs of production and distribution, can naturally account for price differences, and as explained in the following sections, retail and institutional investors are purchasing decidedly different products with large differences in services and distribution costs. However, even for the same product sold to different groups of buyers, price differences are commonplace, such as airline seats (Internet reservations vs. airline phone agents, advance ticket vs. last-minute purchase); hotel rooms (corporate vs. retail, senior rates, and tour group rates); movie theater seats (seniors, students, advance discount purchases, and afternoon vs. evening screenings); a variety of buyer loyalty programs; and discount coupons for supermarkets, restaurants, and other goods. Price competition is not absent, so price differences in these cases have nothing to do with a lack of price competition. To the contrary, price differences exist in these cases because of intense price competition. Firms in price-competitive markets often use differential pricing, when market conditions make it feasible, because it allows them to increase revenues over uniform pricing by taking advantage of differences in buyers' price sensitivity. In these cases, it is not a lack of price competition in one sector that leads to different prices but the very presence of competitive price pressure that forces firms to adopt differential pricing between market segments.[6]

With the same product sold in different market segments, prices can differ as a result of differences in demand and the cost of supply. Thus, to test for price equality between market segments, it is essential that the market conditions of products and services, demands, and costs for each market segment be either virtually identical or controlled for in the statistical test being used. Without such equalities (or statistical controls) between market segments, claims of price inequality are meaningless, as are claims that price differences are due to the absence of price competition in one market segment versus another.

Dissimilar Advisory Products and Fee Disparities

For institutional and retail consumers of investment advisory services, the products and services acquired and the costs of producing the products and services are drastically different, invalidating price comparisons between the two sectors. Mutual fund advisers provide a wide range of services to thousands of shareholders who own shares of stock in a fund's portfolio of assets. In contrast, an institutional investor owns its portfolio's assets directly and an adviser has only a single client (except for commingled pools), such as a public pension fund or university endowment. Advisers to institutional investors are not servicing thousands of individual clients and incurring large marketing and distribution costs, so many activities undertaken by retail mutual funds are not required for institutional investors.

Among major products and services provided primarily to retail fund investors are: full-service Web sites, 24-hour call centers, daily asset pricing, share redemptions, cash management for investor liquidity, exchanges of shares within a complex's funds, tax reporting, custodial services, transfer agency, fund distribution channels, government-required reports and prospectuses based on mutual fund regulations and laws, maintaining the fund's board of directors and producing board-directed studies, and providing education, financial, and retirement counseling to fund investors. These products and services are typically not provided to institutional investors.

Institutional investors are primarily focused on the returns from portfolio management; that is, whether advisers are meeting their contracted-for target returns.[7] External portfolio managers for institutional accounts incur the costs of competing to manage institutional money and the costs of portfolio management, compliance with their contract, financial reporting, and periodic meetings and phone calls with clients, but not the costs of distribution and servicing thousands of relatively small individual account holders along with the costs of constant daily customer turnover.

In summary, differences in the products and costs of servicing retail and institutional accounts invalidate comparisons of their respective annual fees.[8] Such price comparisons provide no information about the presence of price competition in the market for retail mutual funds. With substantially more products and services provided to retail investors, their fees are naturally higher than institutional investor fees.

Identical or Closely Similar Products and Fee Disparities

In the case of an identical or closely similar product sold in different market segments, price differences are common and generally have nothing to do with a lack of price competition. Finding such a product to test for price differences in the case of investment advisory services for retail fund and institutional investors is difficult, because buyers purchase a bundle of goods and product features in each market segment, and individual components of the bundle are typically not available to retail fund investors in separate markets.

In an attempt to eliminate pricing differences due to differences in products and the costs of serving different market segments, some mutual fund fee studies have attempted to determine whether estimates of pure portfolio management costs—including research on firms and industries by securities analysts, selecting securities to buy and sell, asset allocation to balance portfolio risk, and trading securities, separate from a retail mutual fund's expenses for securities distribution, transfer agency, administrative, and all other fund operating costs—differ between advising retail and institutional investors.[9] According to fee critics, pure portfolio management fees as a share of assets under management should be identical in the retail and institutional advisory sectors because the activities and costs of pure portfolio management are identical in both sectors.[10]

How to isolate pure portfolio management costs in the mutual fund and institutional segments of advisory services is not obvious. The problem falls into two categories: cost and demand differences in portfolio management between the market sectors and serious problems in measurement.

First, even if portfolio management costs could be isolated with a semblance of accuracy, contrary to the critics' claim, portfolio management costs are not the same in the retail and institutional advisory sectors because the duties required of portfolio managers in each sector differ. Retail mutual fund advisers must engage in cash management activities in running their portfolios to meet the ever-changing liquidity redemption requirements of investors. Managing cash flows requires investing in programs to optimize the amount of cash necessary to cover liquidity demands, similar to firms using programs to optimize inventory requirements under uncertainty. A significant additional cash-based cost is the opportunity cost of holding cash.[11] Advisers to institutions do not face comparable cash management costs. In addition, cash flow demands in mutual funds can be unpredictable, adding to cash management costs. When investor redemption demand is greater than cash available, securities have to be sold, adding further costs to mutual fund portfolio management, because advisers must determine which securities to sell to achieve a new portfolio risk balance. Costs are further incurred when unexpected redemptions occur, requiring fire sales of large numbers of a company's shares. Advising large institutional investors does not incur such costs. In summary, the costs of cash management are virtually zero when dealing with a single-client, institutional investor.

The costs of managing a portfolio can also increase as assets grow, depending on such factors as investment style and the degree of diversification and risk sought by the advisory firm. Assets under management tend to be larger in large mutual fund complexes because institutional advisers typically manage only a small share of an institution's assets. To the extent the number of securities held increases with asset size, retail mutual funds will have higher portfolio management costs. As an example, take advisers specializing in small-cap stocks. Pouring more money into a fixed, small number of small-cap stocks can increase the cost of trading because of potentially thinly traded stocks. It also increases the percentage share of ownership in a small-cap firm, which is generally restricted to no more than 5 percent under current regulations. Hence, with substantial growth in assets, the number of stocks in a small-cap portfolio will grow. As the number of stocks in a portfolio grows, portfolio management costs increase, because it is necessary to follow a growing number of owned stocks, competing firms' stocks, potential new stock purchases, and a larger number of industries. The study of mutual fund fees and expenses by the SEC found that the greater the number of securities in a portfolio, the higher operating expenses.[12]

Second, there are serious measurement problems when attempting to compare the fees for pure portfolio management between retail funds and institutional funds, using either fees to institutional investors or fees for subadvisory services as proxies for pure portfolio management costs. As discussed earlier, subadvisory fees are the fees paid by retail mutual funds when contracting with external advisers to manage their funds.[13] In the case of subadvisory and institutional investor fees, clients are interested primarily in purchasing portfolio management, apart from the many services generally provided to retail investors. However, subadvisory and institutional clients contract for more than pure portfolio management. In both cases, advisers incur costs in addition to pure portfolio management, including the costs of competing for clients, reporting performance, and meeting with clients, as well as possibly incremental overhead costs, which must be covered through fees to clients. The problem then becomes extracting pure portfolio management costs from the annual advisory fees charged by subadvisers or charged to institutional investors.

In its investigation of mutual fund fees and expenses, the SEC reported that there is no standard reporting of expenses across mutual funds.[14] What is included in management costs for one fund can be drastically different from another fund. Mutual fund filings with the SEC divide expenses into management fees, 12b-1 fees, and other expenses, such as transfer agent, securities custodians, legal, accounting, and the costs of a fund's directors. Management fees include investment advisory fees plus potentially other fees paid to the adviser. Some funds limit their definition of management fees to their estimate of pure portfolio management costs, while other funds include administrative and other services in their reporting of management expenses.[15] Some fund complexes, such as American Century Investments, have a unified management fee, which covers all services, including portfolio management.

As an example, American Century Investments Growth Fund and Vista Fund's income statements report management fees, distribution fees by fund class, directors' fees and expenses, and other expenses.[16] Imbedded in management fees along with administrative and other unidentified expenses are pure portfolio management fees, but it is impossible to obtain a meaningful estimate of portfolio management fees given the complex's unified fee structure.[17]

Moreover, even if costs and portfolio management services were hypothetically identical in the two sectors, fee differences would be perfectly compatible with price competition in each sector. This is true even if retail and institutional investors are investing in the identical portfolio. When portfolio management as a subadviser to mutual funds or as an adviser to institutional investors represents a product extension to a new group of buyers, then pricing will be based on attaining incremental revenues and incurring incremental costs relative to managing retail funds. Subadviser or institutional investor fees need to be just sufficient to cover the incremental costs of servicing new buyers. In comparisons of the average cost in managing retail funds to the incremental cost of managing subadvised and institutional assets, the incremental cost will be lower, so it would not be surprising to find lower portfolio management fees for institutional investors. Importantly, retail fund shareholders benefit when their adviser wins contracts for subadvisory and institutional advisory business so long as the fees generate incremental revenues that are larger than incremental costs. The net gain in revenues helps cover joint and common costs, which reduces retail investors' fees. Thus, with incremental pricing to cover the incremental costs of providing subadvisory services to retail funds and advisory services to institutional clients, price differences provide no basis for concluding that higher prices for retail fund investors demonstrate an absence of price competition.

Estimates of Retail and Institutional Portfolio Management Fee Differences

Freeman and Brown compared portfolio management fees between mutual funds and institutional investors, using fees paid by 36 public pension plans as a proxy for institutional portfolio management fees and average management fees paid by 1,318 mutual funds. They found average mutual fund management fees of 0.56 percent of assets versus 0.28 percent of assets in their sample of public pension plans, consistent in their view with a lack of price competition between retail fund advisers.[18] However, the results for retail advisory firms are likely incorrect because the authors failed to measure pure portfolio management costs in retail funds. As they acknowledge, mutual funds do not report management costs on a standardized basis, given that some funds include administrative costs or some portion thereof as part of management costs, and other funds include part of management costs in their reported administrative costs.[19]

In response to Freeman and Brown's study, Collins used subadvisory fees as a superior measure as compared with general management costs.[20] The Vanguard Group of funds, for example, has historically contracted with subadvisory firms to manage all or part of its actively managed mutual funds while managing its many index funds internally.[21] Collins compared subadvisory fees to the public pension plan fees reported by Freeman and Brown. He found for small and medium-size portfolios ($75 million to approximately $400 million) that subadvisory fees were less than fees paid by the public pension plans, and for larger portfolios the pension plans had somewhat lower fees. Overall, the fees for the pension plan sample averaged 0.28 percent of assets, and subadvisory fees averaged 0.31 percent of assets, indicating relatively small differences between portfolio management fees in retail and institutional accounts. Collins's study shows that subadvisory fees and the fees in Freeman and Brown's public pension sample are closely comparable. Using Freeman and Brown's reasoning that institutional portfolio management fees serve as a benchmark for competitive pricing in retail mutual fund sales, Collins's results are consistent with price competition for portfolio management services in both the retail and institutional sectors.[22]

Following Collins's findings, Freeman, Brown, and Pomerantz selected 19 out of 36 subadvisers to Vanguard funds in 2004 and compared the subadvisory fees they charged to Vanguard with the management fees the advisers charged retail investors in their own funds.[23] As in the earlier Freeman and Brown study, which compared public pension plan fees to retail mutual fund advisory fees, the authors found that the advisers' retail portfolio management fees were substantially higher than the subadvisory fees they charged Vanguard.[24] As explained earlier, such a finding is consistent with using incremental pricing to compete for subadvisory business.

In summary, the existence of price differences between retail and institutional investors are hardly sufficient to conclude that price competition is absent in retail mutual funds. Price differences between retail mutual fund and institutional investors, as well as subadvisory services, can occur for various reasons that are consistent with price competition among mutual fund advisory firms. Before such price comparisons are made, care must be taken to ensure that measures of retail fund portfolio expenses prices are measured properly, given the difficulty of extracting such expenses from a mutual fund's total management costs. Pricing policies, such as incremental pricing, also result in different prices. None of these bases for differences in prices rests on an absence of price competition between retail fund investment advisory firms.

Beyond the problems just discussed, the relevance of comparing portfolio management prices between retail funds and institutional investors is unclear. Retail mutual fund investors are concerned with the total annual fee they pay, not in the individual components of the fee, such as marketing, printing, and portfolio management. Just as automobile buyers shop for cars based on total price, not the price of the engine, steering wheel, or exhaust system (except possibly for optional equipment), mutual fund investors shop across funds on the basis of comparing rival funds' total annual fees and a host of other factors. How the total fee is parceled out to individual components of services to investors is of no consequence in addressing whether the total fee is set by competition or not. Moreover, whether retail mutual fund portfolio management costs are above, equal to, or below advisory fees for institutional investors is largely irrelevant to retail mutual fund investors and the question of whether they are paying a competitive price for their bundle of services from advisory firms. Within any mutual fund investment category, as well as asset size class, there is a wide range of fees available to investors, demonstrating price and fund attribute competition between mutual fund advisory firms. The majority of investors select funds in the lower fee ranges, indicating that they are aware of price differences between funds and are responsive to relative prices.

Price Dispersion and Price Competition

Observing price dispersion between mutual funds within investment styles, fee critics conclude that price competition is absent. They assert that if price competition existed between retail mutual fund advisory firms, the law of one price would hold and investors' fees would be close to identical within a fund's investment style. Table 6.1 shows the range of expense ratios by distribution percentiles across various fund investment styles. Note that median expense ratios vary across investment categories, being highest in small-cap growth, specialty, and international funds, and lowest in S&P 500 index funds. The range of fees in each investment category is shown by the last two columns, indicating the ratio of the highest to lowest expense ratios within each investment category. Comparing the 90th to the 10th percentile expense ratios in the last column, S&P 500 index funds have the widest fee range, and small-cap value funds the narrowest fee range. Because fees are far from equal within each investment category, critics conclude that price competition in the sale of mutual funds is either weak or nonexistent.[25]

Fee critics emphasize that the absence of a single price or a narrow band of prices across S&P 500 index funds is especially noteworthy because gross returns vary only slightly across such funds.[26] With nearly identical performance, critics argue that prices should be virtually identical. Instead, S&P 500 index funds have the largest fee range in Table 6.1, contrary to the law of one price.

It is interesting to note that contemporary and earlier (1960s) fee critics reached opposite conclusions on the competitive meaning of mutual fund price dispersion. The Wharton and SEC studies in the 1960s that spawned the debate on excessive fees concluded that mutual fund fees were largely equal to 0.5 percent of assets (or close to that level) in the 1950s and early 1960s, and in the case of some mutual funds, the percentage had remained unchanged for years. They concluded that this relative equality and stability of fees demonstrated an absence of price competition.[27] They implicitly equated approximate fee equality with price collusion among fund investment advisers. With entry and rapid growth of mutual funds in the 1950s, these studies expected price competition to generate a wide range of fees. In contrast, contemporary fee critics, invoking the law of one price, regard a similarity of fees among mutual funds as demonstrating vigorous price competition, while price dispersion allegedly reflects an absence of price competition.

The Modern View of Competition and Price Dispersion

A basic misconception by contemporary mutual fund fee critics is in applying the law of one price to the real world of mutual funds, with thousands of differentiated funds, hundreds of differentiated fund complexes and investment advisory firms, and consumers without perfect, all-knowing information. The law of one price holds in the idealized, textbook model of perfect competition. In that model, products and services to consumers are perfectly identical across rival sellers, profit-maximizing sellers have identical costs, and buyers are perfectly informed about prices, products, and services. These conditions rarely, if ever, exist in the real world. Products, services to buyers, distribution methods, and firms' reputations and performance are generally not identical across competing firms; firms have different costs of production and distribution; and consumers face search and other transaction costs in the real world,

TABLE 6.1 Dispersion of Average Equity Mutual Fund Expense Ratios by Distribution Percentiles and Investment Categories, 2007

Morningstar Investment Category	N	10th Percentile	25th Percentile	Median	75th Percentile	90th Percentile	75th Percentile to 25th Percentile Ratio	90th Percentile to 10th Percentile Ratio
Large Blend	1,187	0.45%	0.83%	1.19%	1.65%	2.00%	1.99	4.43
Large Growth	1,185	0.77%	1.00%	1.29%	1.81%	2.15%	1.81	2.78
Large Value	986	0.72%	0.94%	1.24%	1.76%	2.01%	1.86	2.79
Mid Blend	362	0.75%	1.04%	1.36%	1.85%	2.16%	1.77	2.88
Mid Growth	681	0.90%	1.10%	1.40%	1.95%	2.20%	1.77	2.44
Mid Value	268	0.84%	1.00%	1.27%	1.83%	2.05%	1.83	2.46
Small Blend	468	0.78%	1.04%	1.31%	1.74%	2.16%	1.68	2.76
Small Growth	607	1.00%	1.23%	1.50%	2.01%	2.37%	1.64	2.38
Small Value	284	0.99%	1.17%	1.44%	2.00%	2.22%	1.71	2.25
Specialty	1,921	0.87%	1.11%	1.52%	1.99%	2.33%	1.79	2.68
International	1,910	0.93%	1.18%	1.52%	2.04%	2.34%	1.74	2.51
S&P 500 Index Objective Funds	127	0.10%	0.25%	0.45%	0.86%	1.34%	3.46	13.38
Over All Equity Funds	**9,859**	0.80%	1.05%	1.39%	1.91%	2.22%	1.81	2.77

Source: Strategic Insight, Simfund Mutual Fund Database, 2008.

Note: Eighty-five funds not assigned to a Morningstar category were excluded.

so it is uneconomical for the average consumer to become perfectly informed and always pay the lowest possible price, assuming this was even hypothetically possible. These real-world conditions are assumed away in the textbook model of perfect competition and its implications as embodied in the law of one price.

The model of perfect competition is useful in understanding how prices are determined, given certain conditions of supply and demand. However, using it as the standard for judging whether price competition exists in the real world is misleading because the conditions for perfect competition are largely unattainable.[28] Therefore, rather than trying to meet an unattainable ideal of perfect competition, the nature of price competition must be examined under real-world conditions, acknowledging unequal products, services, distribution, and firms; diversity in buyer demand; and buyers facing transaction costs and imperfect information.

Economic Theory and Evidence on Price Dispersion

Just as differences in fees between retail mutual fund and institutional investors are consistent with price competition, as discussed earlier in this chapter, price dispersion is consistent with price competition. Given widespread product and firm differentiation, differences in demand across buyers, and market frictions, it can hardly be otherwise. Studies show that price dispersion across rival sellers is commonly observed in highly price-competitive markets.[29] As noted, consumers generally have something less than perfectly complete information on all sellers' products, services, and prices, because it is uneconomical in time spent and other search costs to obtain perfect information.

Price dispersion also exists across competing sellers because of such factors as location, buyer transaction costs, quality of services, warranties, seller reputation, inferences of product quality, and other factors depending on the product. As an example, price dispersion exists due to product differentiation in chemically equivalent products, such as aspirin, liquid bleach, and prescription drugs (brand name versus equivalent generic and private label products). Some buyers are willing, for whatever personal reasons, to pay more for one brand over another based on perceived aspects of product differentiation. Hence, prices differ in price-competitive markets because of such factors as seller brand name, frequency of consumers' purchases, and services to buyers.[30]

Similarly, price differences occur across channels of distribution. Prices for an identical product often differ between types of sales outlets, such as discount versus full-service stores (e.g., cameras, home appliances, and food items), retail stores versus Internet sellers, and across Internet sellers (e.g., CDs and best-selling books).[31] In other contexts, as already mentioned, prices can differ across type of customer and by customer preferences (airline seats, motion picture theater seats, buyer loyalty programs, etc.) Such examples illustrate that price dispersion and price competition are ubiquitous. These examples of price dispersion are consistent with economic theories of consumer search costs, including the opportunity cost of consumers' time and consumer heterogeneity in demand.

Product variety and search costs are just as applicable in explaining price dispersion in mutual funds. Fund share buyers with less investment experience are more likely to purchase through a financial adviser, paying for advice through higher fees.[32] More experienced buyers are likely to provide more of their own financial counsel, incurring lower mutual fund fees and load expenses.[33]

Asset Distribution and Price Range

When examining fund price dispersion data, it is important to consider how fund assets are distributed within fund price ranges. As discussed previously, fund assets are not evenly distributed across investor price ranges; that is, the same percentages of assets are not held in low-, medium-, and high-price funds. Rather, investors' assets are concentrated in the lower price ranges.

In the case of S&P 500 index funds, over 90 percent of fund assets are invested in the lowest price funds, consistent with investors being sensitive to price and price competition prevailing in market index funds.[34] The fact that fees paid by investors vary in such fund investment categories—in which, again, assets are concentrated in the lowest fee funds—provides no support for claims that price competition is absent in index funds or mutual funds more broadly. For higher fee S&P 500 index funds to survive, they must offer a uniquely differentiated product, such as in the types of services or other product attributes sought by a relatively small share of index fund investors.

Because price dispersion is completely compatible with price competition, is there nevertheless a point at which price dispersion is so large as to be incompatible with price competition? The study by Wallison and Litan argues that the size of mutual fund price dispersion in the United States is so large relative to other countries, in particular England, that it can be explained only by a lack of price competition between mutual fund advisory firms in the United States.[35] In general, there is no simple standard to refer to when claiming that price dispersion is large enough to cast doubt on the existence of price competition. More importantly, with respect to mutual fund advisers' fees, whatever the fee dispersion in U.S. equity mutual funds is relative to other countries, the average fee of U.S. mutual funds is either the lowest or close to the lowest in the world—a strong indicator of price competition.[36]

The bottom line is that products and services in general are differentiated in many ways—brand name, reputation, outlets, image, consumers' experience, services to consumers, performance, and so forth—leading to a dispersion of prices across rival sellers. In a similar manner, mutual funds and fund complexes are differentiated in many ways, including past returns to investors, investment advisers, sellers' reputation and image, fund investment style, breadth of product offerings, channels of distribution, marketing efforts, and services to shareholders. There will necessarily be price dispersion across mutual funds, including passively managed funds, such as S&P 500 index funds.

In summary, contrary to fee critics' assertions, price dispersion between rival mutual fund advisers offers no evidence that price competition is lacking. Indeed, low prices in a distribution of the prices of comparable products provide direct evidence of price competition. What would be surprising in branded markets like mutual funds, where there are over 8,000 funds and approximately 600 complexes for investors to choose from, would be finding little price dispersion across competing mutual funds.

Economies of Scale in Mutual Funds and Price Competition

Fee Critics' Arguments

Fee critics assert that there is overwhelming evidence of large economies of scale in managing mutual funds, wherein unit-operating costs decline as assets under management increase.[37] For a profit-maximizing firm, as cost per unit declines with increasing output, the firm's price declines, holding demand and other factors constant. Indeed, regardless of whether a market is served by a single or multiple sellers, price will always reflect economies of scale. Assuming economies of scale exist in mutual funds, the remaining issue is whether such cost savings is sufficiently shared with investors, given the law under the Investment Company Act (ICA) of 1940.

Fee critics test their argument regarding the absence of price competition by first assuming the existence of large economies of scale and then examining changes in mutual fund fees over time. Finding that mutual fund fees have increased over time despite the existence of presumably large economies of scale, they conclude that zero cost savings have been passed on to fund investors—again, because of the supposed absence of price competition. This argument has been central to fee critics' claims of excessive investor fees and a lack of price competition among mutual funds since the 1962 Wharton Report. The facts, however, have gone largely unquestioned.[38]

According to the Wharton Report, although substantial growth in the value of funds' assets and cost reductions generated by large economies of scale occurred in the 1950s, fees had more or less remained constant.[39] The report found that in a sample of 163 investment advisers, only 15 percent provided fee breakpoints to investors—with lower fees after certain levels of assets under management had been achieved—leading to the Wharton Report's conclusion that cost savings were not passed on to the majority of fund shareholders.[40] Based on these findings, the Wharton Report concluded that price competition was absent in the mutual fund industry.

The extent of economies of scale in investment adviser operations and the sharing of cost savings with fund investors have also been singled out in the courts as key factors to consider in cases charging a mutual fund with setting excessive fees. The *Gartenberg* decision identified economies of scale as one among the court's list of factors to consider in assessing whether fees are excessive, based on the court's understanding of Congressional intent[41] in passing the amendment that added Section 36(b) to the ICA in 1970.[42] As described in Chapter 3, Section 36(b) imposes a fiduciary duty on investment advisers with respect to their compensation by fund shareholders and grants shareholders the right to sue investment advisers on the grounds that the fiduciary relationship was breached. This engendered the belief that advisers' management of mutual funds is subject to large economies of scale and that lower costs were not being passed on to investors due to a lack of price competition which underlay passage of Section 36(b). As a consequence, plaintiffs in cases under Section 36(b) have charged mutual funds with failing to pass on cost reductions from economies of scale to shareholders through lower shareholder fees.[43] As indicated, despite the seemingly majority view of large economies of scale in investment advisory services, the extent of such economies, as discussed here in the following section, remains an open question. The fee critics' method of testing for economies of scale is suspect, and economies of scale at the individual fund level are impossible to measure with a reasonable degree of accuracy due to joint and common costs. Questions thus remain on whether the evidence on economies of scale is as overwhelming as claimed.

Economies of Scale in the Short-Run and Long-Run

In stating that cost reductions due to economies of scale are pervasive in the mutual fund industry, critics are referring to a decline in long-run average advisory costs per unit of assets as assets under management increase. This claim stands in contrast to a short-run decrease in average cost as output increases for a fixed technology and scale of operations. Short-run economies of scale do not guarantee long-run economies of scale when an advisory firm repeatedly increases its scale of operations. Assuming there are long-run economies of scale initially, at some point average cost ceases to decline.[44] Economies of scale by themselves do not protect firms from incurring increasing operating costs over time. Manufacturing industries characterized by large economies of scale, such as automobiles, commercial aircraft, and major household appliances, still face potential labor, administrative, materials, energy, plant and equipment, and other cost increases from year to year. Rising input costs may offset any cost reductions associated with increasing scale of operations, such that long-run average and marginal costs do not decline.[45] At issue is whether there are long-run economies of scale in managing mutual funds, giving larger firms cost advantages over smaller firms, or whether smaller advisers suffer minimum cost disadvantages because of scale effects, allowing them to remain price-competitive.

Fee critics tend to use the existence of economies of scale as an either/or test of price competition. Lower advisory costs from economies of scale are either passed on to investors due to price competition between funds, or they are not, indicating an absence of price competition. But this artificial split is inconsistent with basic economics. Economic theory shows that profit-maximizing firms subject to economies of scale necessarily pass some portion of economies of scale cost reductions to buyers because profit maximization requires establishing an optimum price based on demand and the costs of operations. Whether the seller is one of many competitors or a single- firm monopoly, facing no close substitutes, cost reductions from economies of scale are reflected in lower prices to buyers. Under competitive market conditions with firms achieving minimum efficient scale, profit-maximization prevents fees from rising above the competitive level. However, under pure monopoly with economies of scale, only a portion of cost reductions from economies of scale is necessarily passed on in order for the firm to maximize its profits. As a matter of pure economics, the critics' claim that (profit-maximizing) mutual funds do not pass on unit cost reductions generated by economies of scale makes no economic sense.

Relative to the competitive case, pricing in the monopoly case could be considered excessive, depending on how *excessive* is defined. As noted earlier, under the law as interpreted in *Gartenberg*, "To be guilty of a violation of § 36(b), therefore, the adviser-manager must charge a fee that is so disproportionately large that it bears no reasonable relationship to the services rendered and could not have been the product of arm's-length bargaining."[46]

A first question in investigating the claim that economies of scale are not passed on to investors in mutual funds is whether, in contrast to what is widely reported, such economies of scale exist? If there are no substantial overall economies of scale in mutual fund operation, the critics' claim of cost reductions not being passed on to investors is moot. A second question is, if economies of scale do exist, what is the extent of such economies? Are they so substantial that, absent price and nonprice competition, investment advisers would earn well above risk-adjusted, competitive profits?

In addition, what constitutes "disproportionately large" has not been defined in mutual fund fee court decisions. In relationship to the fee critics' world of no or weak price competition versus price competition, the concept is unclear. For example, a pure but inefficiently operated monopolist could have a small price markup over cost, such that price does not appear to be "disproportionately large" relative to cost, even though there is no price competition.

A third question, again under the law as described in *Gartenberg*, is to what extent cost savings need to be passed on to defend against a charge of excessive pricing. Congress did not provide guidance on this point, nor has it been made clear in cases alleging excessive investor fees, although the presence of fee breakpoints based on fund asset size has been regarded as a sufficient passing on of cost reductions in some court decisions.[47]

Prior Studies

Studies on economies of scale in mutual fund management generally fall into one of two categories. The most common approach examines fund expense ratios relative to the amount of assets under management, where expense ratios reflect total investor fees. Most studies find expense ratios decline with increases in assets under management up to some level of assets.[48] Faster growth in assets than expenses, however, does not necessarily establish the presence of large economies of scale.

There are serious problems in estimating economies of scale by comparing expense ratios to asset sizes over time. Economies of scale lead to lower cost per unit of output as output grows, but mutual fund asset size is not necessarily equivalent to advisers' output. Adviser output is reflected in a fund's performance, which logically is associated with changes in assets. However, mutual fund assets can appreciate independent of selling one more share of a fund or adding a single new customer, so in periods of rapid stock market increases, fund assets can be a poor proxy for adviser output, giving an unreliable measure of economies of scale.

This traditional approach to testing for economies of scale can also be misleading, depending on how expense ratios are measured. Because investor fees used to cover the cost of adviser operations are based on adviser expenses, which typically include profits to the adviser for running the fund, these studies are measuring the total revenue ratio, or the amount of revenues per dollar of assets managed by the adviser. Measuring expenses plus profits is unambiguous in the case of complexes that contract out for portfolio management with outside subadvisers to run their funds' portfolios. Subadvisers' fees include the profits earned for the advisers' services, so profits are included as an expense in the fund's expense ratio and passed on to the fund's shareholders.

A further problem results when revenues do not closely track costs. With new entrants or relatively small funds, costs are typically greater than revenues, and over time, as the fund adds more investors and assets, revenues will ideally equal or exceed costs. Thus, studies using the expense ratio are in many cases measuring the ratio of revenues and not costs to assets, as a proxy for cost per unit of output, and provide little basis to draw conclusions on the extent of scale economies.

The Wharton Report, which initiated the debate on whether economies of scale are passed on to investors, provides an example of how *not* to test for economies of scale. The Wharton study examined the ratio of adviser expenses to total revenue over different asset size classes for 86 open-end investment companies, finding that expenses fell as a share of revenue as fund assets under management increased up to $300 to $600 million in assets.[49] However, expenses *rose* as a share of assets for funds of $600 million in assets and higher. In other words, profit margins rose with asset size increases up to $600 million and then fell as assets exceeded $600 million. This approach, comparing profit margins by asset size categories, is not a proper measure of economies of scale. The most successful and efficient firms are more profitable and generally grow relative to rivals, but their size and profitability are not necessarily due to economies of scale. The Wharton Report did not test for economies of scale by analyzing cost changes relative to changes in output for a given scale (short-run economies of scale) or over time as the scale of operations increased (long-run economies of scale). Rather, it looked at how profit margins changed relative to funds' asset size, attempting to infer from rising profit margins with larger asset size the existence of economies of scale. As stated, more profitable firms generally grow at the expense of less profitable firms. Whether they are more profitable because of economies of scale or other reasons cannot be known by just looking at profit margins relative to asset size. Moreover, as noted, profit margins are not necessarily correlated with cost per unit of output. A firm can have relatively low profit margins yet be subject to large economies of scale, depending on how efficiently it is managed. The Wharton Report and subsequent studies using a similar methodology offer little credible empirical basis for concluding that there are large economies of scale in managing mutual funds.

The second category of studies on economies of scale in mutual funds uses regression analysis to test for cost changes as output grows, although they also use assets as a proxy for output.[50] The purpose of using regression models is to account for all the other factors that influence expense ratios or total costs, which are ignored in studies that examine just expense ratios relative to assets under management as a determinant of economies of scale. Prior regression-based models include such explanatory variables as number of funds in a portfolio, number of investor accounts, distribution costs, and fund performance as determinants of economies of scale. These studies tend to find evidence of economies of scale at both the complex and fund level; however, their estimates of the size of such economies, relatively large or small, are not in agreement.

Measuring Economies of Scale in Multiproduct Firms

Estimating a true measure of economies of scale for a product within a multiproduct firm—the relevant description of a mutual fund complex—is difficult, if not impossible, in most cases. In a multiproduct firm there are joint and common costs, with the same operating assets contributing to the production of multiple products. True measures of economies of scale and scope in such a setting should not depend on how joint and common costs are allocated to each product because there are multiple ways to allocate such costs, producing different cost measures by product depending on the allocation method adopted. Although accountants regularly allocate joint and common costs to specific products or business lines for managerial accounting and budgetary purposes, such allocations are arbitrary from an economics perspective.

Imagine, for example, a silicon wafer manufacturing facility producing different types of wafers, all in the same ultraclean facility. How can the cost to purify the air be allocated to each type of wafer, except on an arbitrary basis? Cost could be allocated based on a number of alternative methods, such as number of wafers produced, revenues by wafer type, size of wafers, labor-hours required for each wafer, wafer-specific manufacturing space requirements, and so forth. Each allocation basis would yield a different estimate of product-specific joint and common cost, so measures of performance variables that are a function of costs, such as return on capital and economies of scale, could differ drastically based on the cost allocation basis adopted.

An example of the arbitrariness of allocation rules, using data for T. Rowe Price's Prime Reserve Fund (a money market fund), was provided in the 1980s.[51] The authors used five different variables to allocate costs in order to calculate a return on capital. They allocated costs alternatively based on (1) relative mutual fund revenues, (2) relative number of labor-hours, (3) relative amounts spent on wages, (4) relative number of customers served, and (5) a judicious weighting and manipulation of factors (1) through (4) to generate intuitively plausible rates of return. Using data for 1980, return on capital for the fund varied from −125 percent using number of customers to allocate costs to +247 percent using direct labor costs, that is, from a huge loss to substantial profitability. Similar results were found for 1981, when return on capital varied from −111 percent using number of customers to +201 percent using direct labor costs. Alternatively, weighting each allocation variable—number of customers, revenues, direct labor hours, and direct labor costs—in a manner thought best to reflect each department's activity, produced more conservative profit rates of 15.4 percent in 1980 and 6.7 percent in 1981. Alternative bases for cost allocation, using the same allocation rule for each cost category, produced widely different results.

Such a wide range of results would also occur in any attempt to estimate economies of scale for an individual fund within a fund complex. The greater the differences in cost across alternative cost allocation metrics, the wider the estimates of economies of scale. One can, of course, produce estimates of economies of scale and scope given sufficient data. However, the range of estimates is limited only by the range of cost allocation bases applied. True economies of scale at the fund level, if true cost data were theoretically available, could be within the range of the estimated values or, just as likely, outside the range of such estimates.

The arbitrariness of cost allocations might be improved in some cases by using activity-based allocations. For example, rather than using fund revenues to allocate all joint and common costs for a complex, the number of customers can be used to more accurately allocate customer-based costs, such as telephone costs for fund service representatives, mailings to investors, securities transfer fees, and so forth. By linking cost allocations more closely to the cost-generating activities, more accurate allocations can be achieved in some cases. However, this does not remove all arbitrariness. In some cases, activity-based measures are not available, and even when available, they are not necessarily highly correlated with a product's share of joint and common costs.

Estimating Economies of Scale at the Complex and Fund Levels

Given the structure of the mutual fund industry, a first impression might be that economies of scale at the fund or complex level would be relatively small at best. In industries where economies of scale are large relative to aggregate market demand, revenues or assets are concentrated in a few firms. As noted earlier, examples of industries with large economies of scale and high concentration include manufacturers of large commercial aircraft, large commercial jet engines, and major home appliances. In each case, economies of scale are so large relative to total market demand that only a few firms can profitably operate. This is not the market structure of mutual funds. As detailed in Chapter 5, the top 20 to 25 complexes account for the majority of mutual fund assets, but they face competition from hundreds of rival complexes and thousands of funds, as well as nonmutual fund investments. If there are economies of scale in mutual fund management, they appear to be small relative to total market demand and not large enough to dictate the number and size distribution of firms in the industry. If economies of scale were large in mutual funds, the cost disadvantage of being a small fund would not allow it to survive. Instead, small and large funds and complexes coexist, indicating that if economies of scale exist in mutual funds, they are achieved at relatively small asset size levels. The largest funds, with billions of dollars of assets under management, likely exhausted their economies of scale long ago. As a consequence, accepting the fee critics' argument relating economies of scale to fee levels, any cost and price reductions based on economies of scale are likely to be relatively small.

An Alternative Approach to Estimating Scale Economies

A method that avoids measurement problems associated with allocating joint and common costs and in measuring output in financial markets, where measuring output is often ambiguous, is the "survivor" technique.[52] This method assumes that profit-maximizing firms compete to become the most efficient, optimally sized and organized producer, just as firms compete on the demand side of the market by attempting to offer the best combination of price, quality, service, and distribution. When there are economies of scale, the best run firms will grow into the most efficient, optimum firm size range over time. Firms unable to capture the benefits of economies of scale through growth will disappear, leaving the most efficient sized firms. Hence, when technology, learning by doing, and volume effects lead to large long-run economies of scale, large enough to result in a sustainable competitive advantage over smaller rivals, only the largest, most efficient firms will survive. Conversely, if economies and diseconomies of scale are not significant contributors to firm size, then relatively small, medium, and large firms can compete effectively without suffering significant cost disadvantages owing to firm size. By examining shifts in firm sizes over time, the optimum, most efficient firm size should be identifiable, if it exists. If a range of optimum firm sizes is not evident from examining the size distribution of firms over time in an industry, then economies of scale are small at best, are exhausted at relatively low-size levels, and do not play a significant role in shaping the cost and size of individual firms. If the latter is true in the mutual fund industry, the fee critics' claim that mutual funds experience large economies of scale and that scale-generated cost reductions are not passed on to fund investors has little empirical support.

Table 6.2 shows a survivorship analysis for U.S. equity mutual fund complexes over the periods 1985 to 2007 and 1995 to 2007. The results in each period are arrayed by complex asset size deciles, with the lowest decile being 1 and the highest decile 10. Size deciles in the periods studied are adjusted for returns on the market using the S&P 500 index. The percentage of complexes in a decile that survived to 2007 is shown in the fourth column. As an example, starting in 1985 approximately 47 percent of equity complexes in the smallest decile survived to 2007. For complexes in 1995, approximately 31 percent in the smallest decile survived to 2007, and 46 percent in the next larger decile survived.

Of greatest interest, however, is what happened to the size of the surviving complexes. The matrices on the right-hand side of Table 6.2 provide answers for the periods examined. Of the 47 percent of smallest complexes that survived from 1985 to 2007, 11 percent remained in the smallest decile size class, indicating that they did not survive by growing large relative to their rivals to capture economies of scale. Moving to the third decile for the period 1985 to 2007, the results show that 53 percent survived to 2007, but of those surviving, approximately 30 percent either remained the same size or declined in size relative to their initial year size decile. While the majority of 1985 complexes

Initial Year	Initial Complex Size Decile	Percentage of Decile that Did Not Survive to 2007	Percentage of Decile that Survived to 2007	Distribution of Surviving Complexes by Size Deciles as of 2007 (As a Percentage of Survivors)									
				1	2	3	4	5	6	7	8	9	10
1985	1	52.6%	47.4%	11.1%	0.0%	0.0%	22.2%	0.0%	22.2%	22.2%	0.0%	22.2%	0.0%
1985	2	63.2%	36.8%	0.0%	14.3%	0.0%	28.6%	14.3%	14.3%	0.0%	28.6%	0.0%	0.0%
1985	3	47.4%	52.6%	0.0%	20.0%	10.0%	20.0%	10.0%	20.0%	0.0%	10.0%	10.0%	0.0%
1985	4	42.1%	57.9%	0.0%	0.0%	9.1%	0.0%	0.0%	9.1%	18.2%	18.2%	36.4%	9.1%
1985	5	42.1%	57.9%	9.1%	0.0%	9.1%	0.0%	9.1%	0.0%	18.2%	18.2%	9.1%	27.3%
1985	6	21.1%	78.9%	0.0%	0.0%	0.0%	13.3%	20.0%	13.3%	6.7%	13.3%	20.0%	13.3%
1985	7	42.1%	57.9%	0.0%	0.0%	0.0%	0.0%	9.1%	0.0%	9.1%	27.3%	36.4%	18.2%
1985	8	10.5%	89.5%	0.0%	0.0%	0.0%	0.0%	0.0%	5.9%	0.0%	17.6%	17.6%	58.8%
1985	9	15.8%	84.2%	0.0%	0.0%	0.0%	0.0%	0.0%	0.0%	0.0%	18.8%	31.3%	50.0%
1985	10	0.0%	100.0%	0.0%	0.0%	0.0%	0.0%	0.0%	0.0%	0.0%	0.0%	0.0%	100.0%
	Average	33.7%	66.3%										

(continued)

TABLE 6.2 (continued)

Initial Year	Initial Complex Size Decile	Percentage of Decile that Did Not Survive to 2007	Percentage of Decile that Survived to 2007	Distribution of Surviving Complexes by Size Deciles as of 2007 (As a Percentage of Survivors)									
				1	2	3	4	5	6	7	8	9	10
1995	1	68.9%	31.1%	7.1%	0.0%	21.4%	14.3%	7.1%	28.6%	14.3%	7.1%	0.0%	0.0%
1995	2	54.3%	45.7%	19.0%	4.8%	0.0%	19.0%	14.3%	9.5%	4.8%	0.0%	19.0%	9.5%
1995	3	46.7%	53.3%	0.0%	29.2%	8.3%	8.3%	8.3%	16.7%	12.5%	16.7%	0.0%	0.0%
1995	4	50.0%	50.0%	4.3%	0.0%	17.4%	4.3%	26.1%	13.0%	17.4%	13.0%	0.0%	4.3%
1995	5	35.6%	64.4%	0.0%	3.4%	3.4%	13.8%	17.2%	20.7%	10.3%	27.6%	3.4%	0.0%
1995	6	32.6%	67.4%	0.0%	0.0%	3.2%	3.2%	9.7%	19.4%	32.3%	19.4%	12.9%	0.0%
1995	7	31.1%	68.9%	0.0%	0.0%	3.2%	6.5%	6.5%	9.7%	29.0%	22.6%	16.1%	6.5%
1995	8	37.0%	63.0%	0.0%	0.0%	0.0%	0.0%	0.0%	10.3%	13.8%	31.0%	41.4%	3.4%
1995	9	17.8%	82.2%	0.0%	0.0%	0.0%	0.0%	0.0%	2.7%	0.0%	16.2%	43.2%	37.8%
1995	10	2.2%	97.8%	0.0%	0.0%	0.0%	0.0%	0.0%	0.0%	0.0%	4.4%	13.3%	82.2%
	Average	37.6%	62.4%										

Source: Strategic Insight, Simfund Mutual Fund Database, 2008.

Notes: Excludes closed-end funds, ETFs, funds of funds, exchange funds, and variable annuities. Complex size was measured by total assets under management. Decile 10 represents the largest 10% of complexes. A complex in existence in 1985 or 1995 is deemed to have survived if it has positive net assets in 2007. The data set does not distinguish between complexes that were liquidated and those that were merged into other complexes. Strategic Insight data on assets begin in 1985.

that survived to 2007 grew in size, a surprising share of successful survivors either stayed the same size or lost size relative to their size class rivals. Similar findings are evident for 1995–2007. Overall, the surviving complexes tended to grow into higher size deciles but sometimes declined into smaller size deciles. The results show no evidence of optimum firm size or minimum efficient scale of operations required to capture economies of scale, indicating that economies of scale at the mutual fund complex level are relatively small.

Table 6.3 presents a survivor test for economies of scale at the equity fund level. The surviving, initially smallest funds generally grew into larger asset size deciles, but these shifts in size were spread from the lowest to the highest deciles. Similar results appear for the next few higher deciles for each starting year. For the middle-size deciles, again, the surviving funds tended to grow, but some shrank relative to rivals. There is no evidence in the results of surviving funds clustering into one or a few asset size deciles, as would occur if there were significant economies of scale in individual funds that would handicap smaller or possibly even larger funds.

To summarize, the survivor results for complexes and individual equity funds show no clear evidence of large economies of scale. If economies of scale exist in equity complexes and mutual funds, these results indicate they are relatively small, and the largest complexes and funds exhausted their potential economies of scale long ago. The results are consistent with the structure of the mutual fund industry, with hundreds of complexes and thousands of funds of widely varying size competing for investors. As stated earlier, if there were significant economies of scale in mutual funds, cost-disadvantaged, non-optimal size funds and complexes could not survive. Instead, funds and complexes have a long history of successful entry and survival for decades in competition with well-established and much larger rivals.

We are not surprised by these results. Mutual fund complexes and funds can be organized in multiple ways. Some funds are highly vertically integrated, conducting their own research, portfolio management, distribution, marketing, shareholder securities transfers, and so forth. Some are partially integrated, such as Vanguard, which operates its index funds but traditionally has farmed out the portfolio management of its actively managed funds to subadvisory firms. Some funds contract with an outside sales force, such as brokers and financial advisers. Indeed, funds can contract out for most services—investment advice, transfer agent, custodian services, distribution, and so forth. A fund, for example, can serve primarily as a marketing organization, contracting out for all other services. The ability to purchase such services, relying on the seller's economies of scale, helps explain why small funds and complexes can remain cost- and price-competitive relative to larger rivals.

TABLE 6.3 Survival Rate of U.S. Equity Mutual Funds, 1985–2007 and 1995–2007

Initial Year	Initial Fund Size Decile	Percentage of Decile that Did Not Survive to 2007	Percentage of Decile that Survived to 2007	Distribution of Surviving Funds by Size Deciles as of 2007 (As a Percentage of Survivors)									
				1	2	3	4	5	6	7	8	9	10
1985	1	59.4%	40.6%	3.8%	3.8%	11.5%	0.0%	15.4%	19.2%	3.8%	3.8%	26.9%	11.5%
1985	2	50.8%	49.2%	3.1%	9.4%	3.1%	6.3%	18.8%	9.4%	6.3%	12.5%	25.0%	6.3%
1985	3	52.3%	47.7%	3.2%	3.2%	6.5%	12.9%	3.2%	12.9%	9.7%	9.7%	16.1%	22.6%
1985	4	45.3%	54.7%	2.9%	5.7%	2.9%	5.7%	5.7%	14.3%	2.9%	17.1%	22.9%	20.0%
1985	5	49.2%	50.8%	0.0%	3.0%	3.0%	12.1%	3.0%	18.2%	9.1%	9.1%	18.2%	24.2%
1985	6	46.2%	53.8%	2.9%	0.0%	2.9%	2.9%	8.6%	11.4%	11.4%	17.1%	28.6%	14.3%
1985	7	31.3%	68.8%	0.0%	0.0%	4.5%	9.1%	2.3%	9.1%	18.2%	6.8%	13.6%	36.4%
1985	8	40.0%	60.0%	0.0%	2.6%	0.0%	0.0%	5.1%	15.4%	23.1%	10.3%	7.7%	35.9%
1985	9	29.2%	70.8%	0.0%	0.0%	0.0%	2.2%	2.2%	6.5%	8.7%	6.5%	26.1%	47.8%
1985	10	12.3%	87.7%	0.0%	0.0%	0.0%	0.0%	0.0%	0.0%	3.5%	10.5%	15.8%	70.2%
	Average	41.6%	58.4%										

Year	Decile												
1995	1	61.7%	38.3%	10.8%	16.1%	11.8%	4.3%	9.7%	8.6%	8.6%	11.8%	10.8%	7.5%
1995	2	62.3%	37.7%	5.4%	12.0%	13.0%	14.1%	7.6%	12.0%	10.9%	10.9%	8.7%	5.4%
1995	3	52.3%	47.7%	1.7%	9.5%	8.6%	13.8%	19.0%	10.3%	8.6%	15.5%	10.3%	2.6%
1995	4	51.6%	48.4%	0.0%	4.2%	11.9%	16.1%	16.1%	10.2%	11.0%	11.0%	11.0%	8.5%
1995	5	49.8%	50.2%	0.8%	2.5%	11.5%	13.9%	8.2%	13.9%	7.4%	19.7%	15.6%	6.6%
1995	6	38.5%	61.5%	0.0%	3.3%	6.0%	10.0%	8.0%	16.0%	14.0%	14.7%	14.0%	14.0%
1995	7	38.7%	61.3%	0.7%	2.7%	2.0%	4.0%	8.1%	18.1%	20.8%	18.8%	15.4%	9.4%
1995	8	38.1%	61.9%	0.7%	0.0%	1.3%	4.6%	7.3%	14.6%	17.2%	13.2%	22.5%	18.5%
1995	9	23.9%	76.1%	0.5%	0.5%	1.1%	1.1%	3.2%	8.1%	14.1%	15.1%	27.6%	28.6%
1995	10	11.5%	88.5%	0.0%	0.0%	0.0%	0.5%	0.5%	0.9%	4.6%	10.2%	17.1%	66.2%
	Average	42.8%	57.2%										

Source: Strategic Insight, Simfund Mutual Fund Database, 2008.

Notes: Excludes closed-end funds, ETFs, funds of funds, exchange funds, and variable annuities. Fund size was measured by total assets under management. Decile 10 represents the largest 10% of funds. A fund in existence in 1985 or 1995 is deemed to have survived if it has positive net assets in 2007. The data set does not distinguish between funds that were liquidated and funds that were merged into other mutual funds. Strategic Insight data on assets begin in 1985.

Increasing Expense Ratios as Evidence
of No Price Competition

Fee critics contend that investor fees, as represented by mutual fund expense ratios, have risen since the 1970s despite large economies of scale in fund operation accompanying increases in fund assets under management; that is, expenses have risen faster than assets, leading to lower returns for investors.[53] Increasing expense ratios are offered as evidence that price competition in mutual funds is lacking and investment adviser profits have grown at the expense of returns to investors. Writing in 2003, John Bogle, founder and former head of the Vanguard Group of mutual funds stated, "Over the past twenty years, costs have deprived the average equity fund investor of nearly one-half of the stock markets returns."[54] If correct, the gap between actual stock market returns and, for example, net returns to S&P 500 mutual fund investors has been growing, significantly reducing many fund investors' long-term returns. However, if investors' fees and expenses per dollar of fund assets have been declining, then fee and expense levels offer little empirical support for claims of no price competition in mutual funds.

Various studies have examined trends in average mutual fund expense ratios, and the results tend to contradict the critics' claim of increasing ratios. The results vary across studies, depending on the time period reviewed, how expense ratios are measured, and the sample of mutual funds examined. However, when examined carefully, expense ratios have trended downward.

Trends in expense ratios are strongly affected by how they are measured, such as with or without 12b-1 fees. As noted in Chapter 5, these fees are used to cover additional expenses for selling fund shares, such as brokers' commissions and advice to investors, and expenses in servicing shareholders. Mutual funds' use of 12b-1 fees grew slowly at first, after 1980, but became more widespread in the 1990s, increasing investors' fees in funds incorporating 12b-1 fees. As also noted in Chapter 5, during the same time period, front- and back-end sales loads were declining from an average maximum front-end load of 8.0 percent in the 1970s to approximately 5.0 percent in 2007.[55] In percentage point terms, load fees declined far more than 12b-1 fees rose, so the net effect was a decline in investor fees.

In studying trends in expense ratios, the SEC found that the main cause of increasing average expense ratios was the shift by load mutual funds toward 12b-1 fees.[56] It further found that average expense ratios for all classes of funds was 0.73 percent in 1979, when 12b-1 fees did not exist, and 0.94 percent in 1999, when 12b-1 fees were included in expense ratios.[57] However, examining funds absent 12b-1 fees and loads from 1979 to 1999, to neutralize their influence on expense ratios, the SEC found the average expense ratio was 0.75 percent in 1979 and 0.69 percent in 1999, with a peak of 0.80 percent in 1992 and a low of 0.66 percent in 1999.[58] Funds without 12b-1 fees and loads displayed no long-term trend toward increasing expense ratios over the 21-year period, and in fact their average expense ratios declined.

For load funds, the SEC found that the average expense ratio rose over the same period from 0.72 percent to 1.17 percent.[59] However, when sales loads were incorporated as part of investor costs, the SEC found (by amortizing load fees over a five-year period) that the average expense ratio declined from 2.28 percent in 1979 to 1.88 percent in 1999.[60] This is a general finding across studies that examine price trends by adding amortized load fees to expense ratios.[61] The Investment Company Institute (ICI), for example, reports that stock fund expense ratios when adjusted for sales loads declined from 2.32 percent in 1980 to 1.02 percent in 2007, with much of the decline occurring from 1980 to 2000.[62] The ICI's studies of expense ratios also show that the time period examined matters. The ICI found that average expense ratios, excluding annual sales loads, declined from 1.0 percent in 2002 to 0.86 percent in 2007 but rose from 0.94 percent in 1999 to 1.0 percent in 2002. Similar results were found when examining the largest equity funds, where the greatest potential harm to investors from excessive fees exists. In measuring expense ratios for the largest 46 U.S. equity funds in the 1990s, the GAO found that almost 85 percent of the 46 largest equity funds lowered their fees in the 1990s, and two made no changes, with the average fee falling from 0.75 percent in 1990 to 0.65 percent in 1998, and then rebounding in 2001 to 0.70 percent.[63]

In addition to variations in expense ratios due to how they are measured, equity fund expense ratios vary with the composition of equity mutual funds examined. New funds have higher expense ratios than older funds, so periods of large-scale new entry tend to result in higher average equity fund expense ratios. International, specialty sector, and small-cap funds generally have relatively higher expense ratios because of greater costs of managing investments, so shifts in portfolios toward these stocks, as occurred with foreign stocks from 2004 to 2006, tend to raise expense ratios. Conversely, as investors shift to noload funds and lower fee funds more broadly, average expense ratios tend to decline. As the mix of these opposing influences shifts overtime, along with competition between investment advisers to become more cost efficient and reduce expense ratios, the end result has been declining expense ratios when measured by including amortized sales loads over time, and even when loads are not taken into account, equity fund expense ratios declined from the early 1990s to 2007.

To summarize, studies on expense ratio trends by the SEC, GAO, and others contradict the fee critics' assertion that expense ratios have risen since the 1970s owing to a lack of price competition, resulting in investor exploitation by investment advisers. The average fees paid by equity fund investors in no-load and load funds, including sales load fees, have declined from approximately 1980 to the present, contrary to the fee critics' claim. Claims of rising expense ratios despite allegedly large economies of scale in managing mutual funds have little empirical support. When measured properly, expense ratios have not risen since the 1980s. Moreover, the data show that many smaller funds and complexes are not substantially disadvantaged by a relatively small amount of assets under management, and they are able to compete for years at a relatively small size.

Summary and Conclusions

Fee critics claim to have shown that mutual fund investment advisers do not compete on price because (1) institutional clients' fees are lower than retail mutual funds investors' fees, and institutional fees are set by price competition; (2) according to economic theory, in a competitive market, rivals' prices are identical or close to identical, but actual fees vary widely across mutual funds in the same investment category; and (3) with price competition, cost reductions are passed on to buyers, but cost savings in mutual funds from capturing economies of scale are not passed on to fund investors, as shown by long-term increases in equity funds' expense ratios.

The fee differences found between mutual fund investors and institutional clients are consistent with differences in products and costs in serving the two investment advisory sectors, as well as incremental pricing by fund advisers extending their services to institutional clients. Fee differences produced by these factors have nothing to do with a lack of price competition. Moreover, the fee comparisons made by critics of fund advisory firms are fraught with measurement problems, because reported management costs embody different cost components across mutual funds.

Price dispersion between competing sellers is perfectly consistent with price competition. Prices differ between rivals for a host of reasons, including firm and product differentiation; market frictions, such as search costs; and because of distribution through different sales channels. Numerous studies by economists show that price dispersion is commonly observed in highly price-competitive industries.

The claim that large economies of scale exist in mutual funds, long-term costs decline as assets grow, yet expense ratios have increased over time, proves the absence of price competition between fund advisers is not supported by the evidence. There is widespread belief that mutual fund advisers' costs are subject to large economies of scale, but few studies estimate actual cost curves. The structure of the industry, however, with the majority of assets accounted for by the largest 20 to 25 funds and complexes, with hundreds of smaller funds and complexes remaining in competition, implies that to the extent such economies of scale exist, they do not create a sufficiently large cost disadvantage to drive smaller funds and complexes out of business. Our test for economies of scale, using the survivorship approach, found no clear evidence of large economies of scale and a required minimum efficient scale for competitive survival.

Prior studies on changes in equity mutual fund expense ratios over time offer mixed results, depending on the time period tested and how expense ratios are measured. Some studies find declining expense ratios over long periods; some find expense ratios rising in some periods and falling in other periods; and some find little change in expense ratios over select time periods. The critics' assertion that expense ratios have consistently risen over time despite declining costs owing to large economies of scale has no credible empirical support.

CHAPTER SEVEN

Mutual Funds' Organizational Form and Conflicts of Interest

Introduction

As described earlier, fee critics claim that the organizational structure of most mutual funds, with investment advisers and mutual funds operating under separate ownership, necessarily creates a conflict of interest over the level of fees and, with bargaining power favoring investment advisers, represents the root cause of excessive fees.[1] Some critics also imply that mutual fund directors are bought off by advisers to approve excessive fund shareholder fees.[2]

Proposals to resolve the excessive fee problem center on reducing the postulated conflict of interest between fund shareholders and investment advisers. Two proposals are commonly offered. One proposal calls for eliminating the profit incentive for investment advisers. According to Yale University's chief investment officer, David Swensen, eliminating advisers' profit-maximizing motive dissipates their abuse of investors, including charging excessive fees. As he states:

> Overwhelming evidence proves the failure of the for-profit mutual-fund industry.... Not-for-profit organizational structures allow investment management companies to focus solely on fulfilling fiduciary responsibilities.... the absence of profit margins leads to lower costs for mutual-fund shareholders.... In the case of fund management companies organized on a not-for-profit basis, no conflict exists between serving investor goals and generating corporate income ... When the quest for profits disappears, abuse of investors dissipates.[3]

The second solution calls for funds and investment advisers to vertically integrate under a single, common ownership structure. Some argue that giving a fund's board of directors internal control over both the fund and the investment advisory function would mitigate attempts by investment advisers to act contrary to the interests of fund shareholders. Fees to cover investment advisory services would be within the internal control of the integrated mutual fund firm, owned by the fund's shareholders, and the firm would set investors' fees at the competitive level.[4]

Fee critics combine the two proposals to conclude that vertically integrated, not-for-profit mutual fund firms have no incentive to charge excessive fees or to profit from the fees charged to their investors. Such firms' chief, if not sole, interest is said to be to maximize returns for fund shareholders by pricing advisers' services well below the prices charged by for-profit, nonvertically integrated investment advisers.[5]

As quintessential examples of vertically integrated, nonprofit mutual fund companies whose organizational structure leads to low investor fees, critics point to the Vanguard Group of funds and TIAA-CREF. Vanguard was created in 1974–1975 as a traditional front-end, sales-load mutual fund complex through a name change from the long-established Wellington Funds. A few years later it was reorganized into a no-load group of funds. TIAA-CREF was organized decades earlier as an insurance company for educators. TIAA-CREF extended its product line to mutual funds in the 1980s for the retirement accounts held by a variety of professional groups, especially educators. According to fee critics, the two mutual fund complexes are structured to be free from the conflict of interest between fund shareholders and investment advisers because of their nonprofit status and reliance on internal portfolio management, resulting in rock bottom investor fees and maximization of investor returns. By arguably eliminating the conflict of interest, neither complex's advisers, according to fee critics, act to gain profits at the expense of their funds' shareholders.

Assessing Internal Management and Nonprofit Status

If the fee critics' ideal organizational form was economically superior, would it not be in use in the vast majority of funds today? Alternatively, would not Vanguard and TIAA-CREF be in control of the vast majority of mutual fund investments? With respect to the first question, the opposite has occurred. Just as firms compete for buyers on the basis of price, product and service quality, innovations, and reputation, so do they compete against one another for the most efficient organizational form. The most efficiently organized firms are the most productive at the lowest cost, gaining a competitive advantage over less efficiently organized rivals. The two organizational forms at issue for mutual funds, internal versus external investment advisers, or vertically integrated versus nonvertically integrated operations, have been competing against each other in mutual funds for over 80 years. The predominant mutual fund organizational form in the United States since at least the 1950s has been with an external or nonvertically integrated investment adviser. With regard to the second question, while Vanguard is one of the largest fund complexes in the United States, its total assets have frequently been matched or exceeded by American Funds and Fidelity. Vanguard has never come close to having a dominant share of mutual fund assets. TIAA-CREF has a much smaller share of mutual fund assets than Vanguard, but it has traditionally limited its investment base to educators and other professional groups.

The first open-end mutual fund in the United States, Massachusetts Investors Trust (MIT), along with its companion fund formed in 1934, Massachusetts Investors Growth Stock Fund (MIGSF), were vertically integrated, with the funds' trustees and an advisory group serving as the portfolio manager. MIT was the largest U.S. open-end mutual fund from 1936 into the 1950s.[6] From the first diversified, open-end mutual funds in 1924, both internal and external management structures were available to companies creating mutual funds. Over time, however, more and more investment advisers creating mutual funds adopted the nonvertically integrated structure, contracting with the funds to supply investment advisory services, and funds created with internally managed portfolios converted to external administrative and portfolio management.

The shift to a nonvertically integrated structure after 1940 can be explained in part by requirements under the Investment Company Act (ICA) of 1940, which regulated the makeup of a fund's board of directors; required annual shareholder elections for trustees and directors; and regulated the relationship between a fund's board of directors, investment adviser, and underwriting firm. However, if internally advised funds were superior to external advisory services because of lower costs, those organized before the ICA of 1940 would have produced better performance, attracting others to the internal organizational structure. Just as the vertically integrated MIT flourished from the 1930s to the 1950s, others would have attempted to copy its success by adopting MIT's organizational structure.

As of June 1966, some of the largest fund complexes were still internally managed, indicating they were not necessarily superior but certainly competitive with externally managed complexes at that time. The combined two original Massachusetts funds were second in size among the 10 largest mutual fund complexes.[7] Four funds, known as the Broad Street complex and affiliated with the J. & W. Seligman brokerage firm, owned their investment adviser and were seventh overall in complex asset size. However, across all equity fund complexes, internal management was used by a minority of funds. In the Wharton School report's sample of 164 open-end advisory groups at the end of 1960, only 14 funds had internal advisers.[8] Among 68 mutual fund complexes in the mid-1960s with $100 million or more in assets (that is, among the largest complexes of the time), only 11 managed their portfolios internally, and of the 11 only 6 were open-end investment companies, less than 10 percent of the largest fund complexes.[9] Thus, by the 1960s, external advisory management dominated mutual funds organizational form, in use at approximately 90 percent of all funds.

By the early 1970s, most if not all internally managed funds had converted to external investment management. Internally managed fund complexes, in head-to-head competition with externally managed funds for approximately 45 years, all but disappeared, suggesting that their economic and organizational structure was inferior to that of externally managed funds. The 1950s and 1960s were periods of strong mutual fund asset growth. If internal management was less efficient in meeting growth in investor demand, it would be replaced by the external management form. As one example, the MIT group of funds converted from internal to external management starting in 1969. The group stated that the conversion was needed in order to expand the number of funds offered. MIT explained that in 1968 its internal trustees (the portfolio managers) attempted to start a new fund but were blocked by legal problems with the Securities and Exchange Commission (SEC), which would not have occurred if the fund was managed externally.[10] Given that the SEC has long viewed the external management form as the root cause of the alleged conflict of interest between fund shareholders and their investment adviser, it would be ironic if the SEC itself forced internally managed mutual funds to switch to the external organizational form, that is, the form the SEC long blamed for creating the conflict of interest and thus requiring the SEC to expand its regulations of mutual funds to protect fund investors.

Thus, in the competitive arena of most efficient firm organizational form, approximately 45 years of internal investment advisory service had been largely displaced by external advisory management by 1970. Although some internally managed complexes grew to rank with the largest fund complexes as late as the 1960s, far more investor assets from the 1930s onward were invested in externally managed funds and fund complexes. The organizational structure reviled by fee critics, for-profit external investment advisers, proved more efficient in accommodating industry growth. The relative growth and long-term survival of internally versus externally managed funds suggests that attributing superior cost levels and investor returns to internal portfolio management is suspect.[11]

In addition to there being little evidence that internal portfolio management provided lower fees and greater returns during the period when internally managed complexes and funds were more common, internal advisory management, within the fee critics' framework, does not eliminate the claimed conflict of interest between fund shareholders and their portfolio manager. The fee critics' argument centers on a monopolist investment adviser (selling to immobile fund investors) whose monopoly power is neutralized in theory by a vertically integrated ownership structure operated as a nonprofit corporation. Whether hypothetical monopoly investment adviser services are offered by a fund contracting with a separately owned adviser company or as part of a vertically integrated mutual fund company, they remain a monopolized asset, under the fee critics' framework, whose managers have an incentive to exploit the profit potential for their own well-being. Thus, fund shareholder owners of an integrated firm still face a conflict of interest.

As with all publicly held companies, there is a conflict of interest between shareholders, seeking to maximize their returns, and managers, who seek to maximize their own well-being. With the managers in control of a monopoly asset, the two groups' interests do not necessarily coincide. Mutual fund managers may behave in a manner inconsistent with shareholders' interests, such as slacking off in work effort, taking higher risks than shareholders desire, or in this hypothetical case, setting higher than shareholder desired fees given management's alleged monopoly power.

Whether vertically integrated or not, investment advisers want to maximize their compensation. If restricted from doing so within an internally managed fund complex, with competitive markets for capital and labor, investment advisers will shift to a higher compensation organization. In competition between nonintegrated and integrated mutual fund companies, the best advisers, if unable to capture the full value of their expertise within an internal management structure, will start nonintegrated advisory firms if higher compensation is available, resulting in relatively reduced fund performance at vertically integrated versus nonvertically integrated funds.

The argument that conversion of mutual fund administration and management to nonprofit status will eliminate the identified conflict of interest is similarly specious. There is little basis to contend that a nonprofit firm competing against for-profit firms in the market for capital and labor is not interested in maximizing its profits. How those profits are dispersed at the end of the year to show zero firm profits and conform to nonprofit tax status is another matter. Nonprofit firms competing against for-profit firms must compete for resources—capital, labor, facilities, raw materials, technology, and so forth—in competitive markets, by paying competitive prices. Unless subsidized in some way by outside sources, nonprofit firms must earn at least a risk-adjusted competitive rate of return to attract sufficient capital to survive in the long run. For example, capital will not be forthcoming at the lowest risk adjusted rate unless the nonprofit firm earns at least its cost of capital, that is, a rate of return well above zero. Thus, showing zero year-end profits to conform to its nonprofit status does not mean that a nonprofit firm is not motivated to maximize its profits before they are dispersed within the organization to various claimants.

As an example, assume a nonprofit hospital provides health services in a monopoly setting. Facing no close competition in the supply of hospital services, the hospital has an incentive to set monopoly prices to be paid by private insurers. Nonprofit status does not suddenly turn the hospital into a benevolent monopolist. How it distributes profits so as to maintain its nonprofit status, such as covering the cost of indigent patients, higher compensation for executives and department heads, better facilities for patients and medical staff, better on-the-job training of personnel, less stringent cost controls, and so forth, does not detract from its incentive as a monopolist to maximize profits. More profits mean more funds for better facilities, indigent patients, compensation for executives and department heads, and so forth. Granted, without clearly specified property rights to share in the monopoly profits, efforts by hospital management on the margin at profit maximization may be somewhat reduced compared to a for-profit firm, but incentives for monopoly pricing remain strong to satisfy incumbent executives, management, and other employees.

Nevertheless, assume for the sake of discussion that the fee critics' point on organization structure is valid, that having a fund and investment adviser under common, not-for-profit ownership will eliminate the conflict of interest and excessive fees, and produce greater returns to investors. As a consequence, vertically integrated, nonprofit mutual fund complexes should earn higher risk-adjusted returns for their investors than nonvertically integrated, for-profit mutual funds. The remainder of this chapter examines this hypothesis.

The Vanguard Group

As noted, fee critics identify the Vanguard complex of funds as the preeminent example of nonexploitation of fund shareholders by using internal management and nonprofit incentives to eliminate the conflict of interest with external investment managers.[12] Fee critics argue that as an internally managed company, Vanguard funds' boards of directors do not suffer from divided loyalties between fund shareholders and an effectively permanent external fund manager.

According to Vanguard, it provides portfolio management internally, administrative and distribution services to its fund shareholders at cost (earning no profit on such services), and investment management for its index funds at virtually no cost to shareholders. But this characterization is not quite accurate. Vanguard makes extensive use of external adviser portfolio management in its actively managed funds, and the external advisers earn a profit on their portfolio management services to Vanguard. Vanguard states that while it charges advisory fees for services provided by third party subadvisers for its actively managed equity funds, Vanguard strictly controls the extent of such fees.[13] According to Vanguard, its funds' boards of directors are "motivated purely by their desire to secure for Vanguard's shareholders the best quality services at the lowest possible prices"[14] in hiring subadviser investment managers. In short, Vanguard hires and fires investment subadvisers to minimize shareholder costs and maximize shareholder returns.[15] By arguably eliminating the conflict of interest between fund shareholders and investment advisers through internal management and nonprofit status, Vanguard allegedly saves its shareholders billions of dollars annually in fees.[16]

Vanguard's History and Governance Structure

Vanguard was created following an internal management struggle in the 1970s between Wellington Funds and Wellington Management Company, the investment adviser for Wellington Funds. John C. Bogle started at Wellington Management in 1951. He became president and CEO of Wellington Management Company in 1967.[17] Mr. Bogle became chairman of the Wellington Funds in 1970 while continuing as president and CEO of Wellington Management.[18] In a management dispute at Wellington Management, Mr. Bogle was dismissed in January 1974; however, he remained chairman of the Wellington Funds.[19] In July 1974, Wellington Funds proposed a restructuring, in which it would assume administrative and distribution duties from the Wellington Management Company, and the latter would continue as the investment adviser to Wellington Funds.[20] In December 1974, Wellington Funds applied to the SEC for approval of the restructuring and a change in name to the Vanguard Group of Investment Companies.[21] The SEC granted approval in February 1975, and the shareholders approved the name change a few months latter.[22] Mr. Bogle became head of Vanguard, the renamed Wellington Funds, with Wellington Management Company remaining under separate ownership as the investment subadviser, absent its former administrative and distribution duties to shareholders.

Vanguard began as a traditional mutual fund complex, charging an 8.5 percent buyer's load and selling its funds through brokers. However, Vanguard soon pioneered in offering the first indexed mutual fund, First Index Investment Trust, in August 1976, which later became the Vanguard 500 Index fund, its historically largest fund, selling through major brokerage houses at a 5 percent buyer's load fee.[23] Approximately two years after its creation, Vanguard switched to a low-cost sales strategy, offering no-load funds through direct distribution to investors. Vanguard converted its 14 mutual funds to no-load status in early 1977.[24] Although Vanguard provided the administrative and distribution duties that most funds contract for through their outside investment adviser, Vanguard continued to use an external portfolio manager, Wellington Management Company, as its investment adviser.

With its new direct-to-shareholder distribution, no-load status, and emphasis on selling index funds, the Vanguard Group grew rapidly. Vanguard grew from $1.3 billion in 1974, its founding assets under the Wellington Funds' name, to $450 billion in 1998,[25] and to over one trillion dollars in 2007.

Again, Vanguard is not a wholly internally managed mutual fund complex. Vanguard does manage its mutual funds' administrative and distribution functions as well as its index funds internally. But managing index funds requires no significant investment in stock research and portfolio management, as in an actively managed fund. We examined 47 Vanguard equity mutual funds, including 22 passive and 25 active funds, as listed in Table 7.1, along with each fund's investment adviser(s). Out of 22 actively managed funds, all but one, Strategic Equity Fund, indicated the use of one or more external investment advisers. Based on assets under management, Vanguard outsourced advisory services for over 95 percent of the assets in these 22 actively managed funds. Eighteen different subadvisers were used by Vanguard in 2005.[26] Vanguard's claim that profits are not earned on the fees that it charges for investment advisers is thus somewhat misleading for its subadvised funds, because the outside advisory firms price their services to earn a profit.[27]

More centrally, Vanguard's statement that it prices its services to investors (fund administration, distribution, and portfolio management from outside advisers) at cost with no profit built in raises the question of how it has continued in business since the 1970s. Vanguard—like any other firm—must earn a competitive return in the long run to remain in business, and the profit must

TABLE 7.1 Vanguard Equity Funds and Subadvisers

Fund Name	Active/Passive	Type	Number of Subadvisers	Adviser(s)
500 Index Fund Inv	Passive	Domestic Stock—General	0	Vanguard
Calvert Social Index Inv	Passive	Domestic Stock—General	0	Vanguard
Developed Markets Index	Passive	International/Global Stock	0	Vanguard
Diversified Equity Inv[1]	Passive	Domestic Stock—General	0	Vanguard
Emerging Mkts Stock Index	Passive	International/Global Stock	0	Vanguard
European Stock Index Inv	Passive	International/Global Stock	0	Vanguard
Extended Mkt Index Inv	Passive	Domestic Stock - More Aggressive	0	Vanguard
Growth Index Fund Inv	Passive	Domestic Stock—General	0	Vanguard
Large-Cap Index Fund Inv	Passive	Domestic Stock—General	0	Vanguard
Mid-Cap Index Fund Inv	Passive	Domestic Stock - More Aggressive	0	Vanguard
Pacific Stock Index Inv	Passive	International/Global Stock	0	Vanguard
REIT Index Fund Inv	Passive	Domestic Stock—Industry-Specific	0	Vanguard
Small-Cap Growth Index	Passive	Domestic Stock - More Aggressive	0	Vanguard
Small-Cap Index Fund Inv	Passive	Domestic Stock - More Aggressive	0	Vanguard
Small-Cap Value Index	Passive	Domestic Stock - More Aggressive	0	Vanguard
Tax-Managed Cap Apprec Inv[2]	Passive	Domestic Stock—General	0	Vanguard
Tax-Managed Gr & Inc Inv[3]	Passive	Domestic Stock—General	0	Vanguard
Tax-Managed International[4]	Passive	International/Global Stock	0	Vanguard
Tax-Managed Small-Cap[5]	Passive	Domestic Stock - More Aggressive	0	Vanguard

TABLE 7.1 (*continued*)

Fund Name	Active/ Passive	Type	Number of Subadvisers	Adviser(s)
Total Int'l Stock Index	Passive	International/Global Stock	0	Vanguard
Total Stock Mkt Idx Inv	Passive	Domestic Stock—General	0	Vanguard
Value Index Fund Inv	Passive	Domestic Stock—General	0	Vanguard
Capital Opportu- nity Inv	Active	Domestic Stock - More Aggressive	1	PRIMECAP Management Company
Capital Value Fund	Active	Domestic Stock - More Aggressive	1	Wellington Management Co
Convertible Securities	Active	Domestic Stock—General	1	Oaktree Capital Management LLC
Dividend Growth Fund	Active	Domestic Stock—General	1	Wellington Management Co
Energy Fund Investor	Active	Domestic Stock—Industry- Specific	1	Wellington Management Co
Equity Income Fund Inv	Active	Domestic Stock—General	2	John A. Levin & Co; Wellington Management Co; Vanguard
Explorer Fund Investor	Active	Domestic Stock - More Aggressive	5	Granahan Investment Management; Wellington Management Co; Vanguard; Grantham, Mayo, Van Otterloo & Co; Chartwell Investment Partners; Kalmar Investment Advisers
Global Equity Fund	Active	International/ Global Stock	2	Marathon Asset Management; Acadian Asset Management
Growth and Income Inv	Active	Domestic Stock—General	1	Franklin Portfolio Associates

(*continued*)

TABLE 7.1 *(continued)*

Fund Name	Active/ Passive	Type	Number of Subadvisers	Adviser(s)
Growth Equity Fund	Active	Domestic Stock - More Aggressive	1	Turner Investment Partners
Health Care Fund Inv	Active	Domestic Stock—Industry-Specific	1	Wellington Management Co
International Growth Inv	Active	International/Global Stock	2	Schroder Investment Management; Baillie Gifford Overseas, Ltd
International Value Fund	Active	International/Global Stock	2	Hansberger Global Investors; Sanford C. Bernstein & Co.
International Explorer Fund	Active	International/Global Stock	1	Schroder Investment Management
Mid-Cap Growth Fund	Active	Domestic Stock - More Aggressive	1	Provident Investment Counsel
Morgan Growth Fund Inv	Active	Domestic Stock—General	2	Wellington Management Co, LLP; Franklin Portfolio Associates, LLC; Vanguard
Precious Metals & Mining	Active	Domestic Stock—Industry-Specific	1	M&G Investment Management Limited
PRIMECAP Core Fund	Active	Domestic Stock—General	1	PRIMECAP Management Company
PRIMECAP Fund Investor	Active	Domestic Stock - More Aggressive	1	PRIMECAP Management Company
Selected Value Fund	Active	Domestic Stock - More Aggressive	2	Barrow, Hanley, Mewhinney & Strauss, Inc; Donald Smith & Co
Strategic Equity Fund	Active	Domestic Stock - More Aggressive	0	Vanguard

TABLE 7.1 (*continued*)

Fund Name	Active/ Passive	Type	Number of Subadvisers	Adviser(s)
U.S. Growth Fund Investor	Active	Domestic Stock—General	2	Alliance Capital Management; William Blair & Co
U.S. Value Fund	Active	Domestic Stock—General	1	Grantham, May, Van Otterloo & Co
Windsor Fund Investor	Active	Domestic Stock—General	2	Wellington Management Co; Sanford C. Bernstein & Co.
Windsor II Fund Inv	Active	Domestic Stock—General	4	Barrow, Hanley, Mewhinney & Strauss, Inc; Equinox Capital Management; Hotchkis and Wiley Capital Management; Tukman Capital Management; Vanguard

Sources: Annual Reports, Statements of Additional Information, and Prospectuses for Vanguard; www .vanguard.com, accessed in July 2005.

Notes:

[1] The fund is a "fund of funds" that invests in a diversified group of other Vanguard stock mutual funds.

[2] The fund purchases stocks that pay lower dividends and are included in the Russell 100 Index. The fund uses statistical methods to sample the index.

[3] The fund purchases stocks included in the S&P 500 index. The fund will hold substantially all of the S&P 500 index stocks in approximately the same proportion.

[4] The fund purchases stocks included in the Morgan Stanley Capital International Europe, Australasia, Far East Index. The fund uses statistical methods to "sample" this index.

[5] The fund's adviser is The Vanguard Group. The fund invests in small- and mid-cap domestic stocks based on the adviser's assessment of the securities relative return potential.

come largely from its shareholders, either through direct fees on shareholders' accounts or from taking a share of the net asset value owned by the shareholders. How profits are distributed so that Vanguard shows no profits at the end of the year is a separate matter.

Vanguard competes for investment inflows against thousands of for-profit, nonvertically integrated mutual funds and other investment and savings opportunities for consumers. To be sustainable in the long run, Vanguard must pay market prices for its resources including capital, labor, and technology; cover its costs; and earn at least a competitive return on its investment. Thus, in one way or another, Vanguard must take a share of its funds' net asset value from fund shareholders to compensate for its costs of doing business and earn a profit on its invested capital.[28] Vanguard may be more adept at managing administrative and distribution costs through internal management than some mutual fund complexes or funds that contract out for such services via their investment adviser, giving it a cost advantage over some rivals, but this does not provide the basis for Vanguard to earn zero profits on services to its fund shareholders.

TIAA-CREF

TIAA-CREF mutual funds are managed by Teachers Advisors, a wholly owned indirect subsidiary of TIAA. Teachers Advisors also manages the investments of TIAA-CREF's Institutional Mutual Funds, Life Funds, College Retirement Equities Fund, and life insurance investments. TIAA-CREF's investment portfolios are thus internally managed and shareholders in TIAA-CREF's retail and institutional mutual funds are indirect owners of their funds' investment adviser.

TIAA was founded in 1918 by the Carnegie Corporation as a stock life insurance company. CREF was founded in 1952 as a nonprofit firm to provide retirement annuities based on common stock. TIAA and CREF are separate companies with different boards of trustees. They are in turn monitored by the TIAA and CREF Boards of Overseers. In the 1980s, CREF registered with the SEC as an investment company under the ICA of 1940. CREF offers both retail and institutional mutual funds, and in some cases the same fund is offered to both institutional and retail investors. Between TIAA and CREF, a range of products and services are offered, including insurance, educational savings accounts, and both retail and institutional mutual funds, primarily marketed to teachers and other professional groups.[29]

As with Vanguard, TIAA-CREF's nonprofit structure does not free it from earning a competitive rate of return in the long run in order to survive. To attract resources—labor, capital, and technology—it must pay competitive prices, which means earning a competitive rate of return. TIAA-CREF's fees and access to shareholders' net asset value must be high enough to cover operating expenses, including a competitive rate of return.

TIAA-CREF's nonprofit status does not grant it license to earn zero or negative profits each year. In 2005, TIAA-CREF determined that its wholly owned investment advisor, Teachers Advisors, was losing money and asked its institutional fund shareholders to approve an adviser fee increase from 0.08 percent to 0.48 percent of total assets, a 600 percent increase. Coupled with other fund expenses, TIAA-CREF estimated that this would approximately double operating expenses to about 1.00 percent of assets.[30] Some of its equity funds—growth, international, large-cap value, small-cap, and social choice funds—did not approve the fee increase, but other TIAA-CREF funds did, including its growth and income, mid-cap value, and mid-cap growth funds. The latter funds are also retail funds, indicating that both institutional and retail shareholders in these funds would incur substantial fee increases.[31] In January 2006, TIAA-CREF's institutional mutual funds approved the new fee agreement. The agreement did not affect fees for the college retirement equity fund.[32] At the time, TIAA-CREF was also planning to merge five of its retail investor mutual funds into several of its institutional funds that commanded higher fees, thereby increasing fees on its individual retail investors.[33] The initial shareholder rejection of the fee increase demonstrates that conflicts of interest between advisers and fund shareholders are not eliminated by internal control of investment advisory services and that internal control does not necessarily protect fund shareholders from substantial fee increases. Just as internal pricing conflicts exist in multidivision firms when goods are transferred between divisions of the same firm, so do conflicts of interest over fee levels exist in vertically integrated mutual fund complexes, contrary to the view that internal management eliminates conflicts over fee levels.

Performance Comparisons: Vanguard, TIAA-CREF, and Rival Funds

Returns to Mutual Fund Shareholders: Univariate Results

As investors, mutual fund shareholders are interested primarily in their net returns given the fund product and risk involved. Holding risk constant, low fees coupled with low investor net returns are of little interest to investors compared to higher fees and higher net returns. If, as some contend, vertically integrated, nonprofit mutual fund complexes have the lowest fees, because they earn no profit in servicing their funds' shareholders and internalize the claimed conflict of interest, do the low fees translate into high investor net returns relative to higher-fee, for-profit, nonvertically integrated funds? For example, in the case of equity index funds, if funds are relatively homogeneous, as fee critics claim, and earn the same gross returns, net returns should be correlated with investor fees, with low-fee complexes, such as Vanguard and TIAA-CREF earning higher returns than higher-fee equity index funds. However, in the case of actively managed equity funds, do Vanguard and TIAA-CREF earn higher returns than rivals because they have arguably resolved the conflict of interest between fund shareholders and investment advisers?

Equity Funds

We examine risk-adjusted returns for Vanguard and TIAA-CREF equity funds relative to rival for-profit funds that use the traditional organizational structure—contracting with a separate, independently owned investment adviser. For each December, for the years 2000 through 2003 (and February 2004), we calculate risk-adjusted returns for Vanguard, TIAA-CREF, and all other equity funds using the prior 36 months of returns data. To measure whether, for a given level of risk, a fund was performing better, the same as, or below marketwide returns (known as alpha in finance parlance), we regress funds' monthly returns plus dividends less the risk-free rate, measured by the three-month Treasury Bill rate, over the 36-month period on excess returns for the market as a whole in a three-factor model, using the S&P 500, S&P mid-cap 400, and S&P small-cap 600 for market returns.[34] Returns measured this way that are statistically significantly greater than zero indicate a return to fund investors above the market for the level of risk.

Table 7.2 presents the results based on pooling the data over time and also by separating the funds into large-cap, mid-cap, and small-cap funds.[35] In each case, the results first show the return measure alpha as a relative measure of return, followed by the standard error of the estimated coefficient, and below that the number of funds in the sample tested. Vanguard's equity funds' returns show mixed results over the 36-month periods tested. Vanguard's equity funds did no better than the market as a whole at the end of 2000, 2002, and 2003, but better than the market in one year, 2001. Vanguard's results differ somewhat for year-end periods when looking at results by fund size categories. In large-cap funds, Vanguard did no better than the market at year-end in 2000, 2001, and 2002, and worse than the market in 2003. For mid-cap funds, Vanguard did better than the market in 2001, 2002, and 2003, and worse than the market in 2000. In small-cap funds, Vanguard did better than the market in 2000 and 2001 and no better than the market in 2002 and 2003.

Over this period, among all equity mutual funds, Vanguard was in the lowest decile of mutual fund fees to investors. Nevertheless, Vanguard's investor return performance was mixed—equaling market returns in some years,

TABLE 7.2 Average Multifactor Alpha per Domestic Equity Fund
Category (large-, mid-, and small-cap)
(standard error in parentheses and number of observations below)

Categories	December 2000	December 2001	December 2002	December 2003	February 2004
All	0.0029	−0.0006	−0.0373	−0.0355	−0.0329
	(0.0006)	(0.0005)	(0.0005)	(0.0003)	(0.0003)
	1183	2346	2211	2494	2542
TIAA-CREF All	0.0177	−0.0064	−0.0334	−0.0233	−0.0254
	(0.0083)	(0.0087)	(0.0097)	(0.0035)	(0.0033)
	2	2	2	4	4
Vanguard All	−0.0087	0.0129	−0.0017	−0.0001	−0.0001
	(0.0050)	(0.0028)	(0.0034)	(0.0014)	(0.0012)
	8	26	18	39	46
Large	−0.0055	−0.0144	−0.0360	−0.0344	−0.0312
	(0.0006)	(0.0005)	(0.0005)	(0.0003)	(0.0003)
	703	1399	1312	1449	1458
TIAA-CREF Large	0.0177	−0.0064	−0.0334	−0.0233	−0.0254
	(0.0083)	(0.0087)	(0.0097)	(0.0035)	(0.0033)
	2	2	2	4	4
Vanguard Large	−0.0025	0.0003	−0.0055	−0.0038	−0.0027
	(0.0041)	(0.0034)	(0.0037)	(0.0019)	(0.0015)
	6	14	14	23	28
Medium	0.0338	0.0162	−0.0509	−0.0584	−0.0549
	(0.0018)	(0.0013)	(0.0013)	(0.0007)	(0.0007)
	230	465	474	549	566
Vanguard Medium	−0.1238	0.0426	0.0156	0.0161	0.0105
	(0.0268)	(0.0067)	(0.0088)	(0.0038)	(0.0035)
	1	7	3	7	8
Small	−0.0020	0.0231	−0.0261	−0.0134	−0.0133
	(0.0017)	(0.0013)	(0.0014)	(0.0007)	(0.0007)
	250	482	425	496	518
Vanguard Small	0.0694	0.0065	−0.0004	−0.0031	−0.0013
	(0.0159)	(0.0063)	(0.0177)	(0.0023)	(0.0020)
	1	5	1	9	10

beating the market in some years, and earning less than the market in other year-end periods. Vanguard's relatively low fees, regardless of their basis, did not translate into consistently above-average returns to investors, as some studies argue should occur because Vanguard has arguably solved the supposed conflict of interest problem leading to excessive fees. Vanguard and its relatively low investor fees did no better than the average equity fund in various years.

TIAA-CREF also fell into the lowest decile of mutual funds fees to investors in equity mutual funds during the period examined. As we show in Table 7.2, TIAA-CREF's risk-adjusted returns were below market returns for the 36-month periods ending in 2002 and 2003, and at the market in the periods ending in 2000 and 2001. The same pattern held in the large-cap segment of the market. Again, TIAA-CREF's relatively low investor fees did not produce systematically superior returns relative to nonvertically integrated, for-profit equity funds.

Passively Managed Funds

Vanguard's primary growth historically has been in equity and bond index, or passively managed funds. Vanguard promotes these and other funds by emphasizing their low fees to investors and implying that its equity index funds outperform rival equity index funds due to low fees. Results from our analysis of passive equity funds are presented in Table 7.3. Vanguard's passive equity funds were significantly below the market for the period ending in February 2004, did no better than the market for the periods ending in 2001, 2002, and 2003, and beat the market for the period ending in 2000 (although we had data on only two Vanguard funds for 2000). TIAA-CREF is represented by a single index fund in Table 7.3, which generated returns below the market in the periods ending in 2003 and 2004. In summary, Vanguard's lowest fees are in its index funds, yet its equity index fund returns generally did not beat the market.[36]

TABLE 7.3 Average Multifactor Alpha, Passively Managed Vanguard and TIAA-CREF Funds Versus Other Passively Managed Funds for All Domestic Equity Categories

(standard error in parentheses and number of observations below)

Categories	December 2000	December 2001	December 2002	December 2003	February 2004
Other	−0.0047 (0.0008) 53	−0.0065 (0.0005) 101	−0.0205 (0.0025) 54	−0.0071 (0.0006) 140	−0.0083 (0.0006) 141
Vanguard	0.0016 (0.0001) 2	−0.0005 (0.0031) 14	0.0036 (0.0034) 6	−0.0020 (0.0014) 21	−0.0024 (0.0011) 28
TIAA-CREF				−0.0060 (0.0012) 1	−0.0050 (0.0013) 1

Vanguard's low fees are of little value per se to fund shareholders if they do not produce returns superior to rivals' funds, and similarly for TIAA-CREF. An internal portfolio management structure for index funds and nonprofit status at these two complexes, which according to fee critics eliminates the conflict of interest over fees between shareholders and investment adviser and leads to lower fees, did not result in investor returns being consistently above for-profit index funds, which supposedly charge investors excessive fees.

Actively Managed Equity Funds

Return comparisons for actively managed funds, the funds that Vanguard contracts with external subadvisers to manage and TIAA-CREF manages internally, are shown in Table 7.4. For actively managed funds, Vanguard's funds underperformed the market in 2000, beat the market for the period ending 2001, and were at the market for the 36-month periods ending in 2002 and 2003. TIAA-CREF's returns for actively managed funds beat the market in 2000, were at the market for 2001, and were significantly below the market in 2002 and 2003. As with Vanguard's and TIAA-CREF's passive funds, low fees on actively managed funds did not consistently translate into risk-adjusted returns superior to the market.

These results provide little support for claims by fee critics that nonprofit status and internal management of portfolios, as epitomized by Vanguard and TIAA-CREF, produce the lowest fees and highest returns to mutual fund investors. Vanguard and TIAA-CREF frequently performed no better than or worse than the market as a whole or in specific investment categories, including passively and actively managed funds.

We report the results using a more complete regression model in the Appendix to this chapter. The results are consistent with the findings described above. Being a Vanguard or TIAA-CREF fund was not related to higher investor returns. Using data on fund rankings based on returns to investors, being a Vanguard or TIAA-CREF fund had a low probability of having a high ranking, indicating relatively poor net return performance for their funds' investors, even with low fees.

Summary and Conclusions

Fee critics offer Vanguard and TIAA-CREF as fund complexes that are free from the alleged conflict of interest over investor fees because they are

TABLE 7.4 Average Multifactor Alpha, Actively Managed Vanguard and
TIAA-CREF Funds Versus Other Actively Managed Funds for All Domestic
Equity Categories
(standard error in parentheses and number of observations below)

Categories	December 2000	December 2001	December 2002	December 2003	February 2004
Other	0.0032	−0.0004	−0.0377	−0.0372	−0.0343
	(0.0006)	(0.0005)	(0.0005)	(0.0003)	(0.0003)
	1130	2245	2157	2354	2401
Vanguard	−0.0121	0.0284	−0.0044	0.0022	0.0034
	(0.0066)	(0.0050)	(0.0047)	(0.0026)	(0.0025)
	6	12	12	18	18
TIAA-CREF	0.0177	−0.0064	−0.0334	−0.0291	−0.0322
	(0.0083)	(0.0087)	(0.0097)	(0.0046)	(0.0044)
	2	2	2	3	3

nonprofit firms and their investment portfolios are internally managed. If their governance structure and nonprofit status results in low fees and higher returns relative to for-profit and nonvertically integrated complexes, it should be evident in tests to determine whether Vanguard and TIAA-CREF earn higher returns than for-profit, nonvertically integrated complexes. The evidence shows the opposite. First, if Vanguard's low fees resulted in consistently high returns, then most investors would select Vanguard funds. Although Vanguard is one of the largest fund complexes in the United States, others, some of which charge higher fees, have long rivaled or exceeded Vanguard in asset size. Second, in the period for which we have data, 36-month returns ending in 2000 through 2003, while Vanguard and TIAA-CREF beat the market as a whole in some years, they also underperformed the market in other years and generally did not perform better than the average, for-profit, nonvertically integrated fund complex. If our results can be extrapolated, mutual fund investors can do as well if not better in numerous for-profit rival funds than by investing in Vanguard's and TIAA-CREF's funds. Finally, conflicts of interest over fees between investment advisers and fund investors are not eliminated by shifting to internal portfolio management and nonprofit status, as the 2005–2006 conflict over fee increases at TIAA-CREF demonstrated.

These empirical results are strongly inconsistent with the view that by investing in vertically integrated, nonprofit fund complexes, where there is allegedly no conflict of interest between fund shareholders and investment advisers because of wholly internal management, investors will pay far lower fees and earn substantially greater returns. The results are consistent with the view that for most mutual funds, there is no differentially greater conflict of interest between fund shareholders and investment advisers at for-profit funds that allegedly allows advisers to profit at the expense of returns to fund shareholders. Faced with noncompetitive fees, investors will move to alternative, competitively priced funds and complexes. The results are thus consistent with price competition in the mutual fund industry, as supported by the results we presented in Chapter 4, showing that the demand for equity mutual funds is price-elastic and that cross-price elasticity between funds is consistent with substitutability between mutual fund investments.

CHAPTER EIGHT

What Have We Learned?

Introduction

Studies by the Securities and Exchange Commission (SEC) on competition in the 1960s mutual fund industry concluded that fund investment advisers did not compete on price, resulting in years of overcharges to investors. This conclusion has informed the law and regulations directed at mutual fund pricing from 1970 to the present, resulting in numerous lawsuits charging investment advisers with breaching their fiduciary duty to investors and imposing excessive fees on fund shareholders.

We have examined the nature of competition in the mutual fund industry, with specific attention to retail equity mutual funds. We sought to determine whether current industry conditions and investor behavior are more consistent with the SEC's 1960s finding or with what the present structure of the industry implies—vigorous price competition. Regardless of the merits of the SEC's 1960s studies, if the evolution of the mutual fund industry has led to competitively priced fees, the current panoply of laws and regulations directed at mutual fund pricing, passed under the belief that price competition in the industry did not exist and would never fully develop, serve only to reduce industry efficiency and raise investors' fees. If the post-1960s laws and regulations against excessive fees serve no procompetitive purpose, they necessarily raise costs and reduce industry efficiency, harming mutual fund investors.

The Excessive Fee Hypothesis

According to critics of the mutual fund industry, investors' fees are excessive because investment advisers do not engage in price competition to attract and retain fund investors. Investment advisers are reportedly shielded from price competition because mutual funds rarely replace their advisers, giving advisers a superior bargaining position in negotiating fees relative to funds' boards of directors and shareholders. According to this view, mutual fund investors do not extricate themselves from this position because they are either unaware of the fees they pay each year due to obfuscation by investment advisers, the fees are so small relative to returns that investors pay almost no attention to the size of fees, or the cost to investors of switching funds is too high relative to the potential savings on fees.

Principal Findings

In contrast to the claim that U.S. retail equity mutual fund investment advisers do not engage in price competition, using recent data, we found abundant evidence of price competition. Our research shows that fund investors are in fact sensitive to the fees they pay, such that investment advisers use price, among other product attributes and services, to compete for investors' assets. The evidence includes our findings that: (1) investors on average are strongly sensitive to the price they pay for owning mutual funds; (2) price increases above the competitive level result in investors switching to lower price funds, both within a complex and between complexes; (3) the vast majority of mutual fund assets are invested in the lowest price funds; (4) mutual fund investment advisers commonly compete on price by various means, such as by waiving all or a portion of their published fee to meet or undercut rivals' prices; and (5) when the measure of mutual fund expense ratios include the amortized value of sales loads, expense ratios have been declining for approximately 30 years.

The inability of investment advisers to shield themselves from price competition is a direct result of the ability of mutual fund investors to switch assets across funds and complexes. Equity mutual fund investors can easily move their assets from higher to lower fee mutual funds or complexes, as demonstrated by the fact that most assets are invested in lower price funds. A substantial share of mutual fund assets are redeemed each year, and our mutual fund demand analysis shows that investors substitute between mutual funds. The ability of investors to shift between funds has been enhanced by the relative growth of no-load equity mutual funds since the 1960s, such that the majority of fund assets are now invested in no-load funds. The maximum levels of front- and back-end load fees, which may have inhibited moving assets between funds in the 1960s, have fallen by approximately half since that time, further reducing the cost of shifting assets when dealing with load funds. With ample product choice and availability to investors from existing and new funds, as has now existed for years, investment advisers have little ability to sustain prices above the competitive level. Given investor sensitivity to price and easy, low-cost asset redemption, price competition must follow unless restrained by government regulation.

Price competition between fund advisory firms is further heightened by the threat of new entry. There are no significant barriers to fund and advisory firm entry, expansion of existing funds and investment advisers, or to exit from the mutual fund industry. There has been a large increase in the number of funds since the 1960s and many examples of rapid expansion by new entrants when their performance gained quick favor with investors. Conversely, there are numerous examples of funds that failed to remain competitive and disappeared. With easy new entry, incumbent investment advisers cannot remain lax in pricing competitively. Existing investment advisers and new entrants are always present to draw away the customer base of rival mutual funds that do not maintain competitive prices.

Investment advisers are generally fixated on the amount of money flowing into and out of their funds on a daily basis, for that determines an adviser's competitive success or failure. Without providing long-term competitive pricing for the performance and services provided to investors, a fund's shares will be redeemed and the fund will go out of business, either by being merged into a more successful fund or by liquidating its assets to shareholders.

The entry of new products competing against mutual funds also enhances competition. Most recently, new products included various types of exchange traded funds (ETFs). The largest ETFs, with billions of dollars in assets since their origin in 1993, are essentially stock market–traded index funds. As index fund–based financial instruments, they have low expense ratios and thus relatively low investor fees. As low-cost investment alternatives to conventional mutual funds, ETFs provide further pressure on investment advisers to price their services competitively.

Anecdotal evidence of price competition between investment advisers reinforces the presence of price competition, such as the well publicized price war between Vanguard and Fidelity in 2005 and 2006 on equity index mutual funds. Indeed, it is curious that those proclaiming the absence of price competition in mutual funds always point to Vanguard as an exception, the fund complex that is best known for having persistently competed on price to investors since the late 1970s. Fee critics bifurcate the industry into Vanguard on one side (some also include TIAA-CREF), competing on price, and all others who somehow manage to survive by ignoring the growth and lower prices of Vanguard. More specifically, Vanguard has certainly not been reducing its investors' fees over time to compete against itself, so its pricing actions inevitably pressure rival mutual funds to price competitively. Vanguard's dramatic asset growth since the late 1970s provides a clear example that price competition flourishes in the mutual fund industry.

Facing a low-cost competitor, such as Vanguard, rival mutual funds have little choice but to compete on price for the most profitable investors, or by offering better product quality for the same price, thereby lowering price per unit of quality. Alternatively, some investment advisers and their funds can offer more and better quality attributes for higher fees than lower price funds, choosing not to compete directly for investors searching for the lowest price funds. For example, if Vanguard is the Wal-Mart or Target of the mutual fund industry, then some funds may distinguish themselves by becoming the Bloomingdale's or Neiman Marcus of mutual funds, and thus not attempt to compete directly with the lowest fee funds. However, that does not free them from price competition. A high-price luxury automobile may not compete directly with lower price subcompacts, but it certainly competes on price and product attributes against other luxury automobile brands.

Some take the position that what distinguishes competitive fees from excessive fee-setting is the profit motive of investment advisers, or for-profit versus not-for-profit organizational structures. They contend that when mutual fund complexes are organized as not-for-profit firms, as in a mutual stock company, in which fund shareholders own the investment adviser and all administrative services, the conflict of interest between fund shareholders and investment advisers is eliminated and provides fund shareholders with the lowest fees and highest returns.

Whatever the merits of a fund adviser's not-for-profit status and its ability to reduce investor fees, it is of little consequence to fund investors unless it translates into superior annual net investor returns. We find that Vanguard and TIAA-CREF, identified by fee critics as low-fee, not-for-profit, vertically integrated organizations that are free from the conflict of interest that plagues for-profit, nonvertically integrated investment advisers, do not produce investor returns superior to for-profit funds. Vanguard and TIAA-CREF have relatively low fees, although some for-profit mutual funds have comparably low fees. More importantly, Vanguard and TIAA-CREF perform no better on average in generating investor returns than for-profit, nonvertically integrated equity mutual funds. This indicates that investors in for-profit, nonvertically integrated mutual fund advisers earn returns on average little different from mutual funds with a governance structure that allegedly protects them from price exploitation by their investment adviser. Moreover, this calls into question the entire debate about an inherent conflict of interest resulting in excessive fees due to the separation of mutual fund from investment adviser ownership. If the so-called excessive fees do not produce inferior returns to fund investors, they can hardly be classified as excessive. And without excessive fees, the claim of an inherent conflict of interest has no merit.

Excessive Fees and Mutual Fund Regulation

From the 1960s to the present, studies have called for the SEC to institute new regulations to protect mutual fund investors from the claimed excessive fees of investment advisers. Proposals often call for an expansion of long established SEC policies: greater dominance of funds' boards of directors by independent directors and more transparent disclosure of each fund's fees and expenses. This follows the federal government's position since the 1930s that largely ill-informed, individual mutual fund investors need to be protected from profit-maximizing investment advisers.

The Investment Company Act (ICA) of 1940 called for mutual fund boards of directors, separate from the ownership of investment advisory firms, where the fund's independent directors negotiated fee levels with investment advisers. This separation was intended to prevent expropriation of individual retail investors' returns by investment advisers, strengthen the mutual fund's board in negotiating fee levels, and lessen the likelihood that a fund's board would be captured and controlled by the investment adviser. The SEC has often proposed a greater proportion of independent members on a fund's board of directors. The government's latest proposal to restructure fund boards of directors, following the market timing scandal of 2003 and 2004, called for 75 percent of a board to be composed of independent directors, as well as requiring that the board chairperson be an independent director. The ICA of 1940 required that 40 percent of a fund's board members be independent (later raised to 50 percent). Independent members have been a ruling majority on most equity mutual funds' boards for years, yet studies continue to charge investment advisers with setting excessive fees due to the lack of bargaining power of funds' boards or because the boards have been captured by the investment advisers.

There is some irony in the government's preferred mutual fund–investment adviser organizational structure. It was established to a large extent by the

SEC and Congress in the ICA of 1940 to help neutralize the power of investment advisers to abuse fund investors. However, in the 1960s, the SEC faulted the organizational structure it called for in the ICA of 1940, contending that the conflict of interest between fund shareholders and investment advisers, because of the independence of investment advisers and their bargaining power, made fund shareholders more vulnerable to excessive fees.

In addition to more independent directors, the SEC has long sought reforms to generate better fee disclosure, so that fund investors can make more informed investment decisions. It is unquestioned that buyers and sellers must have sufficient information to gain the efficiencies of a competitive market. The debate covered whether sufficient information on fees was being provided in funds' prospectuses and whether it was in a form readily understood by fund investors. Our results show that price competition is ever present, indicating that investors are receiving and acting on pricing information.[1]

Are there alternative means to address concerns over a conflict of interest between fund shareholders and investment advisers? If the current organizational structure of mutual funds and investment advisers, present in the majority of mutual funds, is regarded as necessary to keep investment advisers in check on issues other than pricing, then meaningful reforms should concentrate on bringing the interests of fund shareholders and investment advisers into closer alignment.

Contrary to the conflict-of-interest school of thought, there has long been an alignment of interests between fund shareholders and their investment advisers. Both parties have a mutual self-interest in maximizing fund returns. The higher the fund returns, the greater the flow of assets into the fund and the greater the potential profits to investment advisers, based on their fees being set as a percentage of total assets. However, as discussed earlier, a fund may possibly grow too large, beyond some optimal, return-maximizing size, as inferred from the many funds that at some point close themselves to new investors to prevent growing so large as to reduce investor returns.[2] If fund size becomes so large that returns and growth decline, both fund shareholders and advisers suffer in the long run. However, in the short run, if investors are slow to redeem assets, hoping for fund returns to rebound to higher levels, investment advisers may continue for a limited time to earn large revenues given a nonoptimal asset size.

Assuming, as critics argue, that excessive fees are possible and advisers can grow funds so large that investor returns diminish, are there further ways to better align the interests of fund shareholders and investment advisers? One way to address both issues is to provide stronger financial incentives so that investment advisers, by acting in their own self-interest, also satisfy the interests of fund shareholders. Instead of discouraging or restricting investment adviser ownership of their funds' shares, it could be encouraged. With sufficient ownership of a fund's shares, investment advisers have no incentive to reduce their returns by imposing excessive fees on themselves and their fund's shareholders. Similarly, with sufficient ownership of a fund's shares, advisers have no incentive to grow a fund beyond its return-maximizing level, reducing the value of their fund shares and the shares of all other shareholders. In like manner, if funds' board members are sufficiently invested in the fund, they have little incentive to approve fees above the competitive level.

However, if the industry is actively engaged in price competition, as our findings demonstrate, both existing and proposed regulations to reduce investment advisers' fee levels are a social waste. Section 36(b) of the ICA of 1940, limiting investment advisers' compensation to an ill-defined, fiduciary level, serves little useful purpose in holding down fee levels when price competition exists. Advisers that do not act in a proper fiduciary manner should be held accountable, but with price competition they have no ability to price monopolistically. As long as fund investors have choice among good substitute funds, which they have, advisers must price competitively.

In contrast, 36(b) has generated numerous lawsuits against investment advisers, with their attendant costs, raising the expenses of fund operations and investor fees. Abundant evidence shows that the law has served little purpose other than to generate lawsuits. Numerous cases have been filed against advisers under 36(b) in the over 25 years since *Gartenberg*. In all the cases to date, plaintiffs have never won because of their failure to produce credible evidence of excessive fees. Given the existence of price competition among fund advisory firms this is not surprising. However, what is the purpose of a law that was intended to protect investors from the absence of price competition when price competition flourishes? Given this record of defeats in the courts, it is doubtful whether the alleged benefits of 36(b) outweigh the costs it has imposed on investors.

Furthermore, it makes little difference to fee levels whether funds' boards are dominated by independent directors or they are in the minority if investment advisers are already disciplined by price competition. Indeed, it would make little difference to fund investors whether the fund had a separate board of directors or not as long as price competition exists, except for the added costs to investors created by the existence and operation of the board. With no mandate for a separate fund board, with its costs for personnel, legal services, investigating proposed fees, and all other costs, expense ratios and investor fees could be reduced, to the benefit of fund shareholders.

Conclusions

With price competition in the mutual fund industry, there is little justification for having laws specific to the industry to control monopoly pricing. Concerns over noncompetitive pricing in the mutual fund industry, as in all nonexempt industries, can be addressed under the antitrust laws, where the courts and government antitrust agencies have over 100 years of experience with monopoly power and allegations of above competitive pricing.

The laws and regulations passed to protect mutual fund investors from anticompetitive pricing are based on 1960s SEC studies that have no claim of pertinence decades later. Investors and consumers in the financial services sector, such as banks, investment banks, and brokerage firms, are all subject to the antitrust laws and enforcement against anticompetitive practices and pricing. There is little that sets the mutual fund industry apart, such that charges of anticompetitive pricing to its customers should be guided by a separate set of laws, limited to mutual fund pricing. If competition has failed fund investors, an appropriate venue for remedy lies in the antitrust laws and their remedies. Moreover, if price competition exists in mutual funds, as our analysis indicates, then the current investment company laws to investigate charges of excessive fees in mutual funds serve little useful purpose.

Finally, we return to the theme of the Introduction and Chapter 1 on the importance of returns to retirement accounts and the increasing importance of mutual funds in investing for retirement. Are mutual fund returns being penalized, as many critics contend, by excessive fees due to an absence of price competition among mutual fund investment advisers? Paying above the competitive price reduces investors' returns and the ability to reach retirement financial goals. Our results show, however, that whatever investors' concerns over their long-term mutual fund returns, such as the large stock market downturn in 2008 and early 2009, being forced to pay excessive fees due to a lack of price competition among funds should not be a serious concern. Our results support the view that mutual fund fees are set by price competition, given the products and features offered, as investors are free to switch to rival funds offering lower fees for the same or better performance. We find that mutual fund investors are in fact sensitive to the fees they pay and take investment actions accordingly. Investment advisers charging above the competitive level for the package of services and product attributes offered will not retain a sufficient number of existing customers and generate sufficient new customers to remain profitable.

The existence of price competition, however, does not mean that in selecting mutual funds, investors can usefully ignore fees. Investors need to shop the market and stay abreast of changes in market conditions, just as they would for any financial commitment, such as monitoring interest rates on savings accounts and certificates of deposit, searching for the best mortgage rates, and purchasing individual stocks and bonds. Sellers' prices differ for the package of product attributes offered. Mutual funds are no different. Fund investors can select low-fee or higher fee funds in the same investment category depending on their preferences for customer services, convenience, financial risk, and returns on investment. However, concern over a lack of price competition is misplaced. Whatever the long-term return on an investor's mutual funds turns out to be, it is not a consequence of the absence of price competition among mutual funds.

Appendix to Chapter Four

This appendix presents the structural models of demand and supply and the methodologies used to generate the empirical results reported in Chapter 4. We use these models to investigate the economic process in the mutual fund market that leads to equilibrium prices and sellers' market shares. The simple simulation model is based on the assumptions that producers maximize profits, offering multiattribute, differentiated products, and that investors maximize utility in their investment choices. In addition, we present the discrete-choice model of demand and the estimation methodologies used to test for price competition between investment advisers.

Discrete-choice models applied to mutual funds permit analysis of investor behavior in the selection of funds along product dimensions, such as within and between rival complexes and within and between channels of distribution. As discussed in Chapter 4, investors are more likely to shift assets from one fund to another within a complex than across complexes, and similarly for distribution channels and other identified market segments. In other words, funds sharing the same market dimension are closer substitutes than funds in other market dimensions. Changes in the demand for mutual funds are thus clustered along specific market dimensions. In such a setting, modeling investor choice is best done using a discrete-choice model, in which each market dimension can be treated separately and several dimensions can be nested.

The Analytical Framework

Underlying the discrete-choice approach is a model of random utility maximization. Assume investor i is faced with J fund choices and will choose a fund that provides the greatest utility. Utility is assumed to be a linear function of fund characteristics X_j and fund price p_j, and has an unobservable mean-zero component ξ_j, which accounts for unobserved product attributes that add to the investor's utility. There is an investor-specific component of utility as well. Because data on individual preferences are not available, this investor-specific component is a random variable η_{ij}.

Investor i selects fund j that maximizes utility:

$$\max_{j \in \{0,\ldots,J_t\}} Vij = X_j^T \beta + \alpha p_j + \xi_j + \eta_{ij}$$

Utility is based on multiple fund attributes, such as expected return, customer service, and complex and fund brand name.

We present two models. The first, a single-nested model, considers only funds within their complexes. Accordingly, we use a nested logit model with one segment, the complex, in our numerical simulation, based on an industry with only two complexes, each with two funds. The second model, a two-nested model, is a generalization of the singled-nested model to two segments, complex and distribution channel, which serves as the basis for the demand estimation model. The latter model, developed with techniques introduced by Nobel laureate Daniel McFadden, uses the "principles of differentiation generalized extreme value model."[1] This model has important advantages over the nested logit model, as discussed here later. We begin with the single-nested demand model and the simulation model of demand and supply.

The Single-Nested Model

The single-nested model is used to examine the substitutability of funds within and between complexes, as well as to investigate the nature of market equilibrium. We examine four different funds and two complexes, with each complex having two funds.

In the nested logit model, investors make two choices in sequence: First, they select a complex and then a fund within the complex. This follows the nested logit model and empirical testing presented by Berry.[2] Although funds are substitutable within and between complexes, a given fund is a closer substitute to a fund within the same complex than a fund from another complex. Consequently, once invested in a complex, investors are more likely to select substitutes from funds within the same complex than funds in other complexes.

As discussed, investors select funds to maximize their personal utility based on a variety of possible factors, such as a fund's past performance, expected net returns, complex and fund reputation, investor fees, and the extent and quality of services to shareholders. Beyond the common services across all funds, such as custodial care, ownership transfers, and SEC-required reporting, investor services might include financial advice, estate planning, ease of buying and selling shares, and alternative distribution channels. As we noted in the chapter, fund and complex reputation are constructed over time based on performance, price, longevity, freedom from financial scandal, brand name capital, and other product characteristics valued by investors.

Complexes invest in earning above their funds' benchmark return level by adding resources until the marginal cost of doing so equals the marginal revenue from increased sales produced by the additional resources. A fund's investment adviser, in conjunction with the fund's board of directors, sets each fund's fees given an awareness of rivals' fees. Those setting fees take into account that fee increases today will reduce net returns and therefore both current as well as future demand, by affecting the fund's reputation for high expected returns.

Complexes maximize the present value of profits and compete in a differentiated Bertrand style, setting price or fees by taking rivals' fees as given. Profits are measured as the difference between fees levied and total costs. The cost function adopted is flexible enough to account for both economies of scale and scope.

The Demand for Complexes and Funds: The Single-Nested Model

The dynamic economic model used to examine the mutual fund market in the single-nested case proceeds as follows.

The demand for fund i in complex j at time t can be represented by the following functional form:

$$y_{i,j,t} = s_{j,t} \cdot \exp[\mu + \lambda_i P_{i,j,t} + \gamma_i P_{3-i,j,t}] \tag{0.1}$$

where, for $i, j = 1, 2, t = 1, 2, \ldots, T$: $y_{i,j,t}$ is the demand (in dollars) of holding fund i from complex j in period t; $s_{j,t}$ is the market share of complex j in period t; $P_{i,j,t}$ is the price of fund i from complex j in period t; and μ, λ_i, and γ_i are fund demand parameters to be estimated. More precisely, λ_i and γ_i are respectively the semi-own (because the demand equation is semi-log) and cross-price elasticities, and μ is a demand shifter.[3]

Note that with two funds in each complex, if a given fund in complex j has price $P_{i,j,t}$, then the price of the "other fund" in that complex can be expressed as $P_{3-i,j,t}$.

This demand function is presented in two parts. The first part determines parameters associated with the market share of complex j at time t. It is parameterized with a standard logistic function:

$$ s_{j,t} = \frac{\exp[\theta_1 P_{1,j,t} + \theta_2 P_{2,j,t} + \phi m_{j,t}]}{\displaystyle\sum_{k=1}^{2} \exp[\theta_1 P_{1,k,t} + \theta_2 P_{2,k,t} + \phi m_{k,t}]} \tag{0.2} $$

where, for $i, j = 1, 2, t = 1, 2, \ldots, T$; $s_{j,t}$ is the market share of complex j in period t; $P_{i,j,t}$ is the price of fund i from complex j in period t; $m_{j,t}$ represents goodwill, reputation, and services; the θ_i's and ϕ are parameters to be estimated. The θ_i's are parameters that measure the sensitivity of complex market share to changes in fund prices. The ϕ term is a parameter that measures the market share sensitivity to changes in services provided by the complex $m_{j,t}$. Thus, it measures the effect that a complex's reputation has on determining a fund's market share.

Complex market share is common to all the funds in the complex. All else equal, it determines the complex's aggregate market share, that is, the sum of the market shares of the funds that belong to the complex. If the market consists of a single complex, the monopoly case, the market share is 1.0 or 100 percent, and equation (0.1) simplifies to:

$$ y_{i,j,t} = \exp[\mu + \lambda_i P_{i,j,t} + \gamma_i P_{3-i,j,t}] \tag{0.3} $$

In this demand function, the own-price elasticity of fund i from complex j is given by:

$$ \varepsilon_{i,j} = \lambda_i \overline{P}_{i,j}, \tag{0.4} $$

where $\overline{P}_{i,j}$ is the average price of fund i in complex j over the period of observation.

The cross-price elasticity of fund i from complex j with respect to the other fund $(3–i)$ in the same complex is given by:

$$\eta_{i,j} = \gamma_i \overline{P}_{3-i,j},\qquad(0.5)$$

where $\overline{P}_{3-i,j}$ is the average price of the "other fund" (than i) in complex j over the period of observation.

The net price of fund i in complex j at time t to the investor is defined by:

$$P_{i,j,t} = f_{i,j,t} - (r_{i,j,t} - \overline{r}_{i,t})\qquad(0.6)$$

where $f_{i,j,t}$ represents the fees charged by the investment adviser of fund i in complex j at time t, and $(r_{i,j,t} - \overline{r}_{i,t})$ equals the fund's return in excess of its contracted for benchmark. Net price is defined as investor fees less the fund's return relative to a benchmark return. Thus, the price to examine for consumer investment decisions is a measure of the extent to which investor fees are above the investor's returns relative to a benchmark return. Nothing restricts this concept of investor price to be positive. We express price as a percentage of net assets invested in the fund rather than in dollars. We do so because of the identity $ER \times TNA = \$fees$, where ER is the expense ratio and TNA represents total net assets.

The last variable embedded in the market share component of the demand function, $m_{j,t}$, represents services to clients provided by the complex, the reputation those services earn the complex, and the perceived goodwill of the complex. The larger $m_{j,t}$, the larger complex j's market share. This variable is dynamic in the sense that, as discussed, increases or declines in goodwill today influence future demand. Table A4.1 presents the parameters of the demand function along with their interpretation.

The Complex Goodwill

In the model, goodwill follows a specific law of motion. As discussed, all else equal, investors select funds based on past and contemporaneous net excess returns, as well as reputation and services to shareholders. The goodwill law of motion is defined as:

$$m_{j,t} = -(P_{1,j,t-1} + P_{2,j,t-1}) + \Omega_{j,t-1} + (1-\delta)m_{j,t-1}\qquad(0.7)$$

TABLE A4.1 Parameters of the Demand Function

Parameter	Interpretation
θ_1 and θ_2	Measure complex market share sensitivity to changes in fund prices.
ϕ	Measures market share sensitivity to changes in complex services m.
λ	Semi-own-price elasticity.
γ	Semi-cross-price elasticity.
μ	Demand shifter.

where $P_{i,j,t}$ is fund price; $\Omega_{j,t-1}$ is residual goodwill of complex j at time t not explained by net past performances of the complex; and δ is the decay rate of goodwill and services or investors' expectations over time.[4] Lower prices, or conversely higher excess returns, imply greater goodwill or better services.

Cost Function

Each complex has technological constraints represented by a cost function. For simplicity, we use a standard quadratic cost function defined as:

$$C(y_{1,j,t}, y_{2,j,t}, q^*)$$
$$= mc(q^*) \cdot \left[\alpha_1 y_{1,j,t} + \alpha_2 y_{2,j,t} + \frac{1}{2}(\xi_{1,1} y_{1,j,t}^2 + \xi_{1,2} y_{1,j,t} y_{2,j,t} + \xi_{2,2} y_{2,j,t}^2) \right] \tag{0.8}$$

where $mc(.)$ is a marginal cost shifter that determines the scale of marginal cost; q^* represents prices of the production factors used in mutual funds, which are assumed to be used optimally at all levels of output; $y_{i,j,t}$ is as defined previously in the demand for assets; and the α_i's and the $\xi_{i,k}$'s are parameters to be estimated.

The cost function as specified in equation (0.8) is flexible enough to incorporate economies of scale and economies of scope. Recall that economies of scale occur when a firm can lower its average cost by increasing production capacity and output, or equivalently a proportional increase in the quantity produced results in a less than proportional increase in total cost. Economies of scope occur when it is more cost-effective for a firm to produce two different goods together rather than separately.

To test for the extent of economies of scale, we examine whether the average cost function decreases as the quantity of production expands. Suppressing the complex and time subscripts for the moment, we seek to determine whether the following inequality holds:

$$C(ty_1, ty_2, q^*) < tC(y_1, y_2, q^*), \text{ or}$$

$$\frac{C(ty_1, ty_2, q^*)}{tC(y_1, y_2, q^*)} < 1 \tag{0.9}$$

That is, we want to know whether a proportional increase in demand leads to a less than proportional increase in a complex's cost as demand increases. If the inequality holds for all fixed combinations of y_1 and y_2, there are economies of scale over the entire range of demands. In practice, we are interested in knowing whether for some fixed values of y_1 and y_2 there are economies of scale. We can test for economies of scale by using the scale elasticity, which represents the proportionate change in cost resulting from a change in output.

$$\frac{dC(ty_1, ty_2, q^*)}{dt} \frac{t}{C(ty_1, ty_2, q^*)}, \text{ which is equal to}$$

$$\frac{y_1 \times \dfrac{dC(y_1, y_2)}{dy_1} + y_2 \times \dfrac{dC(y_1, y_2)}{dy_2}}{C(y_1, y_2)} \tag{1.0}$$

This derivation generates the following definition of economies of scale, which is the reciprocal of (1.0):[5]

$$\text{Scale} = \frac{C(y_{1,j,t}, y_{2,j,t}; q^*)}{\displaystyle\sum_{i=1}^{2} y_{i,j,t} \times \dfrac{\partial C(y_{1,j,t}, y_{2,j,t}; q^*)}{\partial y_{i,j,t}}} \tag{1.1}$$

Based on equation (1.1) we derive:

$$\text{Scale} = \frac{\left[\alpha_1 y_{1,j,t} + \alpha_2 y_{2,j,t} + \dfrac{1}{2}(\xi_{1,1} y_{1,j,t}^2 + \xi_{1,2} y_{1,j,t} y_{2,j,t} + \xi_{2,2} y_{2,j,t}^2)\right]}{[\alpha_1 y_{1,j,t} + \alpha_2 y_{2,j,t} + (\xi_{1,1} y_{1,j,t}^2 + \xi_{1,2} y_{1,j,t} y_{2,j,t} + \xi_{2,2} y_{2,j,t}^2)]}, \tag{1.2}$$

which reduces to

$$Scale = 1 - \frac{1}{2} \frac{(\xi_{1,1}y_{1,j,t}^{2} + \xi_{1,2}y_{1,j,t}y_{2,j,t} + \xi_{2,2}y_{2,j,t}^{2})}{[\alpha_{1}y_{1,j,t} + \alpha_{2}y_{2,j,t} + (\xi_{1,1}y_{1,j,t}^{2} + \xi_{1,2}y_{1,j,t}y_{2,j,t} + \xi_{2,2}y_{2,j,t}^{2})]}. \tag{1.3}$$

Based on equation (1.3), economies of scale exist when the scale variable is greater than 1.0.

An intuitive way of viewing this is presented in Figure A4.1. Economies of scale exist, by definition, when average and marginal costs are decreasing with greater production capacity and output. In equation (1.0), the numerator is simply average cost times output. In the denominator of equation (1.1) the marginal cost of producing each fund is multiplied by output and summed. Because output in the numerator and denominator cancels, our definition tests whether marginal cost is less than average cost; in other words, whether equation (1.1) is greater than 1.0.

Different combinations of parameters and plausible values for $y_{i,j,t}$ can be used with the above specifications to test for economies of scale. The marginal cost shifter mc in equation (0.8) determines the scale of marginal cost, and q^{*} is the vector of mutual fund production factors.

A similar analysis applies for economies of scope. Instead of considering expansion in output, we consider product extensions. Over the past 20 years

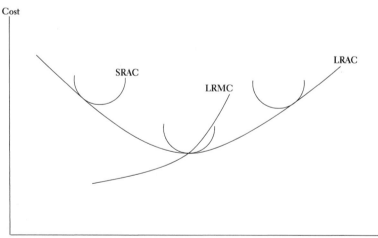

SRAC = Short-Run Average Cost
LRMC = Long-Run Marginal Cost
LRAC = Long-Run Average Cost

FIGURE A4.1 Economies of Scale: Short-Run and Long-Run Cost Changes

or so, besides adding funds, complexes have added fund classes. If economies of scope exist and are not offset by rising input prices, fees would decrease in a perfectly competitive market. Generally, economies of scope are examined by calculating the cost of producing each output separately, compared to the cost of producing them jointly, and setting the prices of the production factors (vector q^*) at their mean or median values.

Accordingly:

$$Scope = \frac{C(y_{1,j,t}, 0; q^*) + C(0, y_{2,j,t}; q^*)}{C(y_{1,j,t}, y_{2,j,t}; q^*)} \qquad (1.4)$$

which gives:

$$Scope = \frac{mc(q^*) \cdot \left[\alpha_1 y_{1,j,t} + \alpha_2 y_{2,j,t} + \frac{1}{2}(\xi_{1,1} y_{1,j,t}^2 + \xi_{2,2} y_{2,j,t}^2) \right]}{mc(q^*) \cdot \left[\alpha_1 y_{1,j,t} + \alpha_2 y_{2,j,t} + \frac{1}{2}(\xi_{1,1} y_{1,j,t}^2 + \xi_{1,2} y_{1,j,t} y_{2,j,t} + \xi_{2,2} y_{2,j,t}^2) \right]} \qquad (1.5)$$

or:

$$Scope = 1 - \frac{\xi_{1,2} y_{1,j,t} y_{2,j,t}}{2 \left[\alpha_1 y_{1,j,t} + \alpha_2 y_{2,j,t} + \frac{1}{2}(\xi_{1,1} y_{1,j,t}^2 + \xi_{1,2} y_{1,j,t} y_{2,j,t} + \xi_{2,2} y_{2,j,t}^2) \right]} \qquad (1.6)$$

For economies of scope to exist, the scope variable in (1.4) will be greater than 1; that is, it costs less to produce two products jointly than separately.

Simulation of Competition Between Two Complexes with Four Funds

We analyze two levels of competition: a one-period, static competition, ignoring the impact of a complex's goodwill; and multiperiod competition, where pricing and performance today affect future demand for funds and complexes and economies of scale are possible. In the static case, each complex maximizes its profit function, given by:

$$\pi_j = f_{1,j} y_{1,j} + f_{2,j} y_{2,j} - C(y_{1,j}, y_{2,j}; q^*), \qquad (1.7)$$

where π_j is the profit function of complex j; $f_{i,j}$ is the fee charged for fund i from complex j; $C(.)$, $y_{i,j}$, and q^* are, respectively, as previously defined, the cost function, the total net assets (output), and the vector of input prices, associated with optimal factor employment.

We obtain the Bertrand-Nash static equilibrium by solving the following system, consisting of equations corresponding to all $i, j = 1, 2$:

$$\partial \pi_j / \partial f_{i,j} = 0 \qquad (1.8)$$

Each complex maximizes its profits by choosing a level of fund fees, taking the fund fees charged by its rival complex as given. The resulting optimization solution yields a set of prices (the fees) that maximize the static profits of the complex.

In the multiperiod case, complexes compete over time by choosing a fee level, taking into consideration their expected ability to provide above benchmark level returns. Each complex solves recursively, beginning in the last period, for $t = 1, \ldots, T$:

$$V_{j,t}(m_{1,t}, m_{2,t}) = \pi_{j,t} + \beta V_{j,t+1}(m_{1,t+1}, m_{2,t+1}) \qquad (1.9)$$

where $V_t(.)$ is the value of discounted profits at time t; β is the discount factor; $\pi_{j,t}$ and $m_{i,t}$ are, respectively, as defined previously the profit and goodwill/reputation/services of complex j in period t.

Assuming the terminal value of discounted profits equals zero, or:

$$V_{j,T+1}(m_{1,T+1}, m_{2,T+1}) = 0 \qquad (2.0)$$

The multiperiod profit function is given by:

$$\pi_{j,t} = f_{1,j,t} y_{1,j,t} + f_{2,j,t} y_{2,j,t} - C(y_{1,j,t}, y_{2,j,t}; q^*). \qquad (2.1)$$

The present value discount factor is given by $\beta = \dfrac{1}{1+r}$ where r is the real rate of interest. The complexes start by maximizing profits at T, the terminal period, and given the optimal prices obtained, maximize profits backward at $T - 1$, the previous period before termination, $T - 2$, and so on. This ensures that the equilibrium is subgame perfect and the complexes have no incentive to deviate from the optimal price path.

Empirical Estimation of the Nested Logit Demand Model

In the nested logit case, we assume that the decision to buy a fund follows a two-step process: first, the investor chooses the fund complex and, second, chooses a fund within the complex. In this framework, the model to be estimated can be represented as:

$$\ln(s_{i,j,t}) - \ln(s_{0,t}) = x_{i,j,t}\,\beta - \alpha p_{i,j,t} + \sigma \ln(\bar{s}_{i|j,t}) + \varepsilon_{i,j,t} \qquad (2.2)$$

where, for $i, j = 1, 2, t = 1, 2, \ldots, T$; s_{ijt} is the market share of fund i in complex j at time t, and $\bar{s}_{i|j,t}$ is the (conditional) market share of fund i in complex j at time t. Table A4.2 presents the variables of the nested logit model.

In discrete-choice modeling, the alternative to purchasing any of the goods under investigation is purchasing the outside good. Without the outside good, consumers are modeled as having to choose among a bundle of goods that do not represent the entire market. The outside good expands the analysis to include the prices of all alternatives so that demand does not depend only on the relative prices of the goods being investigated. In our estimations, the outside good is defined as the funds belonging to smaller complexes. The model is estimated using the two-stage least squares method in order to take into account the possible endogeneity of prices and the within-complex market share.

Empirical Estimation of Own-Price and Cross-Price Elasticities

Given the functional form in equation (2.2), the semi-own-price elasticity is defined as:

$$\frac{\partial \ln(s_{i,j,t})}{\partial p_{i,j,t}} = \alpha\left(s_{i,j,t} + \frac{\sigma}{1-\sigma}\bar{s}_{i|j,t} - \frac{1}{1-\sigma}\right) \quad \text{where } \alpha > 0, \qquad (2.3)$$

The within-complex semi-cross-price elasticity is defined as:

$$\frac{\partial \ln(s_{i,j,t})}{\partial p_{3-i,j,t}} = \alpha\left(s_{3-i,j,t} + \frac{\sigma}{1-\sigma}\bar{s}_{3-i|j,t}\right) \quad \text{where } \alpha > 0, \qquad (2.4)$$

TABLE A4.2 Nested Logit Model Variables

Variable	Interpretation
$s_{i,j,t}$	Market share of fund i in complex j at time t.
$s_{0,t}$	Market share of the outside good at time t.
$\bar{s}_{i|j,t}$	Market share of fund i in the fund complex j at time t.
$p_{i,j,t}$	Price of fund i in complex j at time t.
$x_{i,j,t}$	Other confounding factors of fund i in complex j at time t.
$\varepsilon_{i,j,t}$	Random noise.

To obtain the complex price elasticity, the individual fund elasticities are aggregated by complex.

Using the following identity:

$$S_{j,t}(p_{1,j,t}, p_{2,j,t}) = s_{1,j,t}(p_{1,j,t}, p_{2,j,t}) + s_{2,j,t}(p_{1,j,t}, p_{2,j,t}) \qquad (2.5)$$

where $S_{j,t}$ is the total complex j market share at time t and $s_{i,j,t}$ is the market share of fund i in complex j at time t.

Then,

$$
\begin{aligned}
S_{j,t}(p_{1,j,t} + h, p_{2,j,t} + h) = {} & S_{j,t}(p_{1,j,t}, p_{2,j,t}) \\
& + \left(\frac{\partial s_{1,j,t}(p_{1,j,t}, p_{2,j,t})}{\partial p_{1,j,t}} h + \frac{\partial s_{1,j,t}(p_{1,j,t}, p_{2,j,t})}{\partial p_{2,j,t}} h \right) \\
& + \left(\frac{\partial s_{2,j,t}(p_{1,j,t}, p_{2,j,t})}{\partial p_{1,j,t}} h + \frac{\partial s_{2,j,t}(p_{1,j,t}, p_{2,j,t})}{\partial p_{2,j,t}} h \right) \qquad (2.6)
\end{aligned}
$$

or,

$$
\begin{aligned}
\frac{\Delta S_{j,t}(p_{1,j,t}, p_{2,j,t})}{h} = {} & \left(\frac{\partial s_{1,j,t}(p_{1,j,t}, p_{2,j,t})}{\partial p_{1,j,t}} + \frac{\partial s_{1,j,t}(p_{1,j,t}, p_{2,j,t})}{\partial p_{2,j,t}} \right) \\
& + \left(\frac{\partial s_{2,j,t}(p_{1,j,t}, p_{2,j,t})}{\partial p_{1,j,t}} + \frac{\partial s_{2,j,t}(p_{1,j,t}, p_{2,j,t})}{\partial p_{2,j,t}} \right) \qquad (2.7)
\end{aligned}
$$

Therefore, the derived fund complex price elasticity is:

$$\frac{\Delta S_{j,t}(p_{1,j,t}, p_{2,j,t})}{h} \frac{h}{S_{j,t}(p_{1,j,t}, p_{2,j,t})} \tag{2.8}$$

These formulas can be generalized for complexes with more than two funds.

The Two-Nested Model

The principles of differentiation generalized extreme value model extends the nested logit model to a market with two or more segments, as described in Bresnahan, Stern, and Trajtenberg.[6] Their article extends the theory of random utility maximization underlying discrete-choice models and shows the differences between nested logit models and the principles of differentiation generalized extreme value model approach when examining multiple market segments. We apply their approach to our fund sample. In our principles of differentiation generalized extreme value model, investors make three choices: complex, channel of distribution, and fund. In contrast to the nested logit model, no sequential order in selections is imposed. Investors can assign different weights to the relative importance of complex, channel, and fund, and the three decisions can be made simultaneously. Funds are substitutable across complexes and channels of distribution and within each segment. As with the nested logit model, a given fund is more likely to be a closer substitute for a fund within the same complex and/or the same distribution channel than a fund from another complex and/or channel.

The same general assumptions underlying the nested logit model apply to the principles of differentiation generalized extreme value model. Funds are selected based on performance and expected returns, reputation, and services to shareholders. Complexes maximize their profits by investing in earning returns above their benchmark level until the marginal cost of investing equals the marginal revenues from investing. The consequences of current fee changes on current and future demand are taken into account in setting fees. Firms compete in a differentiated Bertrand-style, taking rivals' prices as given and maximizing the present value of profits.

The Demand for Funds

Without loss of generality and for simplicity, we assume the mutual fund industry is composed of two complexes, two distribution channels, and two funds per channel in each complex. The demand for funds in the principles of differentiation generalized extreme value model is expressed as follows:

$$y_{i,j,k,t} = s_{j,t} \cdot s_{k,t} \cdot \exp[\mu_{i,j,k} + \lambda_{i,k}P_{i,j,k,t} + \gamma_{i,k}P_{3-i,j,k,t}] \tag{2.9}$$

where, for $i, j, k = 1, 2, t = 1, 2, \ldots, T$; $y_{i,j,k,t}$ is the demand of asset (in dollars) for fund i from complex j sold through channel k at time t; $s_{j,t}$ is the market share of complex j in period t; $s_{k,t}$ is the market share of channel k in period t; $P_{i,j,k}$ is the price of fund i from complex j sold through channel k at time t; $\mu_{i,j,k}$, $\lambda_{i,k}$, and $\gamma_{i,k}$ are fund demand parameters to be estimated. More precisely, $\lambda_{i,k}$ and $\gamma_{i,k}$ are the semi-own and cross-price elasticities, respectively, and $\mu_{i,j,k}$ is a demand shifter.

In the monopoly case, when there is one complex and one distribution channel, equation (2.8) simplifies to a semi-log demand function. In that case, the own-price elasticity of fund i from complex j sold through channel k is:

$$\varepsilon_{i,j,k} = \lambda_{i,k}\overline{P}_{i,j,k}$$

The cross-price elasticity of fund i is given by:

$$\eta_{i,j,k} = \gamma_{i,k}P_{3-i,j,k}.$$

We define the "marginal" market share of complex j at time t by:

$$s_{j,t} = \frac{\exp\left[\sum_{i=1}^{2}\sum_{k=1}^{2}\theta_{i,k}P_{i,j,k,t} + \phi m_{j,t}\right]}{\exp\left[\sum_{i=1}^{2}\sum_{k=1}^{2}\theta_{i,k}P_{i,j,k,t} + \phi m_{j,t}\right] + \exp\left[\sum_{i=1}^{2}\sum_{k=1}^{2}\theta_{i,k}P_{i,3-j,k,t} + \phi m_{3-j,t}\right]} \tag{3.0}$$

where i indexes the fund and k the distribution channel. For example, $P_{1,2,1,t}$ is the price of fund 1 in complex 2, sold through distribution channel 1 at time t.

Using the same notation, the "marginal" market share of distribution channel k at time t is defined by:

$$s_{k,t} = \frac{\exp\left[\sum_{i=1}^{2}\sum_{j=1}^{2}\psi_{i,j}P_{i,j,k,t} + \upsilon n_{k,t}\right]}{\exp\left[\sum_{i=1}^{2}\sum_{j=1}^{2}\psi_{i,j}P_{i,j,k,t} + \upsilon n_{k,t}\right] + \exp\left[\sum_{i=1}^{2}\sum_{j=1}^{2}\psi_{i,j}P_{i,j,3-k,t} + \upsilon n_{3-k,t}\right]} \tag{3.1}$$

The complex "market share" is common to all the funds in the complex. All else equal, it determines the complex's aggregate market share, that is, the sum of the market shares of the respective funds in the complex. With a single complex in a market, the numerator and denominator of equation (3.0) are equal, and the complex market share equals 1.0 or 100 percent. The same reasoning applies to the distribution channel market share.

Again, we define the net price of fund i in complex j sold through distribution channel k at time t by:

$$P_{i,j,k,t} = f_{i,j,k,t} - (r_{i,j,k,t} - \bar{r}_{i,t}) \tag{3.2}$$

The variables are defined as in the single-nested case in equation (0.6).

Similarly, the last variables embedded in the market share components of the demand function are the goodwill/reputation/services that the complexes and distribution channels have built over time ($m_{j,t}$, $n_{k,t}$). All else equal, the larger $m_{j,t}$ and $n_{k,t}$ are, the larger will be the market share of the complex and distribution channel.

Table A4.3 describes the parameters of the demand function.

TABLE A4.3 Parameters of the Demand Function

Variable	Interpretation
$s_{i,j,t}$	Market share of fund i in complex j at time t.
$s_{0,t}$	Market share of the outside good at time t.
$\bar{s}_{i|j,t}$	Market share of fund i in the Fund Complex j at time t.
$p_{i,j,t}$	Price of fund i in complex j at time t.
$x_{i,j,t}$	Other confounding factors of fund i in complex j at time t.
$\varepsilon_{i,j,t}$	Random noise.

Complex and Distribution Channel Goodwill

As in the nested logit model, the variables are dynamic in the sense that good-will built or diminished today has an effect on future demand and evolves following a specific law of motion. The law of motion of the complex and distribution channel goodwill is defined by:

$$m_{j,t} = -\left(\sum_{i=1}^{2} \sum_{k=1}^{2} P_{i,j,k,t-1} \right) + \Omega_{j,t-1} + (1 - \delta)m_{j,t-1} \qquad (3.3)$$

$$n_{k,t} = \Theta_{k,t-1} + (1 - \delta)n_{k,t-1} \qquad (3.4)$$

where, for $i, j, k = 1, 2, t = 1, 2, \ldots, T$; $P_{i,j,k,t}$ is the price as defined above; $\Omega_{j,t-1}$ is the residual goodwill/reputation/services not explained by the net past per-formances of the complex; $\Theta_{k,t-1}$ is the exogenous value attributed to the good-will, reputation, and services of the distribution channel by investors; and δ is the decay rate of goodwill/reputation/services over time or the level of investor patience. Lower prices, or conversely higher returns above the benchmark level, imply greater goodwill/reputation/services.

Cost Function

In addition to the demand function, each complex has technological con-straints represented by a cost function. For simplicity, we use a standard qua-dratic cost function defined by:

$$C(y_{1,j,t}^*, y_{2,j,t}^*, q^*)$$
$$= mc(q^*)\left(\alpha_1 y_{1,j,t}^* + \alpha_2 y_{2,j,t}^* + \frac{1}{2}(\xi_{1,1} y_{1,j,t}^{*2} + \xi_{1,2} y_{1,j,t}^* y_{2,j,t}^* + \xi_{2,2} y_{2,j,t}^{*2}) \right) \qquad (3.5)$$

where $y_{i,j,t}^* = \sum_{k} y_{i,j,k,t}$, which is the sum of the outputs of all funds in complex j.

As in the single-nested model, we specify a representation of economies of scale and scope. We define scope as:

$$\text{Scope} = \frac{C(y_{1,j,t}^*, 0; q^*) + C(0, y_{2,j,t}^*; q^*)}{C(y_{1,j,t}^*, y_{2,j,t}^*; q^*)}$$

In this case, economies of scope exist if $\xi_{1,2} < 0$.

Economies of scale can be defined as:

$$\text{Scale} = \frac{C(y^*_{1,j,t}, y^*_{2,j,t}; q^*)}{\sum_{i,j,t} y^*_{i,j,t} \times \dfrac{\partial C(y^*_{1,j,t}, y^*_{2,j,t}; q^*)}{\partial y^*_{i,j,t}}}$$

Economies of scales exist when the scale measure is greater than unity, that is, when total cost is greater than the cost of producing everything at marginal cost. The difference between this case and the single-nested case is that there are now more funds to account for. However, the same intuition applies as was used previously.

Competition Between Complexes

We look at the static competition case, ignoring the dynamic impact of complex goodwill, and also at a pseudodynamic version of the model. In the latter case, the two complexes/distribution channels model starts with different levels of goodwill. The static equilibrium is computed and the output of period t is used as an input for the static equilibrium of period $t + 1$. In the static formulation each complex maximizes its profits function given by:

$$\pi_j = \sum_k (f_{1,j,k} y_{1,j,k} + f_{2,j,k} y_{2,j,k}) - C(y^*_{1,j}, y^*_{2,j}; q^*) \tag{3.6}$$

The Bertrand-Nash static equilibrium is obtained by solving the following system:

$$\partial \pi_j / f_{i,j,k} = 0 \quad \text{For all } i, j, k \tag{3.7}$$

Each complex maximizes its profits taking the other complex's fee level as given. The result of the optimization is a set of prices that maximize the static profits of the complexes. Because complexes maximize profits, the Bertrand-Nash system is formally identical to the system in the single-nested model; the only difference is that four funds are considered instead of two.

Estimation of the Principles of Differentiation Generalized Extreme Value Model

Beyond parameters defining the utility of funds' observable and unobservable characteristics, the key parameters are the segmentation parameters. Each dimension considered is assigned such a parameter, which lies on the unit interval. As the parameter approaches 1.0, segmentation along the corresponding dimension is weaker and investors feel less compelled to substitute among products in the same "category" along that dimension. If all segmentation parameters are equal to 1.0, for example, the model collapses to a regular multinomial logit model in which the ratio of the choice probability of any two funds is independent of the utility of other funds. Intuitively, these parameters are a measure of market segmentation along the dimensions considered.

Theoretical Aspects of the Principles of Differentiation Generalized Extreme Value Model

As a first step, we define the utility of fund j to investor i as $v_{i,j} = x_j\beta + \alpha p_j + \xi_j + \eta_{i,j}$ where x_j are observed fund characteristics, p_j is the price of the fund, ξ_j is the unobserved characteristics of the fund and $\eta_{i,j}$ are the investor specific preferences. This last term is assumed to be a mean-zero error that captures the effects of investors' random tastes.

The mean utility level for product j becomes a linear function of the price of fund j along with the characteristics of that fund. It is defined as: $\delta_j = x_j\beta + \alpha p_j + \xi_j$, for $j = 0 \ldots J$. There are $J + 1$ elements in vector δ: J funds and an outside good ($j = 0$) whose mean utility level is normalized to zero, or $\delta_0 = 0$. The need for normalization arises because utility levels are relative. It is the difference between two levels of utility that is important rather than its absolute value. The choice of normalizing the mean utility level of the outside good to zero is particularly convenient for calculations.[7]

McFadden shows that for a well defined function G, the market share of product j is:[8]

$$s_j = \frac{e^{\delta_j} G_j(e^{\delta_0}, \ldots, e^{\delta_J})}{G(e^{\delta_0}, \ldots, e^{\delta_J})} \tag{3.8}$$

where $G_j(.)$ is a partial derivative and δ_j is the mean utility of fund j.

The principles of differentiation generalized extreme value framework defines G as a function of the dimensions which segment the market. We use fund complexes and distribution channels as segmenting dimensions. In that case, the principles of differentiation generalized extreme value framework defines the function G as:

$$G(e^\delta) = a_f \left[\sum_{f=1}^{F} \left(\sum_{j \in \text{family } f} e^{\delta_j/\rho_f} \right)^{\rho_f} \right] + a_d \left[\sum_{d=1}^{D} \left(\sum_{j \in \text{distribution } d} e^{\delta_j/\rho_d} \right)^{\rho_d} \right] + e^{\delta_0} \quad (4.0)$$

where $a_f = \dfrac{1 - \rho_f}{2 - \rho_f - \rho_d}$ and $a_d = \dfrac{1 - \rho_d}{2 - \rho_f - \rho_d}$. ρ_f and ρ_d are the segmentation parameters mentioned previously. They are a measure of the substitutability of funds in the same complex/channel of distribution compared to other funds.

Market shares are defined as:

$$s_j = \frac{a_f \dfrac{e^{\delta_j/\rho_f}}{\displaystyle\sum_{k \in \text{family } j} e^{\delta_k/\rho_f}} \left(\displaystyle\sum_{k \in \text{family } j} e^{\delta_k/\rho_f} \right)^{\rho_f} + a_d \dfrac{e^{\delta_j/\rho_d}}{\displaystyle\sum_{k \in \text{distribution } j} e^{\delta_k/\rho_d}} \left(\displaystyle\sum_{k \in \text{distribution } j} e^{\delta_k/\rho_d} \right)^{\rho_d}}{G(e^\delta)}$$

$$(4.1)$$

Because

$$s_0 = \frac{1}{G(e^\delta)}$$

we can rewrite the market shares equation relative to the outside good:

$$\frac{s_j}{s_0} = a_f \dfrac{e^{\delta_j/\rho_f}}{\displaystyle\sum_{k \in \text{family } j} e^{\delta_k/\rho_f}} \left(\displaystyle\sum_{k \in \text{family } j} e^{\delta_k/\rho_f} \right)^{\rho_f}$$

$$+ a_d \dfrac{e^{\delta_j/\rho_d}}{\displaystyle\sum_{k \in \text{distribution } j} e^{\delta_k/\rho_d}} \left(\displaystyle\sum_{k \in \text{distribution } j} e^{\delta_k/\rho_d} \right)^{\rho_d} \quad (4.2)$$

This formulation is an extension of the well known nested logit model. For example, assuming no distribution channel clustering ($\rho_d \to 1$, which implies that $a_d \to 0$), this expression becomes:

$$\frac{s_j}{s_0} = e^{\delta_j} s_{j|family}^{1-\rho_f} \tag{4.3}$$

where $S_{j|family}$ is the share of fund j within its own fund complex. This last equation is equivalent to:

$$\ln(s_j) - \ln(s_0) = \delta_j + (1 - \rho_f)\ln(s_{j|family}) \tag{4.4}$$

This expression can be used to derive the segmentation parameters and estimate the parameters defining the mean utilities of the funds in the nested logit framework.

Solving the Principles of Differentiation Generalized Extreme Value Equation

The general expression for market share does not have as compact a form for regular segmentation parameters. In this case, parameters have to be estimated directly from equation (4.2). To estimate the different parameters of the model, we proceed in two iterative steps. In the first step, we fix the segmentation parameters ρ_d and ρ_f. Given these parameters, we use a contraction mapping theorem to compute $\hat{\delta}_j(\hat{\rho}_d, \hat{\rho}_f)$ numerically from equation (4.4). We denote the right-hand side of equation (4.2) by $\hat{s}(\rho_f, \rho_d, \delta)$. Then, as shown in Berry, Levinsohn, and Pakes, as modified in Moul (2006),[9] the operator T: $\delta^j \to \delta^j$ is defined by:

$$T(s, \rho_f, \rho_d)[\delta_j] = \delta_j + \ln\left(\frac{s_j}{s_0}\right) - \min(\rho_f, \rho_d) * \ln(\hat{s}(\rho_f, \rho_d, \delta)) \tag{4.5}$$

Equation 4.5 is a contraction mapping. It is necessary to weight the contraction by the minimum of the segmentation parameters, $\min(\rho_d, \rho_f)$, to ensure the contraction mapping converges.[10] The contraction mapping theorem therefore applies and δ can be estimated recursively by starting with some initial guess δ and iteratively replacing it by the value of the right-hand side of equation (4.5) until convergence.

In the second step, we use the generalized method of moments (GMM) and run the following regression:

$$\hat{\delta}_j(\hat{\rho}_d, \hat{\rho}_f) = x_j\beta + \alpha p_j + \xi_j \tag{4.6}$$

with instruments for the prices of funds and the within distribution channel/ complex market shares. The instruments used for this purpose are the average price of other funds in the complex, the number of funds in the complex and the number of funds in the channel of distribution. These steps are then repeated using an improved grid search on the parameter space defined by ρ_d and ρ_f in order to find the combination that minimizes the objective function of the second step GMM. The improvement on a regular grid search is obtained through the application of a simplex algorithm, which, at each step, evaluates feasible directions for the next step and selects the one that achieves the greatest decrease in the objective function. The variables included in x are the same as those included in the previous specification of the simple-nested logit model.

TABLE A4.4 Regression Results for Two-Nested Model, Two-Stage Least Squares, 2001–2007

	2001	2002	2003	2004	2005	2006	2007
Dependent Variable: Nonlinear Transformation of Market Share							
Constant	-3.180 [0.565]	-3.369 [0.550]	-5.822 [0.427]	-4.795 [0.412]	-3.889 [0.244]	-3.317 [0.200]	-2.518 [0.199]
Current Month Return	-0.535 [1.930]	1.940 [1.977]	-4.569 [2.812]	0.964 [2.020]	1.802 [0.951]	-5.496 [2.163]	1.376 [0.745]
Morningstar Rating (Base = 1 Star)							
2 Stars	-0.504 [0.249]	-0.280 [0.252]	0.010 [0.195]	-0.176 [0.177]	-0.275 [0.124]	-0.047 [0.094]	0.039 [0.087]
3 Stars	-0.182 [0.157]	0.011 [0.147]	0.311 [0.117]	0.158 [0.099]	0.182 [0.068]	0.106 [0.054]	-0.013 [0.050]
4 Stars	0.268 [0.141]	-0.088 [0.137]	0.321 [0.112]	0.344 [0.096]	0.201 [0.069]	0.144 [0.056]	0.123 [0.049]
5 Stars	0.540 [0.181]	0.471 [0.177]	0.481 [0.171]	0.123 [0.149]	0.146 [0.108]	0.215 [0.080]	0.252 [0.069]
Turnover Ratio	-0.001 [0.001]	-0.001 [0.001]	-0.003 [0.001]	-0.003 [0.001]	-0.003 [0.000]	-0.001 [0.000]	0.000 [0.000]
Fund Age	0.023 [0.007]	0.030 [0.006]	0.046 [0.005]	0.035 [0.005]	0.025 [0.003]	0.013 [0.003]	0.002 [0.003]

Investment Objective - Size (Base = Large Cap)

	(1)	(2)	(3)	(4)	(5)	(6)
Mid Cap	-0.200 [0.140]	-0.035 [0.138]	0.126 [0.107]	0.057 [0.096]	-0.053 [0.052]	-0.019 [0.047]
Small Cap	-0.534 [0.186]	-0.432 [0.166]	-0.073 [0.123]	0.013 [0.107]	-0.017 [0.060]	0.003 [0.054]
Passive Management Dummy	-0.438 [0.320]	-0.246 [0.320]	0.171 [0.261]	0.003 [0.270]	0.101 [0.141]	-0.332 [0.129]
Deferred Load Dummy	0.105 [0.117]	0.080 [0.113]	0.230 [0.100]	0.281 [0.088]	0.145 [0.054]	0.154 [0.048]
Strategic Insight Distribution Channel (Base = Noninstitutional)						
Institutional	-1.892 [0.253]	-1.619 [0.236]	-1.029 [0.190]	-1.311 [0.164]	-0.652 [0.072]	-0.686 [0.065]
Price	-189.253 [31.021]	-166.119 [27.984]	-87.079 [21.008]	-116.407 [21.509]	-78.604 [10.788]	-113.909 [10.304]
Observations	762	903	1,046	1,161	1,409	1,606
Adjusted R-squared	0.296	0.243	0.330	0.355	0.270	0.146

Appendix to Chapter Seven

Multivariate Results

The empirical analysis is extended here by using a more inclusive regression equation. To enhance the model, we add explanatory variables, including shareholder fees, fund turnover ratios, fund asset sizes, whether a fund was passively or actively managed, and the fund's investment style by size category, such as large-cap value, large-cap growth, mid-cap blend, and so forth. Holding these variables constant, we conduct tests to determine whether being a Vanguard or TIAA-CREF fund was positively, negatively, or statistically unrelated to above-market returns. The results, in Table A7.1, show that on a pooled basis over the time period examined, high fees and high turnover ratios were statistically significantly related to low alphas; large asset size was related to high alphas; being a passive fund was related to lower alphas; and being a Vanguard fund was related to lower alphas. Although low fees were related to high alphas, being a Vanguard fund was not related to high alphas. Being a TIAA-CREF fund was also not significantly related to higher alphas. The results, after holding constant various determinants of alphas, are consistent with the univariate results reported in Chapter 7: the relatively low fees of Vanguard and TIAA-CREF are not related to consistently superior returns relative to for-profit, nonvertically integrated equity funds that supposedly charge investors excessive fees.

We also use a regression model to examine the relationship between the variables identified above and the probability of being ranked highly by Morningstar. Morningstar rankings are based on returns to fund shareholders and

TABLE A7.1 Multifactor Alpha Regressions from 2000 to 2004, for December of Each Year from 2000 to 2003, and for February 2004 (standard error of coefficients in parentheses and time dummies omitted)

	Pooled	2000	2001	2002	2003	2004
Intercept	−0.0493	−0.0453	−0.0464	−0.0185	−0.0216	−0.0104
	(0.0015)	(0.0089)	(0.0057)	(0.0056)	(0.0041)	(0.0037)
Fee Ratio	−0.7295	−0.9703	−0.3493	−1.3910	−0.9679	−1.3429
	(0.0318)	(0.3060)	(0.2075)	(0.1687)	(0.1079)	(0.0986)
Turnover Ratio	−0.0022	0.0134	−0.0011	−0.0034	−0.0019	−0.0021
	(0.0002)	(0.0033)	(0.0008)	(0.0008)	(0.0005)	(0.0005)
Log of Net Assets	0.0063	0.0073	0.0076	0.0040	0.0029	0.0023
	(0.0001)	(0.0010)	(0.0007)	(0.0008)	(0.0005)	(0.0005)
Vanguard Dummy	−0.0117	−0.0308	−0.0153	−0.0060	−0.0056	−0.0056
	(0.0027)	(0.0231)	(0.0129)	(0.0166)	(0.0090)	(0.0077)
TIAA-CREF Dummy	−0.0020	−0.0130	−0.0089	0.0001	−0.0004	−0.0073
	(0.0079)	(0.0455)	(0.0442)	(0.0481)	(0.0267)	(0.0245)
Passive Dummy	−0.0043	0.0005	−0.0072	−0.0127	−0.0027	−0.0088
	(0.0014)	(0.0097)	(0.0066)	(0.0094)	(0.0047)	(0.0043)
Large Gr. Dummy	−0.0180	0.0490	0.0026	−0.0632	−0.0499	−0.0525
	(0.0008)	(0.0063)	(0.0042)	(0.0044)	(0.0033)	(0.0030)
Large Val. Dummy	0.0073	−0.0259	0.0031	0.0393	0.0321	0.0369
	(0.0008)	(0.0059)	(0.0041)	(0.0048)	(0.0036)	(0.0033)
Mid-Cap Bl. Dummy	0.0226	−0.0111	0.0251	0.0404	0.0393	0.0354
	(0.0014)	(0.0105)	(0.0075)	(0.0079)	(0.0054)	(0.0049)
Mid-Cap Gr. Dummy	−0.0179	0.1001	0.0320	−0.0962	−0.0817	−0.0780
	(0.0009)	(0.0076)	(0.0048)	(0.0052)	(0.0038)	(0.0034)
Mid-Cap Val. Dummy	0.0323	−0.0316	0.0487	0.0875	0.0675	0.0642
	(0.0013)	(0.0092)	(0.0063)	(0.0069)	(0.0060)	(0.0054)
Small Bl. Dummy	0.0356	−0.0065	0.0383	0.0453	0.0450	0.0421
	(0.0013)	(0.0095)	(0.0062)	(0.0073)	(0.0050)	(0.0044)
Small Gr. Dummy	0.0082	0.0531	0.0499	−0.0494	−0.0330	−0.0354
	(0.0010)	(0.0075)	(0.0051)	(0.0056)	(0.0041)	(0.0037)
Small Val. Dummy	0.0371	−0.0443	0.0384	0.0738	0.0868	0.0805
	(0.0013)	(0.0090)	(0.0060)	(0.0075)	(0.0058)	(0.0051)
Adj. R-Squared	0.1337	0.3766	0.1258	0.4375	0.4766	0.5265
N	93,384	1,193	2,374	2,231	2,537	2,592

TABLE A7.2 Ordered Probit Results from 2000 to 2004, for December of Each Year from 2000 to 2003, and for February 2004 (standard error of coefficients in parentheses and time dummies omitted)

	Pooled	2000	2001	2002	2003	2004
Intercept	1.5526	2.6208	2.2030	1.5357	2.1876	2.5437
	(0.0228)	(0.1916)	(0.1230)	(0.1115)	(0.1129)	(0.1136)
Multifactor Alpha	7.8773	18.2926	17.9159	10.1826	15.7005	20.2681
	(0.0511)	(0.7259)	(0.5232)	(0.3873)	(0.4939)	(0.5719)
Fee Ratio	−18.5621	−22.7392	−21.4722	−16.2988	−35.9183	−37.0498
	(0.6514)	(7.0289)	(4.6471)	(4.4025)	(3.9552)	(3.9775)
Turnover Ratio	−0.0178	−0.1695	−0.0385	0.0046	−0.0221	−0.0210
	(0.0022)	(0.0600)	(0.0156)	(0.0128)	(0.0115)	(0.0120)
Log of Net Assets	0.0974	0.1135	0.0524	0.1176	0.0867	0.0672
	(0.0019)	(0.0182)	(0.0128)	(0.0124)	(0.0117)	(0.0114)
Vanguard Dummy	−0.1630	−0.4599	−0.1485	0.0339	−0.2611	−0.1276
	(0.0372)	(0.3985)	(0.2300)	(0.2589)	(0.1851)	(0.1759)
TIAA-CREF Dummy	−0.5827	−0.3107	−1.3613	−0.4635	−0.0598	−0.0361
	(0.1071)	(0.7752)	(0.8308)	(0.7450)	(0.5368)	(0.5416)
Passive Dummy	−0.0890	0.0341	−0.1327	−0.0687	−0.4567	−0.4424
	(0.0191)	(0.1676)	(0.1168)	(0.1493)	(0.1089)	(0.1092)
Large Gr. Dummy	0.0981	−0.6288	−0.8107	0.7304	0.9104	1.1275
	(0.0111)	(0.1134)	(0.0759)	(0.0744)	(0.0726)	(0.0748)
Large Val. Dummy	0.0145	0.2360	0.5386	−0.4341	−0.3868	−0.7538
	(0.0114)	(0.1030)	(0.0725)	(0.0767)	(0.0758)	(0.0775)
Mid-Cap Bl. Dummy	0.0288	0.0149	0.5453	−0.1185	−0.4443	−0.5040
	(0.0187)	(0.1815)	(0.1344)	(0.1245)	(0.1117)	(0.1122)
Mid-Cap Gr. Dummy	0.3169	−1.7287	−0.5068	1.2020	1.5136	1.8381
	(0.0131)	(0.1527)	(0.0874)	(0.0921)	(0.0883)	(0.0913)
Mid-Cap Val. Dummy	0.0797	0.0964	1.0327	−0.6570	−0.7560	−1.0035
	(0.0175)	(0.1630)	(0.1222)	(0.1126)	(0.1262)	(0.1257)
Small Bl. Dummy	0.0237	−0.9899	0.9875	−0.0260	−0.4074	−0.5853
	(0.0177)	(0.1672)	(0.1166)	(0.1163)	(0.1041)	(0.1025)
Small Gr. Dummy	−0.0964	−2.5659	−0.5417	0.6613	0.9732	1.1497
	(0.0138)	(0.1536)	(0.0957)	(0.0917)	(0.0876)	(0.0891)
Small Val. Dummy	−0.0158	−0.2465	1.4474	−0.8564	−1.3925	−1.6662
	(0.0176)	(0.1628)	(0.1162)	(0.1214)	(0.1260)	(0.1255)
Limit 1 (μ_1)	1.0656	1.4475	1.3740	1.1431	1.2890	1.3546
	(0.0063)	(0.0816)	(0.0518)	(0.0425)	(0.0430)	(0.0459)
Limit 2 (μ_2)	2.1530	2.8803	2.8041	2.3534	2.5206	2.7540
	(0.0076)	(0.0977)	(0.0632)	(0.0522)	(0.0524)	(0.0569)

(continued)

TABLE A7.2 (*continued*)

	Pooled	2000	2001	2002	2003	2004
Limit 3 (μ_3)	3.2318	4.3335	4.1649	3.4970	3.9062	4.1865
	(0.0095)	(0.1198)	(0.0808)	(0.0667)	(0.0715)	(0.0769)
McFadden's LRI	0.1289	0.3205	0.3076	0.1535	0.1922	0.2377
N	92,923	1,183	2,361	2,231	2,505	2,549

Morningstar's measure of a fund's risk.[1] We regress the same variables in Table A7.1 on each fund's Morningstar ranking, with the results shown in Table A7.2. The coefficients in Table A7.2 reflect the probability of being top ranked by Morningstar. For example, a negative coefficient for a variable, such as investor fees, implies that the probability of having a 5-star Morningstar ranking decreases with an increase in that variable.

On a pooled basis over the years examined, a high alpha was statistically significantly positively related to an increased probability of being highly ranked by Morningstar, and the fund fee expense ratio was negatively related to the rankings, indicating that the probability of having a high fund ranking decreases with higher fees. Nevertheless, the results also show that being Vanguard or TIAA-CREF, although both are relatively low-fee complexes, is negatively related to a high fund ranking based on return to investors, meaning that a Vanguard or TIAA-CREF fund had a low probability of a high Morningstar ranking. In other words, Morningstar, which ranks mutual funds based on performance and risk, found both Vanguard and TIAA-CREF provided relatively poor net performance. The results are consistent with those in Table A7.1, showing that being a Vanguard or TIAA-CREF fund is not consistently related to producing a high, risk-adjusted return to investors.

Notes

Foreword

1. *Irving L. Gartenberg v. Merrill Lynch Asset Management Inc. et al.*, 694 F.2d 923 (2d Cir. 1982).
2. *Jerry N. Jones et al. v. Harris Associates L.P.*, 527 3d. 627 (7th Cir. 2008).

Introduction

1. Goldman, "Product Differentiation and Advertising: Some Lessons from Soviet Experience," pp. 346–356.
2. Mutual funds allow investors to pool their money and obtain professional money management in stocks, bonds, and money market investments. This pooling provides the benefits of asset diversification and risk management at a lower cost than what most individuals can achieve by creating and managing their own equivalent portfolios.
3. For convenience we use *price* and the annual *fees* mutual fund investors pay interchangeably. Price competition in this sense refers to the fees paid by investors.
4. Bogle, "The Mutual Fund Industry 60 Years Later: For Better or Worse?" pp. 15–24.
5. U.S. Securities and Exchange Commission (SEC), *Investment Trusts and Investment Companies* (1939–1941); and Farina, Freeman, and Webster, "The Mutual Fund Industry: A Legal Survey," pp. 732–983.
6. For a review of pertinent cases up to 1982, see Rogers and N. Benedict, "Money Market Fund Management Fees: How Much Is Too Much?" pp. 1059–1125.

7. SEC, *Report on the Public Policy Implications of Investment Company Growth*; and Wharton School, A *Study of Mutual Funds* (hereinafter called Wharton Report).

8. In addition to the 1930s, Congress held hearings in the 1960s and 1990s to solicit testimony on mutual funds charging excessive fees. Hearings on S. 3550 Before the Subcomm. of the Senate Comm. on Banking and Currency, 76th Cong. 3d sess. (1940); Hearings on S. 34 and S. 296 Before the Senate Comm. on Banking and Currency, 91st Cong. 1st sess. (1969); and Hearing Before the SubComm. on Finance and Hazardous Materials, H.R. 105th Cong., 2d sess. (September 29, 1998). For a review of more recent cases see Benedict, Murphy, and Robertson, "The Aftermath of the Mutual Fund Crises," 261–280.

9. The 19 funds represent those with assets over $500,000. Closed-end funds dominated investment companies during that era, with open-end funds representing only 2 percent of investment company assets in 1929. Wharton Report, pp. 37–38.

10. Investment Company Institute (ICI), *2008 Investment Company Fact Book*, p. 9.

11. ICI, *2007 Investment Company Fact Book*, p. 57.

12. ICI, *2008 Investment Company Fact Book*, pp. 86, 91.

13. A defined benefit plan promises to pay a specified amount upon retirement, generally based on an employee's years of service and latest year's level of salary. A defined contribution plan makes no promise of specific payment. Rather, the employee, employer, or both make a tax-deferred contribution that the employee invests in an individual account, which is available at the time of retirement.

14. A fund complex is also known as a fund family. The number of funds within a complex range from two or three to well over 100.

15. There are a few exceptions. After the economic model for this book was developed and tested, a similar model was presented in Zhang, "Mutual Fund Expense Ratios in Market Equilibrium." For an earlier study, see Baumol et al., *The Economics of Mutual Fund Markets: Competition Versus Regulation.*

16. *Irving L. Gartenberg v. Merrill Lynch Asset Management et al.*, 694 F. 2d 923 (1982) and 528 F. Supp. 1038 (1981).

17. *Jerry N. Jones et al. v. Harris Associates L.P.*, 527 3d 627 (7th Cir. 2008). In 2009, the eighth circuit ruled that there was merit to both the seventh and second circuits' approaches to analyzing mutual fund excessive fee cases. *John E. Gallus et al. v. Ameriprise Financial* 561 F.3d 816 (8th Cir. 2009).

18. The decision distinguished between investment advisers competing on price to manage mutual funds versus competing on price to attract fund investors. The court concluded that only the former was of interest and that advisers did not compete on price to manage mutual funds. *Gartenberg*, 694 F. 2d at 929.

19. *Jones et al.* 527 3d at 929.

1. Mutual Fund Industry Growth and Importance in Retirement Plans

1. Investment Company Institute (ICI), 2008 *Fact Book*, p. 70.
2. Ibid., pp. 20, 22; and ICI, 2007 *Fact Book*, pp. 17, 93.
3. This figure excludes funds that invest in other funds. ICI, 2008 *Fact Book*, p. 110.
4. ICI, 2007 *Fact Book*, p. 16; and ICI, 2008 *Fact Book*, p. 14.
5. ICI, 2007 *Fact Book*, pp. 3–4.
6. ICI, 2008 *Fact Book*, pp. 88, 92.
7. Traditional IRAs were created under the Employee Retirement Income Security Act of 1974 (ERISA). SEP IRAs were created under the Revenue Act of 1978. SAP SEP IRAs were created under the Tax Reform Act of 1986, but new SAP SEP IRA plans were prohibited in the Small Business Job Protection Act of 1996 and replaced by SIMPLE retirement plans. ICI, "The Role of IRAs in U.S. Households' Savings for Retirement, 2008."
8. ICI, 2008 *Fact Book*, p. 87.
9. Stephanie L. Costo, "Trends in Retirement Plan Coverage Over the Last Decade," pp. 58–64. Another study found that workers with only defined benefit plans declined from 62 percent in 1983 to 20 percent in 2004, and workers with defined contribution plans increased from 12 percent in 1983 to 63 percent in 2004. The remaining workers were covered by both types of plans. "You Might Switch to a 401(k) Plan B," *Los Angeles Times*, (November 16, 2008), p. A1.
10. IRAs also benefit from rollovers as employees switch employment or retire.
11. ICI, "U.S. Retirement Market, 2006," *ICI Research Fundamentals* (July 2007).
12. ICI, 2007 *Fact Book*, p. 91.
13. *Kathi Cooper et al. v. IBM Personal Pension Plan and IBM Corporation*, 7th Cir. (August 7, 2006), and 274 F. Supp. 2d 1010 (S.D. Ill. 2003).
14. Report of the Audit Committee of the City of San Diego, July 2006.
15. Wilshire Consulting, 2008 *Report on State Retirement Systems Funding Levels and Asset Allocation* (2008), pp. 1–2; and Wilshire Consulting, 2007 *Report on State Retirement Systems Funding Levels and Asset Allocation* (2007), pp. 1, 3.
16. Wilshire Consulting, 2007 *Report on City & County Retirement Systems: Funding Levels and Asset Allocation* (2007), pp. 1, 5.
17. "Public-Sector Anger Builds as Public Pension Cost Rise," *Los Angeles Times* (October 2, 2006), p. A1.

2. Mutual Funds and Charges of Excessive Fees

1. Swensen, *Unconventional Success*; Bogle, "Mutual Fund Industry Practices and Their Effect on Individual Investors"; Freeman and Brown, "Mutual Fund Advisory Fees," pp. 609–674; U.S. General Accounting Office, *Mutual Funds: Information on Trends in Fees and Their Related Disclosure*, GAO-03-551T

(March 12, 2003); U.S. General Accounting Office, *Mutual Funds: Greater Transparency Needed in Disclosures to Investors*, GAO-03-763 (June 2003); U.S. General Accounting Office, *Mutual Fund Fees: Additional Disclosure Could Encourage Price Competition*, GAO/GGD-00-126 (June 7, 2000); SEC, *Report on the Public Policy Implications of Investment Company Growth*, (1966); and Wharton School, *A Study of Mutual Funds*.

2. Swensen, *Unconventional Success*, p. 219.
3. This structure resulted from the IAA of 1940 and the ICA of 1940. However, this type of organizational structure was not always the case. The first open-end mutual fund in this country, the Massachusetts Investors Trust (MIT), provided investment management internally from 1924 to the late 1960s. Near the end of the 1950s, about 10 percent of mutual funds provided investment management internally. Wharton School, *A Study of Mutual Funds*, p. 6. MIT and other internally managed funds converted to external portfolio management in the 1960s. By the early 1970s, most if not all funds used external investment advisers. Thus, in direct competition for investors over an approximately 45-year span, external portfolio management proved more economically efficient for the vast majority of funds and investment advisers.
4. SEC, *Staff Report, Protecting Investors: A Half-Century of Investment Company Regulation*, p. 251.
5. SEC, *Report on Mutual Funds Fees and Expenses*, p. 9.
6. SEC, *Investment Company Governance*, Proposed Rule, Release No. IC-26323, File No. S7-03-04 (January 15, 2004).
7. Swensen, *Unconventional Success*, p. 221.
8. This reasoning can be applied to advisers as well. If the adviser rejects a fee offer as too low, how can it credibly threaten to terminate its agreement and manage a rival fund? It could start a new fund, but not likely displace a rival adviser. The adviser and the fund are generally committed to each other on a long-term basis and must reach a mutually beneficial agreement on fees.
9. Sirri and Tufano, "Competition and Change in the Mutual Fund Industry." Using large yearly samples of actively and passively managed equity and bond funds from 1993 to 2002, Kuhnen reports the incident of investment adviser hiring and firing. In 1994, approximately 6 percent of the funds' fired an adviser and in the peak year, 2001, approximately 16 percent fired an adviser. Over the entire period, approximately 21 percent of the funds changed advisers at least once, and some changed two or more times. However, the study did not distinguish between replacing primary and secondary advisers. Kuhnen, "Dynamic Contracting in the Mutual Fund Industry."
10. Freeman and Brown, "Mutual Fund Advisory Fees," p. 662, and *Gartenberg*, 694 F. 2d at p. 929.
11. The SEC found that investors are deterred from switching to rival funds by having to pay another sales load and possibly a capital gains tax. SEC, *Report on the Public Policy Implications of Investment Company Growth*, p. 126.

12. Ibid., p. 10.
13. Farina, Freeman, and Webster, "The Mutual Fund Industry," p. 782.
14. Baumol et al., *The Economics of Mutual Fund Markets*, p. 8.
15. Farina, Freeman, Webster, "The Mutual Fund Industry," pp. 787–793.
16. Baumol et al., *The Economics of Mutual Fund Markets*, pp. 47–54; and Farina, Freeman, and Webster, "The Mutual Fund Industry," p. 782.
17. Farina, Freeman, and Webster, "The Mutual Fund Industry," p. 790.
18. The 2003 mutual fund market-timing and late trading scandal, in which preferred customers were allowed to trade at favorable prices after the market closed, was not the first time some mutual funds engaged in this type of selling. Mutual fund timing and other cases in recent years are discussed in Benedict, Murphy, and Robertson, "The Aftermath of the Mutual Fund Crises," p. 261.
19. Farina, Freeman, and Webster, "The Mutual Fund Industry," p. 769.
20. Public Utility Holding Company Act of 1935, § 30, 15 U.S.C.
21. SEC, *Investment Trusts and Investment Companies*, Part One, H.R. Doc. No. 707, 75th Cong. 3d. Sess. (1939); Part Two, H.R. Doc. 70, 76th Cong. 3d Sess. (1939); Part Three, H.R. Doc. No. 279, 76th Cong., 3d Sess. (1940); Parts Four and Five, H.R. Doc. No. 246, 77th Congress., 1st. Sess. (1941).
22. Hearing Before SubComm. of the Committee on Banking and Currency United States Senate, 76th Cong., 3rd. Sess. On S. 3580 part 2, 1940, p. 797; and Farina, Freeman, and Webster, "The Mutual Fund Industry," p. 768.
23. Farina et al., "The Mutual Fund Industry," pp. 787–793.
24. ICI, *2007 Fact Book*, p. 93.
25. Wharton School, *A Study of Mutual Funds*, p. 39.
26. Wharton School, *A Study of Mutual Funds*.
27. SEC, *Report on the Public Policy Implications of Investment Company Growth*, p. 83. Most of the cases were settled after the courts dismissed three cases. In some cases, the adviser agreed to a modest reduction in fees based on a sliding scale related to fund asset size.
28. Wharton School, *A Study of Mutual Funds*, p. 29.
29. SEC, *Report on the Public Policy Implications of Investment Company Growth*.
30. Hearings on H.R. 9510 and H.R. 9511 Before the Subcommittee on Commerce and Finance of the House Comm. on Interstate and Foreign Commerce, 90th. Cong., 1st Sess. (October 10, 1967), pp. 37–38.
31. SEC, *Report on the Public Policy Implications of Investment Company Growth*, p. 126.
32. Ibid., p. 52.
33. Ibid., p. 144.
34. Section 36(b) of the ICA of 1940 states that "the investment adviser . . . shall be deemed to have a fiduciary duty with respect to the receipt of compensation of services, or of payments of a material nature, paid by such registered investment company, or by the security holders thereof, to such investment

adviser or any affiliated person of such investment adviser. An action may be brought under this subsection by the Commission, or by a security holder of such registered investment company on behalf of the company, against such investment adviser, . . . for breach of fiduciary duty in respect of such compensation or payments."

35. Courts have defined or described fiduciary duty in various ways; for example (1) undivided loyalty implicit in the fiduciary bond, *Galfand v. Chestnut Corp.*, 545 F.2d 807, 811 (2d Cir. 1976); (2) the standard of fiduciary duty "is concerned with fairness and equity," *In re Gartenberg*, 636 F. 2d 16, 17 (2d Cir. 1980), cert. denied, 101 S. Ct. 1979 (1981); (3) a fiduciary test is "whether or not under all the circumstances the transaction carries the earmarks of an arm's-length bargain," *Pepper v. Litton*, 208 U.S. 295, 306–307 (1939); and (4) in the context of the law of trusts, "A trustee owes an obligation of candor in negotiation, and honesty in performance," *Jones v. Harris*, 527 3d at p. 632.

36. Senate Report, No. 184, 91st Cong. 1st Sess. (1969), p. 7.

37. GAO, *Mutual Funds: Greater Transparency Needed in Disclosures to Investors*.

38. Swensen, *Unconventional Success*, p. 341; and Bogle, "Mutual Fund Industry Practices and Their Effect on Individual Investors," p. 3.

3. Mutual Fund Excessive Fees and the Courts

1. *Irving L. Gartenberg v. Merrill Lynch Asset Management et al.*, and *Simone C. Andre v. Merrill Lynch Ready Assets Trust et al.*, 528 F. Supp. 1038 (1981) and 694 F. 2d 923 (1982).

2. *Gartenberg*, 528 F. Supp. at p. 1042.

3. *Gartenberg*, 694 F. 2d 923.

4. *Gartenberg*, 528 F. Supp. 1038 (1981).

5. Ibid., pp. 1043–44.

6. Ibid., p. 1044.

7. The appellate court concluded that the difference between using a reasonableness or fiduciary duty test was more semantics than a substantive difference in tests. *Gartenberg*, F. 2d. at 929.

8. *Pepper v. Litton*, 208 U.S. 295, 306–307 (1939), and *Gartenberg*, 528 F. Supp. 1038, 1046 (1981).

9. *Gartenberg*, 528 F. Supp. at 1049.

10. Ibid.

11. *Gartenberg*, 694 F.2d at 929.

12. Securities and Exchange Commission (SEC), *Report on the Public Policy Implications of Investment Company Growth*, p. 131.

13. Ibid.

14. *Gartenberg*, 694 F. 2d at 930.

15. Ibid. The court subsequently retreated in part from this position when discussing rivals' lower fees due to economies of scale by stating the following: "We do not suggest that rates charged by other adviser-managers to other similar funds are not a factor to be taken into account. . . . However, the existence in most cases of an unseverable relationship between the adviser-manager and the fund it services tends to weaken the weight to be given to rates charged by advisers of other similar funds."

16. SEC, *Report on the Public Policy Implications of Investment Company Growth*, p. 131.

17. There is, however, a market for subadvisers, external portfolio management firms who provide portfolio management services to other funds. At present the use of subadvisers is relatively widespread. The extent of subadviser services at the time of *Gartenberg* is unclear. Chen, Harrison, and Kubik, "Outsourcing Mutual Fund Management: Firm Boundaries, Incentives and Performance."

18. *Gartenberg*, 694 F. 2d at 930.

19. The appellate court based its claim of small and competitively insignificant money market fees on the SEC's 1966 report, which states, "Cost reductions in the form of lower advisory fees or other cost considerations do not figure significantly in the battle for investor favor" (SEC, *Report on the Public Policy Implications of Investment Company Growth*, p. 126). As discussed earlier, the SEC's investigation of equity mutual funds in the 1960s found that most funds charged a 0.50 percent fee and there was little variation about that level. Finding that fees were similar across the equity mutual funds it examined, the SEC concluded that fee differences were not significant to investors' choices.

20. Bogle, "Mutual Fund Industry Practices and Their Effect on Individual Investors," Exhibit II.

21. *Gartenberg*, 694 F. 2d at p. 930.

22. Ibid. As noted earlier, the court stated that all factors must be considered, implying that the seven factors are merely a starting point.

23. SEC, *Report on the Public Policy Implications of Investment Company Growth*, pp. 143–144.

24. The *Schuyt* court further rejected the economic experts' testimony because they did not fully address the *Gartenberg* list of factors for determining the disproportionality of fees. *Gertrude B. Schuyt v. Rowe Price Prime Reserve Fund et al.*, 663 F. Supp. 962, 974, n37, n38, and n39 (1987), affirmed, 835 F. 2d 45 (2d. Cir. 1987).

25. *Gartenberg*, 694 F. 2d at 930, quoting from Investment Company Amendments Act of 1970, Senate Report No. 91-184, 91st Cong. 2d Sess. (1970), reprinted in [1970] U.S. Code Cong. & Ad News at 4910.

26. *Gartenberg*, 694 F. 2d at 932.

27. The dispute over fall-out benefits arose again in a second suit filed by Mr. Gartenberg against the Merrill Lynch fund and adviser a few days after he lost

in the original appellate decision. *Irving Gartenberg v. Merrill Lynch Asset Management et al.*, 573 F. Supp. 1293 (1983), 740 F. 2d 190 (2d Cir. 1984). For the second suit, Merrill Lynch hired Peat Marwick, Mitchell & Company to calculate fall-out benefits from commissions, float income, and free credit balances (balances in accounts before being reinvested). Peat Marwick estimated benefits from float and free credit balances, but concluded that it was impossible to estimate commission income attributable to fall-out benefits, which the plaintiff's expert concurred with (Ibid., p. 1313). Mr. Gartenberg was unable to prove that the measurable fall-out benefits exceeded what would be negotiated through arm's length bargaining.

28. The SEC argued that capital gains and sales loads prevent mutual fund investors from switching funds. However, capital gains taxes are generally not an issue in short-term money market funds, and money market funds generally carry no sales loads. SEC, *Report on the Public Policy Implications of Investment Company Growth*, p. 126.

29. Schumpeter, *History of Economic Analysis*, pp. 61–62.

30. This is distinguished from legal monopoly pricing, as may occur occasionally from superior business skill, luck, or government-granted monopolies. Conversely, price can be unfair when it is set too low, below the competitive level, as under monopsony market conditions.

31. Senate Report (1969), No. 184 91st Congress, 1st Session, p. 6.

32. *Gartenberg*, 740 F.2d 190 (2d Cir. 1984); *Schuyt v. Rowe Price Prime Reserve Fund et al.*, 663 F. Supp. 962 (1987); *Krinsk v. Fund Asset Management, Inc. et al.*, 875 F. 2d 404 (2d Cir. 1989); and *Krantz v. Prudential Investments Fund Management LLC et al.*, 77 F. Supp. 2d 559 (U.S.D.C. 1999), 305 F. 3d 140 (2002).

33. Benedict, Murphy, and Robertson, "The Aftermath of the Mutual Fund Crises," pp. 261–280.

34. *Yampolsky v. Morgan Stanley Investment Advisers Inc.*, 2004 WL 1065533 (S.D.N.Y. May 12, 2004), and *In re Eaton Vance Mutual Funds Fee Litigation*, 380 F. Supp. 2d 222 (S.D.N.Y. 2005).

35. *Strigliabotti v. Franklin Resources, Inc.*, 2005 WL 645529 (N.D. Cal., March 7, 2005), and *John E. Gallus et al. v. American Express Financial Corporation*, 370 F. Supp. 2d 862 (D. Minn. 2005).

36. *Jerry N. Jones et al. v. Harris Associates L.P.*, 527 F. 3d 627 (7th Cir. 2008). In a motion to rehear the case *en banc*, which was denied, a strong dissent arguing in favor of retaining the *Gartenberg* framework was submitted by five judges. *Jerry N. Jones et al. v. Harris Associates L.P.*, 537 F. 3d 728 (7th Cir. 2008).

37. *John E. Gallus et al. v. Ameriprise Financial, Inc.*, 561 F.3d 816 (8th Cir. 2009).

38. U.S. Supreme Court No. 08-586, *Jerry N. Jones et al. v. Harris Associates L.P.*, On Petition for a Writ of Certiorari to the U.S. Court of Appeals for the 7th Cir. (Nov. 2008) and U.S. Supreme Court, No. 08-586, Grant of Certiorari, 2009 WL 578699 (March 9, 2009). The plaintiffs-respondent in *Jones* argued

that the proper measure of whether the defendant breached its fiduciary duty is not *Gartenberg's* proportionality test, but the difference between the fees Harris's retail fund investors pay and the fees paid by Harris's institutional clients. This measure of proposed excess fees is discussed in Chapter 6.

39. The seventh circuit's *Jones* decision recognizes that with thousands of mutual fund investment alternatives, ease of entry into mutual funds, and ease of investor mobility between funds, mutual funds come closer to the requirements of an atomistically competitive market than most markets. *Jones*, 527 F. 3d at 634.

4. Price Competition and the Demand for Mutual Funds

1. Consumer price sensitivity implies consumer choice because evidence of price sensitivity would not exist without consumers' ability to choose between similar products. Hence, evidence of price sensitivity is generally sufficient to establish the existence of price competition.

2. These include the SEC, *Report on the Public Policy Implications of Investment Company Growth*, and Wharton School, *A Study of Mutual Funds*, as well as more recent studies by Swensen, *Unconventional Success: A Fundamental Approach to Personal Investment*; Bogle, "Mutual Fund Industry Practices and Their Effect on Individual Investors"; Freeman, Brown, and Pomerantz, "Mutual Fund Advisory Fees: New Evidence and a Fair Fiduciary Duty Test"; Freeman and Brown, "Mutual Fund Advisory Fees: The Cost of Conflicts of Interest"; and the GAO, *Mutual Fund Fees: Additional Disclosure Could Encourage Price Competition*.

3. Bergstresser, Chalmers, and Tufano, "Assessing the Costs and Benefits of Brokers in the Mutual Fund Industry"; and Zhao, "The Role of Brokers and Financial Advisors Behind Investments into Load Funds."

4. Sirri and Tufano, "Costly Search and Mutual Fund Flows," pp. 1589–1622.

5. Gallaher, Kaniel, and Starks, "Madison Avenue Meets Wall Street: Mutual Fund Families, Competition and Advertising."

6. Economists measure the sensitivity or responsiveness of buyers' demand to changes in a product's price by the (own) price elasticity of demand. Price elasticity is measured by the percentage change in quantity demanded relative to a percentage change in price, holding other factors constant. When demand is price-elastic, demand changes more than proportionately to the change in price, so price elasticity is greater than 1. When demand is price-inelastic, demand changes less than proportionately to a change in price, so price elasticity is less than 1. The more price-elastic demand, or the more price elasticity is greater than 1, the more responsive buyers are to price changes; conversely, the more price-inelastic demand (that is, less than ·1), the less responsive buyers are to price changes. When demand is price-elastic, a firm will find that by raising its price relative to the price of a substitute product, it will lose customers and

its profits will fall, and therefore will refrain from doing so in the future. The converse is true when demand is price-inelastic.

7. Two exceptions in Panel B are the studies by Walsh, "The Costs and Benefits to Fund Shareholders of 12b-1 Plans," and Zhang, "Mutual Fund Expense Ratios in Market Equilibrium." Walsh properly measures new money growth relative to changes in expense ratios, finding price-elastic demand. However, she does not measure front-end loads and 12b-1 fees in changes, and finds them to be highly price-inelastic. Zhang uses a nested logic model with instrumental variables applied to a sample of growth funds and regresses instrumental changes in market share in assets and changes in money inflows on expense ratios and other variables. He finds a highly price sensitive relationship with expense ratios and both of his dependent variables.

8. Koehn et al., "Do Mutual Fund Investors Care About Fees?"

9. Cross-price elasticity measures the price elasticity or price sensitivity between two products. It measures what happens to the demand for a product when the price of a complementary product (used jointly with the product at issue) or rival product is raised or lowered, holding other factors constant. When cross-price elasticity equals zero, the products are neither substitutes nor complementary to one another. When cross-price elasticity is positive, the products are substitutes because a price rise in one product increases the demand for the second product. Conversely, if the cross-price elasticity is negative, the products are complementary to one another, used jointly, such as bread and butter.

10. Peter, "Evaluating the Performance of Merger Simulation: Evidence from the U.S. Airline Industry," pp. 627–649; Berry, Levinsohn, and Pakes, "Automobile Prices in Equilibrium," pp. 841–890; Nevo, "Mergers with Differentiated Products," pp. 395–421; Bresnahan, Stern, and Trajtenberg, "Market Segmentation and the Sources of Rents from Innovation," pp. S17–S44; and Stern, "Market Definition and the Returns to Innovation."

11. Absent data on individual investor choices, the models must adapt to using marketwide data. In addition, because not all characteristics of a product sought by consumers are observable, nor are all investor preferences, the demand and supply analyses require a model indicating the probability that investors select a given product. Discrete choice models are well suited for use under these conditions. The models are designed to analyze outcomes in markets in which consumers make a series of choices in an attempt to maximize their well-being.

12. Strategic Insight, Simfund, Mutual Fund Database, 2008. See Table 4.2.

13. The economics and finance literature is replete with studies showing that investors seemingly behave at times contrary to their best interest. Bailey, Kumar, and Ng, "Behavioral Biases and Mutual Fund Clienteles." Other studies find mutual fund investors using information efficiently, in their own best interest. Ippolito, "Consumer Reaction to Measures of Poor Quality," pp. 45–70; and

Berk and Green, "Mutual Fund Flows and Performance in Rational Markets," pp. 1269–1295.

14. This premise is in contrast to studies assuming little investor mobility. Evidence of investor fund mobility is presented in Chapter 6, showing substantial annual investor asset redemptions.

15. Fund advisers do not necessarily maximize the asset size of various funds. Funds are frequently closed to new investors when the fund reaches a certain size. One explanation given for closing funds is to maintain their ability to sustain strong performance for existing shareholders. Other funds may remain small by choice based on their investment strategy, such as a specialty sector, specializing in small-cap funds, or serving a narrow niche class of investors.

16. In economists' terms, each firm has its own downward-sloping demand curve that is conditional on the presence of reasonably close substitute funds and complexes.

17. The regression demand equation is a simplified version of the demand model shown in the appendix to this chapter. The economic model in the appendix also incorporates the cost to provide funds. However, lacking cost data on funds, we are limited to estimating the demand for mutual funds.

18. In many cases, deferred load charges are reduced the longer an investor owns a fund, until in five to seven years on average the charges are often reduced to zero. Nevertheless, we used deferred load charges because the data on up-front load charges in the Simfund data set were too incomplete to be used.

19. We derive this number by taking the total number of funds, 1,161, and dividing by 23 complexes and then by two channels per complex, yielding 25.24 as the average number of funds within a complex/distribution channel. The average market share for these funds is the reciprocal of 25.24, or about 4.0 percent. We use two channels in the example because a review of the number of channels used by the top 20 complexes in our sample shows that most concentrate their sales in no more than two channels of distribution, such as the direct and sales force channels.

20. We calculate this amount as follows. When a single fund increases its fees by 1.0 percent, its cluster (complex/distribution channel) loses 0.08 percent in assets. However, the remaining funds in the complex but in other distribution channels gain 0.022 percent because of cross-price elasticity substitution effects, as seen from Table 4.3. Assuming the two distribution channels split the assets 50-50, the profit implication is calculated by multiplying the loss in assets, 0.08 percent, by 50 percent and the gain in assets of 0.022 percent by 50 percent, yielding a net asset loss of 0.03 percent.

21. The way the model is solved (backward-looking) ensures that the price strategy is optimal and each mutual fund cannot increase its profits by unilaterally changing fees once it starts selling fund shares. The firms set their optimal prices at time T and then look back one period, to $T-1$, set optimal prices at $T-1$ that are consistent with the prices set in T, using all the information up to $T-1$, and so

forth, back to the beginning period. This ensures that the firms' actions are in Nash equilibrium, meaning that given the actions of rivals, a firm cannot improve its profits by engaging in other than its equilibrium action. Thus, expected and actual profits are maximized at the outset by selecting the optimal price structure (see Tirole, *The Theory of Industrial Organization,* p. 206).

22. Consistent with this view, Wahal and Wang find strong competition between incumbents and new entrant mutual funds from the late 1990s through 2005, as reflected in price competition, reduced returns to incumbents, and reductions in demand for incumbent firms. This is consistent with the declines in largest firms' market shares seen earlier (see Wahal and Wang, "Competition Among Mutual Funds").

5. Mutual Fund Industry Structure and Indicators of Price Competition

1. As noted earlier, the U.S. Government Accounting Office reached the same conclusion in 2000 with respect to equity and bond funds, but not money market funds.

2. Investment Company Institute (ICI), *2008 Fact Book,* p. 110.

3. See Chapter 1, Table 1.1.

4. U.S. Department of Justice and Federal Trade Commission, *Horizontal Merger Guidelines* (1992), revised (1997).

5. Ibid. The *Merger Guidelines* provides screens for further government investigation of a proposed merger. The Herfindahl-Hirschman Index (HHI) screens are based on judgment (not derived from economics) and are designed to screen out horizontal mergers with very low anticompetitive potential. An HHI of 1,000 is equivalent to 10 equal size competitors, while the mutual fund industry has hundreds of rivals, so the likelihood of anticompetitive harm based on HHI in mutual funds is even more remote.

6. SEC, *Report on the Public Policy Implications of Investment Company Growth,* pp. 45–49. As a fund complex, Fidelity ranked in the top 10 complexes.

7. Bad news for investors, such as poor fund performance or an SEC investigation, can also lead to rapid changes in asset shares through redemptions. Funds exposed during the market timing scandal in 2003 for violating trading rules, such as Janus and Putnam, lost substantial share relative to 2000.

8. Direct purchases from funds have declined in recent years, from 23 percent of purchases in 1990 to 11 percent in 2006, relative to fund sales through third parties and to institutional investors. ICI, *2007 Fact Book,* p. 69. Purchases of fund shares through employer-based retirement plans have increased substantially.

9. ICI, *2008 Fact Book,* p. 73.

10. Ibid., p. 26. The remaining balance was invested in variable annuities.
11. ICI, *2007 Fact Book*, p. 21.
12. SEC, *Report on the Public Policy Implications of Investment Company Growth*, p. 7.
13. ICI, *2008 Fact Book*, p. 58.
14. Reid and Rea, "Mutual Fund Distribution Channels and Distribution Costs." Another study found that the proportion of diversified equity funds using front-end loads declined from 91 percent in 1962 to 35 percent in 1999. Barber, Odean, and Zheng, "Out of Sight, Out of Mind," pp. 2095–2121.
15. ICI, *2008 Fact Book*, p. 66. The SEC authorized 12b-1 fees in 1980, a further class of expenses to be deducted from a fund's assets.
16. ICI, "The Costs of Buying and Owning Mutual Funds," and ICI, *2008 Fact Book*, p. 62.
17. ICI, *2008 Fact Book*, p. 146.
18. Ibid., p. 38.
19. Ibid., p. 39.
20. Ibid., p. 40.
21. Ian Salisbury, "A Tale of Two ETF Trends: Prices Rise, as Prices Fall," *Wall Street Journal* (October 2, 2007), p. R1.
22. "Fidelity Makes Fee Cuts Permanent," *Wall Street Journal* (March 2, 2005), p. C15; and "Firms Slash Fees as Investors Flock to Low-Cost Portfolios," *Los Angeles Times* (July 11, 2006), p. C1.
23. Bogle, "Mutual Fund Industry Practices and Their Effect on Individual Investors"; and F. William McNabb III, "Statement," Hearing before the Subcommittee on Finance and Hazardous Materials of the Committee on Commerce, House of Representatives, 195th Congress (September 29, 1998), pp. 69–75.
24. Salisbury, "A Tale of Two ETF Trends: Prices Rise, as Prices Fall," p. R1.
25. Examining fee waivers in the early 1990s, Christoffersen found that 37 percent of equity funds engaged in fee waivers and 55 percent of money market fund managers waived approximately 67 percent of their listed fees to investors. Christoffersen, "Why Do Money Fund Managers Voluntarily Waive Their Fees?" pp. 1117–1140.
26. ICI, *2008 Fact Book*, p. 60.
27. Ibid., p. 61.
28. ICI, *2008 Fact Book*, p. 64.

6. Mutual Fund Pricing, Excessive Fees, and Empirical Evidence

1. One study asserts that retail mutual fund investment advisers earn long-run monopoly profits due to charging excessive fees, and the study attempts to test for monopoly profits. The study uses stock market returns for five investment

advisory firms from the 1980s through 2006 as evidence of monopoly profits and, by inference, excessive fees. Freeman, Brown, and Pomerantz, "Mutual Fund Advisory Fees: New Evidence and a Fair Fiduciary Duty Test," pp. 83–153. The study asserts that firms earning economic profits in noncompetitive markets, profits above the risk-adjusted competitive level owing to the absence of price competition, will earn excess stock price returns annually until their monopoly power is eliminated. The study does not consider how nonprice competition will affect economic profits and stock market returns. The use of long-term stock price returns as a proxy for monopoly profits is conceptually incorrect. A firm's stock price reflects the discounted value of expected future earnings. If the existence of monopoly power and profits is known, which according to fee critics has been true for investment advisory firms since the 1960s, expected monopoly profits will be capitalized into the value of the firm's stock. Subsequent stock buyers will earn only a competitive return until there are changes in expectations of future earnings. For the authors' reasoning applied to investment advisers to be valid, investors in publicly traded advisory firms must have been chronically wrong about the firms' monopoly power and expected earnings each year for at least 20 to 25 years, which is implausible. Various investment advisory firms may have earned above average stock market returns (adjusted for risk) in the last two decades, as did numerous firms in other industries, but it was not because of monopoly power in negotiating prices. Firms in competitive industries earning above average stock market returns do so because of competitive superiority, not because of an annual awakening to monopoly power and the capitalization of expected monopoly profits year after year, long after monopoly power is known by the investment community.

2. In a commingled pool, a small group of high wealth investors pool their assets to be managed as a single portfolio by an investment adviser. The investors typically contribute a substantial amount individually, such as $5 to $10 million, so total initial assets can be relatively large, depending on the number of investors.

3. The Wharton School report examined the fees charged by 54 investment advisers to mutual and nonmutual fund clients. It found that fees were at a minimum 50 percent higher to mutual fund clients in 39 cases, and much higher in other cases. Wharton School, *A Study of Mutual Funds*, p. 489. The SEC studied six banks, finding that fees on pension and profit-sharing plans were approximately 0.06 percent versus the 0.5 percent then prevailing at mutual funds, although the study acknowledged that fees were lower at banks in part because of their investing more heavily in fixed-income securities. Moreover, the products were not directly comparable because mutual funds faced higher risks and costs of starting and operating a fund. U.S. Securities and Exchange Commission (SEC), *Report on the Public Policy Implications of Investment Company Growth*, pp. 114–121. Based on a survey of the 100 largest pension plans in 1998, with approximately one-third useful responses, Freeman

and Brown concluded that average retail fund fees were double the size of average fees paid by pension plans to external portfolio managers. Freeman and Brown, "Mutual Fund Advisory Fees: The Cost of Conflicts of Interest," pp. 627–640.

4. Freeman and Brown, "Mutual Fund Advisory Fees: The Cost of Conflicts of Interest," pp. 627–640.

5. A survey of 401(k) defined contribution plans by Deloitte & Touche indicates that poorly performing advisers are replaced frequently. The study reports that 70 percent of such plan sponsors replace underperforming funds and 64 percent reported taking such action within the last two years. Deloitte & Touche, *401(k) Benchmarking Survey: 2008 Edition*, p. 22.

6. Baumol, *Regulation Misled by Misread Theory: Perfect Competition and Competition-Imposed Price Discrimination*. For articles on competition and price discrimination see "Symposium: Competitive Price Discrimination," *Antitrust Law Journal*, 70 (2003), pp. 599–696.

7. This is not to say that retail mutual fund investors are not primarily focused on returns to their investment. Rather, it is to distinguish the many aspects of the product bundle purchased by retail investors from the institutional investor's narrower product bundle.

8. The *Gartenberg* appellate court rejected using institutional investor fees as a competitive benchmark because of different services provided to retail investors. According to the court, "The nature and extent of the services required by each type of fund differ sharply." As the court recognized, pension funds do not face the myriad of daily purchases and redemptions throughout the nation which must be handled by the Fund [Merrill Lynch's money market fund], in which a purchaser may invest for only a few days." *Gartenberg*, 694 F. 2d at 930, footnote 2.

9. Freeman, Brown, and Pomerantz, "Mutual Fund Advisory Fees: New Evidence and a Fair Fiduciary Duty Test," p. 95; Freeman and Brown, "Mutual Fund Advisory Fees: The Cost of Conflicts of Interest," pp. 627–640; and Collins, "The Expenses of Defined Benefit Pension Plans and Mutual Funds."

10. Freeman and Brown, "Mutual Fund Advisory Fees: The Cost of Conflicts of Interest," pp. 627–640.

11. Using a sample of diversified domestic equity funds over the period 1992–2001, Yan found the average cash holdings were 5.33 percent of total net assets, with average total net assets of $1.2 billion. Yan, "The Determinants and Implications of Mutual Fund Cash Holdings," pp. 67–91. Luo found average cash ratios in the mid-1990s varied by fund investment category—small cap, growth, equity-income, and so forth—generally falling between 6 and 8 percent. Luo, "Mutual Fund Fee-Setting, Market Structure and Mark-ups," p. 261.

12. SEC, *Report on Mutual Funds Fees and Expenses*, p. 28.

13. Subadvisory services, where the fund accounts for all nonportfolio services, has grown as a share of total mutual fund portfolio management since the

mid-1990s. For a sample of over 4,500 mutual funds in 2004, subadvisory services accounted for 35 percent of small-cap growth funds, 33 percent of aggressive growth funds, and 33 percent of growth and income funds. Chen, Hong, and Kubik, "Outsourcing Mutual Fund Management: Firm Boundaries, Incentives and Performance."

14. SEC, *Report on Mutual Funds Fees and Expenses*, pp. 15–16.

15. Ibid., p. 49, footnote 60.

16. American Century Investments, Growth Fund, Vista Fund, Semiannual Report (April 30, 2008), p. 21.

17. Adding to the measurement problem, what is included in 12b-1 fees can vary widely from fund to fund. According to the SEC, such fees are commonly used to pay distribution expenses, printing costs, and advertising. However, they are also used in some cases to pay other operating costs, including advisory services and administrative costs. SEC, *Report on Mutual Funds Fees and Expenses*, footnote 61.

18. Freeman and Brown, "Mutual Fund Advisory Fees: The Cost of Conflicts of Interest," p. 631. Not only are mutual fund investors allegedly overcharged compared to public pension plans on portfolio management fees, but the authors claim that retail fund advisers have lower costs because they do not have to compete for investors. They assert that competing for institutional clients "necessitates a significant cost that [retail mutual] fund advisers need not pay: The cost of finding business in a competitive marketplace. Fund managers escape paying that cost due to their unseverable tie with the fund." Freeman, Brown, and Pomerantz, "Mutual Fund Advisory Fees: New Evidence and a Fair Fiduciary Duty Test," p. 110.

19. In a letter to the Secretary of the SEC, John Freeman defends their measures of advisory fees. Freeman states that while the data problem exists, it is minor and they adjusted for the problem by eliminating funds that clearly commingled administrative and advisory costs, and included administrative costs in reported 12b-1 fees. Their study, however, only says that they eliminated funds that did not report administrative costs; not that they had a valid method for identifying funds with errors in measuring management or advisory costs. John P. Freeman, Letter to Secretary, U.S. Securities and Exchange Commission (March 13, 2007), p. 5. Freeman, Brown, and Pomerantz state that they refined Freeman and Brown's method of extracting pure portfolio management costs and conclude that any measurement error in their estimates amounted to no more than three basis points. Freeman, Brown, and Pomerantz, "Mutual Fund Advisory Fees: New Evidence and a Fair Fiduciary Duty Test," p. 109, footnotes 90 and 91.

20. Collins, "The Expenses of Defined Benefit Pension Plans and Mutual Funds."

21. Vanguard Stockholders' Reports, released annually.

22. Prior to Collins's 2003 study, Freeman and Brown endorsed the use of subadvisory fees for actively managed equity funds to measure pure portfolio fees.

Using subadvisory fees for ten actively managed Vanguard domestic equity funds in 1999, they found a weighted average base fee (before adjustments for fund performance in 1999) of approximately 0.15 percent, or about half of the 0.28 percent fee they claimed was the competitive price for portfolio management based on their survey of public pension plans. Freeman and Brown, "Mutual Fund Advisory Fees: The Cost of Conflicts of Interest," p. 638. But if the competitive price is 0.28 percent, how could Vanguard pay subadvisory fees at half the competitive level? In Freeman's rebuttal letter to the SEC, he argued that Vanguard receives prices well under the average competitive price because of economies of scale in subadvising its actively managed funds. Freeman, letter to the SEC (2007), pp. 7–8. However, Freeman and Brown's data for Vanguard refute that explanation. Their data for Vanguard's subadvisory fees show no consistency between fund asset size and fees (Freeman and Brown's measure of economies of scale). Vanguard's highest fee funds do not have the lowest total assets, nor do the largest asset Vanguard funds have the lowest fees. Freeman and Brown, "Mutual Fund Advisory Fees: The Cost of Conflicts of Interest," p. 638. Moreover, the base fees Vanguard paid for subadvisory services ranged from 0.09 percent to 0.40 percent (0.04 percent to 0.40 percent after adjustment for fund performance payments). Freeman and Brown claim that portfolio management service is a commodity, so fees for comparable equity funds should be similar, yet their own data refute that claim. Adding to the doubtfulness of Freeman and Brown's data is that in comparing fees for S&P 500 index funds between retail, institutional, and Vanguard's S&P 500 index fund, they claim that Vanguard ran its $91 billion fund for only $100,000 in advisory costs, an advisory fee of about .0001 percent. This amount is factually suspect. In contrast, Vanguard's administrative expenses for the fund, as reported by Freeman and Brown, were approximately $164 million (Ibid., p. 640).

23. Freeman, Brown, and Pomerantz, "Mutual Fund Advisory Fees: New Evidence and a Fair Fiduciary Duty Test," pp. 99–100.

24. Freeman, Brown, and Pomerantz, "Mutual Fund Advisory Fees: New Evidence and a Fair Fiduciary Duty Test," p. 100. The authors claim that subadvisory contracts manage "only a minor fraction of the fund business," and that Collins understated subadvisory fees by failing to include additional charges that funds add to subadvisory fees when compiling investors' annual fees (Ibid., p. 117). The greater than one-third of mutual funds managed by subadvisors in 2004 cannot easily be classified as a "minor" fraction. Chen, Hong, and Kubik, "Outsourcing Mutual Fund Management: Firm Boundaries, Incentives and Performance," pp. 39–41. Their criticism of Collins is misguided. The point of Collins's study was to obtain a more accurate measure of pure portfolio management fees at the retail fund level than Freeman and Brown's attempt to extract such fees when they are imbedded with other costs in a fund's total management costs. Expense ratios and thus investor fees contain markups for profits as well.

25. Wallison and Litan, *Competitive Equity: A Better Way to Organize Mutual Funds*; Brian G. Cartwright, General Counsel, U.S. Securities and Exchange Commission, "Remarks Before the 2006 Securities Law Developments Conference Sponsored by the Investment Company Institute Education Foundation" (December 4, 2006); and Swensen, *Unconventional Success: A Fundamental Approach to Personal Investment*, p. 352.

26. In the case of S&P 500 index funds, fees range from approximately 0.10 percent to over 2.0 percent of assets, even though each fund tracks as closely as possible returns to the S&P 500 index. ICI, *2008 Fact Book*, p. 64; and Hortacsu and Syverson, "Product Differentiation, Search Costs, and Competition in the Mutual Fund Industry," pp. 404–406.

27. The Wharton School report's conclusion that little price dispersion existed across mutual funds in the 1950s and early 1960s is arguably overstated. The study reports that in a survey of 163 advisers in 1960, 49 percent had a 0.5 percent fee; 28.3 percent had fees below 0.5 percent; and 22.7 percent had fees above 0.5 percent. In addition, 9 percent of advisers had fees below 0.14 percent and 9 percent had fees above 1.0 percent, so the full range of fees did not cluster closely around 0.5 percent. Wharton School, *A Study of Mutual Funds*, p. 482. The report did find, however, that for the largest 29 funds in 1958, 23 had a list price of 0.5 percent of assets since 1952 or earlier. With shareholder approval required to raise list price it is not surprising to find list prices upwardly sticky.

28. The perfectly competitive model in market equilibrium eliminates price competition. In a perfectly competitive market equilibrium, pricing above the competitive price results in the loss of a firm's entire sales, driving it out of business, and pricing below the competitive equilibrium price results in unsustainable losses, so firms cannot deviate from the market-determined price without going bankrupt. In addition, under the given technology, there is no incentive for new rivals to enter the industry. Under these conditions there is no price competition.

29. Pratt, Wise, and Zeckhauser, "Price Differences in Almost Competitive Markets," pp. 189–211; Lach, "Existence and Persistence of Price Dispersion: An Empirical Analysis," pp. 433–444; Roberts and Supina, "Output Price, Markups, and Producer Size," pp. 909–921; and Zhao, "Price Dispersion in the Grocery Market," pp. 1175–1192.

30. Carlton and Perloff, *Modern Industrial Organization*, pp. 440–470; and Roberts and Supina, "Output Price, Markups, and Producer Size," pp. 909–921.

31. Even in channels where search costs are relatively low, such as Internet sites, price dispersion prevails in highly price-competitive markets. Ellison and Ellison, "Lessons About Markets from the Internet," pp. 139–158; Baye, Morgan, and Scholton, "Price Dispersion in the Small and in the Large: Evidence from an Internet Price Comparison Site," pp. 463–496; Brown and Goolsbee, "Does the Internet Make Markets More Competitive? Evidence from the Life Insurance

Industry," pp. 481–507; and Clay, Krishnan, and Wolff, "Prices and Price Dispersion on the Web: Evidence from the Online Book Industry," pp. 521–540.

32. Surveys by the ICI found that among households owning mutual funds outside defined contribution pension plans, 80 percent purchased funds through professional financial advisers, which include full service brokers, independent financial advisers, insurance agents, bank or savings institutions investment specialists, and accountants. The ICI reported that 43 percent owned funds solely through advisers, and only 12 percent owned funds solely by direct purchase from funds, fund supermarkets, or discount brokers. ICI, 2008 Fact Book, p. 75.

33. Barber, Odean, and Zheng, in "Out of Sight, Out of Mind: The Effects of Expenses on Mutual Fund Flows," found that more experienced fund investors tend to purchase lower load fee funds.

34. ICI, 2008 Fact Book, p. 64. The relationship between fees and assets invested raises the statistical question of whether large asset size leads to low fees or low fees lead to larger asset investment. Our statistical demand study results, reported in Chapter 4, account for the possibility of causation going from fund size to price rather than price to fund size. The results are consistent with the conventional view that lower price leads to greater demand and fund size. Other studies have controlled for this possibility to prevent bias in the results and report findings consistent with lower price leading to greater demand. Khorana and Servaes, "Conflicts of Interest and Competition in the Mutual Fund Industry."

35. Wallison and Litan find that price dispersion between the lowest and highest fees in U.S. mutual funds is approximately 300 percent versus 100 percent in England. However, average fees in the United States are significantly lower than those in England, a factor of no small consequence to investors. See Khorana, Servaes, and Tufano, "Mutual Fund Fees Around the World" and Wallison and Litan, Competitive Equity: A Better Way to Organize Mutual Funds. Wallison and Litan argue that the cost of doing business in England accounts for England's higher average fees. The cost of doing business cannot explain the price differential between the United States and numerous other countries. In Canada, for example, mutual fund fees are two to three times higher than in the United States and the cost of doing business is roughly equal. In general, average mutual fund fees in the United States are among the lowest in the world compared to fees in Western European and developed Asian countries. Even if price dispersion is greater in the United States than in other countries, with the United States having close to the lowest average fees in the world among developed countries, there is little basis to contend that the relatively low U.S. fees are not a product of price competition among investment advisers.

36. Khorana, Servaes, and Tufano, "Mutual Fund Fees around the World."

37. Freeman and Brown, "Mutual Fund Advisory Fees: The Cost of Conflicts of Interest," pp. 619–627; Swensen, Unconventional Success: A Fundamental Approach to Personal Investment, pp. 237–242; and Bogle, "The Mutual Fund

Industry 60 Years Later: For Better or Worse?" pp. 15–24. The debate over economies of scale and the level of mutual fund fees in academic research, the courts, and Congress generally does not refer to economies of scope. With economies of scope, it costs less to produce two or more products jointly (such as mutual funds within a fund complex) than by producing them separately, on a stand-alone basis. The debate over fee levels and economies of scale should also consider economies of scope.

38. In contrast to this received opinion, in a study 34 years after the 1966 SEC Report, the SEC found no evidence of economies of scale. SEC, *Report on the Public Policy Implications of Investment Company Growth*, p. 11; and SEC, *Report on Mutual Funds Fees and Expenses*, pp. 29–31.

39. Wharton School, *A Study of Mutual Funds* (1962), p. 482.

40. Ibid., p. 480.

41. *Gartenberg*, 694 F. 2d at 930. In debating the Section 36(b) amendment to the ICA of 1940, Congress stated that investors should share in the economies stemming from growth in mutual funds and the general acceptance of funds. Senate Report No. 184, 91st Congress, 1st Session (1970), 4, and 1970 U.S. Code Congressional & Administrative News, p. 4901.

42. 15 U.S.C. §80a-36(b).

43. As explained in Chapter 3, although prices are determined by both supply (cost) and demand, plaintiffs consider cost only in claiming that fees are excessive, relying on the *Gartenberg* decision. However, economies of scale and unchanged nominal fees by themselves do not address whether fees are excessive. Price reductions can be passed on to investors in nonfee form, such as improved product and service quality, so that price per unit of quality declines but nominal price remains unchanged.

44. A rare exception is the case of a "natural monopoly" industry, in which average cost continues to decline with increasing output until only one firm can operate profitably.

45. As examples, technological advances in electronics have led to declining costs and prices over time in personal computers and numerous other electronic products, along with improvements in product quality. However, in many labor-intensive service sectors, such as health care and education, costs have consistently risen in recent decades.

46. *Gartenberg*, 694 F. 2d at 928.

47. *Schuyt v. Rowe Price Prime Reserve Fund et al.*, 663 F. Supp. 962, 980 (U.S.D.C., 1987).

48. Freeman and Brown, "Mutual Fund Advisory Fees: The Cost of Conflicts of Interest"; Bogle, "The Mutual Fund Industry 60 Years Later: For Better or Worse?"; and Swensen, *Unconventional Success: A Fundamental Approach to Personal Investment*.

49. Wharton School, *A Study of Mutual Funds*, p. 503. The 1966 SEC study concurred with the Wharton School report's conclusion on economies of scale,

citing as an example growth in the Dreyfus fund from 1961 to 1965, where operating expenses rose less than proportionately to assets and advisory fees increased significantly. SEC, *Report on the Public Policy Implications of Investment Company Growth*, pp. 94–95.

50. Berkowitz and Yotowitz, "Managerial Quality and the Structure of Management Expenses in the U.S. Mutual Fund Industry," pp. 315–330; Tufano and Sevick, "Board Structure and Fee Setting in the U.S. Mutual Fund Industry," pp. 321–355; Dermine and Roller, "Economies of Scope and Scale in French Mutual Funds," pp. 83–93; and Baumol et al., *The Economics of Mutual Fund Markets: Competition Versus Regulation*, pp. 190–192.

51. Baumol, Koehn, and Willig, "How Arbitrary Is Arbitrary?—or, Toward the Deserved Demise of Full Cost Allocation," pp. 16–21.

52. Stigler, "The Economics of Scale," pp. 71–94.

53. Statement of John Bogle Before the U.S. House of Representatives, Subcommittee on Capital Markets, Insurance, and Government Sponsored Enterprises of the Committee on Financial Services, March 12, 2003, p. 1; and Barber et al., "Out of Sight, Out of Mind: The Effects of Expenses on Mutual Fund Flows."

54. Bogle, "Mutual Fund Industry Practices and Their Effect on Individual Investors," p. 1.

55. ICI, *2008 Investment Company Fact Book*, p. 58.

56. SEC, *Report on Mutual Funds Fees and Expenses*, p. 6.

57. Ibid, pp. 19–20.

58. Ibid, p. 21.

59. Ibid.

60. Ibid, p. 22.

61. Sirri and Tufano, "Competition and Chance in the Mutual Fund Industry"; SEC, *Report on Mutual Funds Fees and Expenses*; Khorana and Servaes, "Conflicts of Interest and Competition in the Mutual Fund Industry"; and ICI, *2008 Fact Book*, p. 59.

62. ICI, *2008 Fact Book*, p. 59.

63. GAO, *Mutual Fund Fees: Additional Disclosure Could Encourage Price Competition*, p. 50; and GAO, *Mutual Funds: Information on Trends in Fees and Their Related Disclosure*, p. 6.

7. Mutual Funds' Organizational Form and Conflicts of Interest

1. Again, at the most basic level there is a counterargument. The counterargument holds that just as shareholders in any publicly held firm who believe there is a conflict of interest between shareholders and management can sell their shares, so can mutual fund shareholders sell their shares if they believe that the investment adviser is not acting in the interests of the fund's

shareholders, thus moving their assets to comparable, lower fee or better performing funds.

2. This argument makes little sense when directors own a nontrivial amount of fund shares, since their interests are closely aligned with fund shareholders. Studies show that approximately two-thirds of directors own shares in the funds they monitor and director ownership is significantly positively related to fund performance. Chen, Goldstein, and Jiang, "Directors' Ownership in the U.S. Mutual Fund Industry"; and Cremers, Driessen, and Weinbaum, "Does Skin in the Game Matter? Director Incentives and Governance in the Mutual Fund Industry." In a test of whether advisers and directors have successfully acted jointly against the interests of fund shareholders, Kuhnen concluded, "Thus while connections [between advisers and directors] are strong determinants of how the manager and director positions are filled in this industry, they do not have an economically significant impact on the investors' bottom line." Kuhnen, "Social Networks, Corporate Governance and Contracting in the Mutual Fund Industry."

3. Swensen, *Unconventional Success: A Fundamental Approach to Personal Investment*, pp. 341, 343. Bogle, in "The Mutual Fund Industry 60 Years Later: for Better or Worse?" argues in a similar manner that until 1958 fund money managers acted as stewards of clients' assets, solely in the interest of fund shareholders and not as profit-maximizing firms. In 1958, the Ninth Circuit and U.S. Supreme Court granted an investment adviser, Insurance Securities, Inc., the right to go public and sell shares, which according to Bogle transformed advisers into profit-maximizing firms, compelling them to act contrary to the interests of fund shareholders. No explanation is given as to why competing privately held investment advisory firms prior to 1958 lacked the motivation and competitive pressure to maximize profits.

4. In reality, the distinction between internal and external portfolio management can be ambiguous. In some cases wherein funds are managed by external advisers, officers of the investment advisory firm are also officers of the fund's board of directors. Moreover, studies find that mutual fund performance increases with increasing investment adviser fund ownership. Khorana, Servaes, and Wedge, "Portfolio Manager Ownership and Fund Performance," pp. 179–204; and Evans, "Portfolio Manager Ownership and Mutual Fund Performance." In such cases, fund shareholder and investment adviser interests are in close alignment, with both seeking to maximize returns to shareholders.

5. Bogle, "The Mutual Fund Industry 60 Years Later: For Better or Worse?" p. 10; and Swensen, *Unconventional Success: A Fundamental Approach to Personal Investment*, pp. 341, 343.

6. Wharton School, *A Study of Mutual Funds*, pp. 38–39.

7. SEC, *Report on the Public Policy Implications of Investment Company Growth*, p. 102.

8. Wharton School, *A Study of Mutual Funds*, p. 442.

9. SEC, *Report on the Public Policy Implications of Investment Company Growth*, p. 102.

10. "Major Reorganization Set at Massachusetts Investors Trust Group," *Wall Street Journal* (July 2, 1969).

11. Both the Wharton and SEC studies in the 1960s reported that expense ratios and management fees were substantially lower in internally as compared to externally managed fund complexes. The fee data reported do not include waivers, so the data may be subject to error. Even so, based on expense ratios, there are some notable exceptions to the claimed superiority of cost levels in internally managed complexes. As of June 30, 1966, the internally managed funds of MIGSF and Century Shares Trust had an expense ratio of 0.38 percent, the same as such externally managed funds as Investors Mutual, Wellington Fund, and Bullock Fund, and above the externally managed Affiliated Fund at 0.34 percent. The SEC reported that internally managed MIGSF had a fee of 0.26 percent and Century Shares 0.28 percent, while externally managed Wellington had a 0.26 percent advisory fee, Affiliated Fund 0.24 percent, Putnam Income Fund 0.27 percent, and Bullock Fund 0.23 percent. Hence, while on average internal portfolio management at the time may have charged lower fees than external portfolio management, there were a number of exceptions, where externally managed funds had comparable or even lower fees. SEC, *Report on the Public Policy Implications of Investment Company Growth*, pp. 102–107. Similarly, the Wharton School report found that operating expenses for externally managed funds, measured in cents per $1,000 managed as of 1960–1961, were lower than management expenses in internally managed funds when comparing funds in the $300 to $600 million size class as well as for funds in the $10 to $50 million size class. The data show that internal portfolio management in the 1960s, by itself, did not assure investors the lowest annual fees. Wharton School, *A Study of Mutual Funds*, p. 525.

12. Freeman and Brown, "Mutual Fund Advisory Fees: The Cost of Conflicts of Interest," pp. 618–619; and Freeman, Brown, and Pomerantz, "Mutual Fund Advisory Fees: New Evidence and a Fair Fiduciary Duty Test," p. 95. Despite their view of Vanguard as the ideal governance form, Freeman and Brown do not call for a universal change in mutual fund governance structure to vertically integrated, not-for-profit status. Rather, the authors ask the SEC to require standardized accounting reporting of shareholder fees to facilitate fee comparisons between retail and institutional funds and a most-favored-nation requirement on investor fees, so that retail shareholders' pay the same lower fees as institutional investors.

13. Ibid., p. 617. Vanguard states that it earns no profit on the fees it charges stockholders. *Vanguard 500 Index Annual Report* (December 31, 2004), note B, p. 24.

14. Ibid.

15. Mutual funds' use of subadvisers is fairly common. The incidence of outsourcing has risen in recent years, with approximately 48 percent of fund

complexes outsourcing to some degree in 2004, up from 39 percent in 1994. Chen, Hong, and Kubik, "Outsourcing Mutual Fund Management: Firm Boundaries, Incentives and Performance," p. 41. In addition, Chen et al. find that investor returns on average are significantly lower for subadvised equity funds.

16. Freeman and Brown, "Mutual Fund Advisory Fees: The Cost of Conflicts of Interest," p. 618.

17. Carlson Elliot, "Wellington Management Names John Bogle President in Reshuffle of Top Officers," *Wall Street Journal* (November 1, 1967), p. 10.

18. "Wellington, Windsor Funds Elect John Bogle Chairman," *Wall Street Journal* (April 24, 1970), p. 24.

19. Richard Teitelbaum, "Vanguard Edge," *Bloomberg Markets* (November 2005), p. 42.

20. Thomas J. Bray, "Wellington Fund to Assume Some Duties of Its Adviser, Resolving Internal Clash," *Wall Street Journal* (July 30, 1974), p. 7.

21. "Wellington Fund Ask SEC to Clear a Change in Name, Restructuring," *Wall Street Journal* (December 10, 1974), p. 22.

22. "Wellington Group Name Change," *Wall Street Journal* (May 5, 1975), p. 27.

23. "Vanguard Unit Offers Two Million Shares," *The Wall Street Journal* (August 4, 1976), p. 22; and Teitelbaum, "Vanguard Edge," p. 43.

24. "Vanguard Group Shifts Funds to No Load Status," *Wall Street Journal* (February 10, 1977), p. 13.

25. Freeman and Brown, "Mutual Fund Advisory Fees: The Cost of Conflicts of Interest," p. 618.

26. A Bloomberg study found that Vanguard had 26 outside managers, up from 19 five years earlier. Teitelbaum, "Vanguard Edge," p. 50.

27. Vanguard has a reputation for reducing outside managers' fees to a minimum. Vanguard has a sliding scale for fees based on the amount of assets under management and a fund performance adjustment fee, where good performance generates a bonus and poor performance generates a reduction in fees. Managers that perform well, such as Primecap, manager of Vanguard's Primecap Fund, did in 2005, can receive an increase in the contracted fee plus a year-end bonus. Primecap's fee was raised in 2005 from 0.18 to 0.22 percent on the $27.4 billion Vanguard Primecap Fund, an $11 million increase in fee revenues. Teitelbaum, "Vanguard Edge," p. 50.

28. Vanguard receives a share of its funds' net asset as a "Contribution to Capital." *Vanguard 500 Index Fund Annual Report* (December 31, 2004), note B, p. 24. Vanguard states in fund prospectuses that the fund may contribute up to 0.40 percent of net asset value to Vanguard's capital. This mechanism is one way that Vanguard can earn profits on the services it provides to fund shareholders. However, as a privately held corporation, Vanguard's profits and profit disbursement to its owners are not reported.

29. http://www.tiaa-cref.org/governance/corp_structure.html.

30. Prospectus, *TIAA-CREF Institutional Mutual Funds Retail Class* (February 1, 2005), p. 20; and Supplement to the Prospectuses Dated February 1, 2005 (September 16, 2005).
31. "TIAA-CREF's Fee Countermove," *The Wall Street Journal* (October 6, 2005), p. C1.
32. http://www.tiaa-cref.org/newsroom/news_articles?newsarticle 166.htm.
33. "Mutual Fund Mergers Jump Sharply," *Wall Street Journal* (March 9, 2006), p. C1.
34. Brealey, Myers, and Allen, *Principles of Corporate Finance*, pp. 199–205.
35. The results use equally weighted returns. Similar conclusions resulted from using weighted-average returns.
36. We also examined returns to Vanguard's Value Index fund over the period January 1993 to March 2009 and Vanguard's Value exchange traded fund (ETF) for the period February 2004 to March 2009. ETFs are marketed as having lower investor fees than traditional mutual funds. Both Vanguard's Value Index and Value ETF underperformed the market (negative and statistically significant alphas), similar to our results for Vanguard and domestic equity funds as a whole and passively managed funds. Again, Vanguard's low fees did not translate into greater returns than Vanguard's mostly for-profit, nonvertically integrated rivals.

8. What Have We Learned?

1. To further improve investors' access to relevant mutual fund information and their ability to compare fund costs across mutual funds, the SEC announced an improved disclosure policy that funds must implement no later than January 1, 2010. Mutual funds must provide a concise summary of relevant information at the beginning of their required prospectus, which discloses in plain English the fund's costs, risks, strategies, and objectives. U.S. Securities and Exchange Commission, "SEC Improves Disclosure for Mutual Fund Investors," Press Release, 2008-275, November 19, 2008.
2. Chen et al., "Does Fund Size Erode Mutual Fund Performance? The Role of Liquidity and Organization," pp. 1276–1302.

Appendix to Chapter Four

1. McFadden, "Econometric Models of Probabilistic Choice," pp. 198–272.
2. Berry, "Estimating Discrete-Choice Models of Product Differentiation," pp. 242–262.
3. To reduce notation, μ is used to represent a demand shift in the model rather than $\mu_{i,j}$. Excessive subscripting is avoided where possible.

4. To avoid confusion in notation, we note that δ is conventionally used to represent both the decay rate of goodwill and mean utility in discrete choice models.

5. Baumol, Panzar, and Willig, *Contestable Markets and the Theory of Industry Structure*, pp. 448–450, and Pulley and Braunstein, "A Composite Cost Function for Multiproduct Firms with an Application to Economies of Scope in Banking."

6. Bresnahan, Stern, and Trajtenberg, "Market Segmentation and the Sources of Rents and Innovation," pp. S17–S44.

7. See appendix in Berry, "Estimating Discrete-Choice Models of Product Differentiation," on inverting the market share function.

8. McFadden, "Econometric Models of Probabilistic Choice."

9. Berry, Levinsohn, and Pakes, "Automobile Prices in Market Equilibrium," pp. 841–890; and Moul, "Consequences of Omitting Advertising in Demand Estimation."

10. Moul, "Consequences of Omitting Advertising in Demand Estimation."

Appendix to Chapter Seven

1. William F. Sharpe, "Morningstar's Risk-Adjusted Ratings."

Bibliography

Bailey, Warren, Alok Kumar, and David Ng. 2009. "Behavioral Biases and Mutual Fund Clienteles." Working paper, Cornell University.

Barber, Brad M., Terrance Odean, and Lu Zheng. 2005. "Out of Sight, Out of Mind: The Effects of Expenses on Mutual Fund Flows." *Journal of Business* 78:2095–2121.

Baumol, William. 2006. *Regulation Misled by Misread Theory: Perfect Competition and Competition-Imposed Price Discrimination.* AEI-Brookings Joint Center, Distinguished Lecture 2005, American Enterprise Institute and the Brookings Institute.

Baumol, William J., Stephen M. Goldfeld, Lilli A. Gordon, and Michael F. Koehn. 1990. *The Economics of Mutual Fund Markets: Competition Versus Regulation.* Boston: Kluwer.

Baumol, William, Michael F. Koehn, and Robert D. Willig. 1987. "How Arbitrary Is Arbitrary?—or, Toward the Deserved Demise of Full Cost Allocation." *Public Utilities Fortnightly* 125:16–21.

Baumol, William J., John C. Panzar, and Robert D. Willig. 1982. *Contestable Markets and the Theory of Industry Structure.* New York: Harcourt Brace Jovanovich.

Baye, Michael R., John Morgan, and Patrick Scholton. 2004. "Price Dispersion in the Small and in the Large: Evidence from an Internet Price Comparison Site." *Journal of Industrial Economics* 52:463–496.

Benedict, James N., Sean M. Murphy, and Andrew W. Robertson. 2005. "The Aftermath of the Mutual Fund Crises." *Securities & Commodities Regulation* 38: 261–280.

Bergstresser, Daniel, John M. R. Chalmers, and Peter Tufano. 2006. "Assessing the Costs and Benefits of Brokers in the Mutual Fund Industry." Review of Financial Studies, forthcoming.

Berk, Jonathan B. and Richard C. Green. 2004. "Mutual Fund Flows and Performance in Rational Markets." *Journal of Political Economy* 112:1269–1295.

Berkowitz, Michael K. and Yehuda Yotowitz. 2002. "Managerial Quality and the Structure of Management Expenses in the U.S. Mutual Fund Industry." *International Review of Economics and Finance* 11:315–330.

Berry, Steven T. 1994. "Estimating Discrete-Choice Models of Product Differentiation." *The RAND Journal of Economics* 25:242–262.

Berry, Steven T., James Levinsohn, and Ariel Pakes. 1995. "Automobile Prices in Equilibrium." *Econometrica* 63:841–890.

Bogle, John C. 2003. "Mutual Fund Industry Practices and Their Effect on Individual Investors." Statement Before the House of Representatives, Subcommittee on Capital Markets, Insurance and Government Sponsored Enterprises of the Committee on Financial Services, Washington D.C. (March 12, 2003).

Bogle, John C. 2005. "The Mutual Fund Industry 60 Years Later: For Better or Worse?" *Financial Analysts Journal* 61:15–24.

Brealey, Richard A., Stewart C. Myers, and Franklin Allen. 2006. *Principles of Corporate Finance*, 8th edition. Boston: McGraw-Hill Irwin.

Bresnahan, Timothy F., Scott Stern, and Manuel Trajtenberg. 1997. "Market Segmentation and the Sources of Rents from Innovation: Personal Computers in the Late 1980s." *The Rand Journal of Economics* 28:S17–S44.

Brown, Jeffrey R. and Austan Goolsbee. 2002. "Does the Internet Make Markets More Competitive? Evidence from the Life Insurance Industry." *Journal of Political Economy* 110:481–507.

Carlton, Dennis and Jeffrey Perloff. 2005. *Modern Industrial Organization*, 4th edition. Boston: Pearson Addison-Wesley.

Chen, Joseph, Harrison Hong, Ming Huang, and Jeffrey D. Kubik. 2004. "Does Fund Size Erode Mutual Fund Performance? The Role of Liquidity and Organization." *American Economic Review* 94:1276–1302.

Chen, Joseph, Harrison Hong, and Jeffrey D. Kubik. 2007. "Outsourcing Mutual Fund Management: Firm Boundaries, Incentives and Performance." Working paper, University of Southern California.

Chen, Qi, Itay Goldstein, and Wei Jiang. 2007. "Directors' Ownership in the U.S. Mutual Fund Industry." Working paper, Duke University.

Christoffersen, Susan. 2001. "Why Do Money Fund Managers Voluntarily Waive Their Fees?" *Journal of Finance* 56:1117–1140.

Clay, Karen, Ramayya Krishnan, and Eric Wolff. 2001. "Prices and Price Dispersion on the Web: Evidence from the Online Book Industry." *Journal of Industrial Economics* 49:521–540.

Coates, John IV and R. Glenn Hubbard. 2007. "Competition in the Mutual Fund Industry: Evidence and Implications for Policy." *Journal of Corporate Law* 33:151–222.

Collins, Sean. 2003. "The Expenses of Defined Benefit Pension Plans and Mutual Funds." *Perspective* 9 (December). Washington, DC: Investment Company Institute.

Costo, Stephanie L. 2006. "Trends in Retirement Plan Coverage over the Last Decade." *Monthly Labor Review* 129:58–64.

Cremers, Maratijn, Joost Driessen, and David Weinbaum. 2006. "Does Skin in the Game Matter? Director Incentives and Governance in the Mutual Fund Industry." Working paper, Yale University ICF.

Deloitte. 2008. *401(k) Benchmarking Survey: 2008 Edition, Deloitte Consulting LLP.*

Dermine, Jean and Lars-Hendrik Roller. 1992. "Economies of Scope and Scale in French Mutual Funds." *Journal of Financial Intermediation* 2:83–93.

Ellison, Glenn and Sara Fisher Ellison. 2005. "Lessons About Markets from the Internet." *Journal of Economic Perspective* 19:139–158.

Evans, Allison L. 2006. "Portfolio Manager Ownership and Mutual Fund Performance." Working paper, University of North Carolina.

Farina, Richard H., John P. Freeman, and James Webster. 1969. "The Mutual Fund Industry: A Legal Survey." *Notre Dame Lawyer* 44:732–983.

Freeman, John P. and Stuart B. Brown. 2001. "Mutual Fund Advisory Fees: The Cost of Conflicts of Interest." *Journal of Corporate Law* 26:609–674.

Freeman, John P., Stuart B. Brown, and Steve Pomerantz. 2008. "Mutual Fund Advisory Fees: New Evidence and a Fair Fiduciary Duty Test." *Oklahoma Law Review* 63:83–153.

Gallaher, Steven, Ron Kaniel, and Laura Starks. 2006. "Madison Avenue Meets Wall Street: Mutual Fund Families, Competition and Advertising." Working paper, University of Texas.

Goldman, Marshall. 1960. "Product Differentiation and Advertising: Some Lessons from Soviet Experience." *Journal of Political Economy* 68:346–356.

Hortacsu, Ali and Chad Syverson. 2004. "Product Differentiation, Search Costs, and Competition in the Mutual Fund Industry." A Case Study of S&P 500 Index Funds, *Quarterly Journal of Economics* 119:403–456.

Investment Company Institute. 2004. "The Costs of Buying and Owning Mutual Funds." *Fundamentals* 13 (February), Investment Company Institute.

Investment Company Institute. 2007. "U.S. Retirement Market." *Research Fundamentals* 17 (July), Investment Company Institute.

Investment Company Institute. 2007. *2007 Investment Company Fact Book*, 47th edition. Washington, DC: Investment Company Institute.

Investment Company Institute. 2008. *2008 Investment Company Fact Book*, 48th edition. Washington, DC: Investment Company Institute.

Investment Company Institute. 2009. "The Role of IRAs in U.S. Households' Savings for Retirement, 2008." *Research Fundamentals* 18 (January), Investment Company Institute.

Ippolito, Richard A. 1992. "Consumer Reaction to Measures of Poor Quality: Evidence from the Mutual Fund Industry." *Journal of Law & Economics* 35:45–70.

Khorana, Ajay and Henri Servaes. 2005. "Conflicts of Interest and Competition in the Mutual Fund Industry." Working paper, Georgia Institute of Technology.

Khorana, Ajay, Henri Servaes, and Lei Wedge. 2007. "Portfolio Manager Ownership and Fund Performance." *Journal of Financial Economics* 85:179–204.

Khorana, Ajay, Henri Servaes, and Peter Tufano. 2009. "Mutual Fund Fees Around the World." *Review of Financial Studies* 22:1279–1310.

Koehn, Michael F., Stanley I. Ornstein, Jimmy Royer, and Marc VanAudenrode. 2007. "Do Mutual Fund Investors Care About Fees?" Working paper, 2007 Canadian Economics Association Meetings.

Kuhnen, Camelia M. 2004. "Dynamic Contracting in the Mutual Fund Industry." Working paper, Stanford Graduate School of Business.

Kuhnen, Camelia M. 2008. "Social Networks, Corporate Governance and Contracting in the Mutual Fund Industry." Working paper, Northwestern University. Retitled as "Business Networks, Corporate Governance and Contracting in the Mutual Fund Industry." *Journal of Finance*, forthcoming.

Lach, Saul. 2002. "Existence and Persistence of Price Dispersion: An Empirical Analysis." *Review of Economics and Statistics* 84:433–444.

Luo, Guo Ying. 2002. "Mutual Fund Fee-Setting, Market Structure and Mark-ups." *Economica* 69:245–271.

McFadden, Daniel. 1981. "Econometric Models of Probabilistic Choice." In *Structural Analysis of Discrete Data*, ed. Charles Manski and Daniel McFadden. Cambridge, MA: MIT Press, 198–272.

Moul, Charles. 2006. "Consequences of Omitting Advertising in Demand Estimation: An Application to Theatrical Movies." Working paper, Washington University, St. Louis.

Nanda, Vikram, Z. Jay Wang, and Lu Zheng. 2004. "Family Values and the Star Phenomenon: Strategies of Mutual Fund Families." *Review of Financial Studies* 17:667–698.

Nevo, Aviv. 2000. "Mergers with Differentiated Products: The Case of the Ready-to-Eat Cereal Industry." *RAND Journal of Economics* 31:395–421.

Peter, Craig. 2006. "Evaluating the Performance of Merger Simulation: Evidence from the U.S. Airline Industry." *Journal of Law & Economics* 49:627–649.

Pratt, John W., David A. Wise, and Richard Zeckhauser. 1979. "Price Differences in Almost Competitive Markets." *Quarterly Journal of Economics* 93:189–211.

Pulley, Lawrence B. and Yale M. Braunstein. 1992. "A Composite Cost Function for Multiproduct Firms with an Application to Economies of Scope in Banking." *Review of Economics and Statistics* 74: 221–230.

Reid, John K. and John D. Rea. 2003. "Mutual Fund Distribution Channels and Distribution Costs." *Perspective* 9 (July). Washington, DC: Investment Company Institute.

Roberts, Mark J. and Dylan Supina. 1996. "Output Price, Markups, and Producer Size." *European Economic Review* 40:909–921.

Rogers, William, and James N. Benedict. 1982. "Money Market Fund Management Fees: How Much Is Too Much?" *New York University Law Review* 57:1059–1125.

Schumpeter, Joseph. 1954. *History of Economic Analysis.* New York: Oxford University Press.

Sharpe, William F. 1998. "Morningstar's Risk-Adjusted Ratings." *Financial Analysts Journal* 54:21–22.

Sirri, Eric R. and Peter Tufano. 1993. "Competition and Change in the Mutual Fund Industry." In *Financial Services, Perspectives and Challenges,* ed. Samuel L. Hayes, III. Boston: Harvard Business School Press, 181–214.

Sirri, Eric R. and Peter Tufano. 1998. "Costly Search and Mutual Fund Flows." *Journal of Finance* 53:1589–1622.

Stern, Scott. 1996. "Market Definition and the Returns to Innovation: Substitution Patterns in Pharmaceutical Markets." Working paper, Massachusetts Institute of Technology.

Stigler, George J. 1968. "The Economics of Scale." In *The Organization of Industry.* Homewood, IL: Irwin, 71–94.

Swensen, David F. 2005. *Unconventional Success: A Fundamental Approach to Personal Investment.* New York: Free Press.

"Symposium: Competitive Price Discrimination." 2003. *Antitrust Law Journal* 70:593–696.

Tirole, Jean. 1997. *The Theory of Industrial Organization.* Cambridge, MA: MIT Press.

Tufano, Peter and Matthew Sevick. 1997. "Board Structure and Fee Setting in the U.S. Mutual Fund Industry." *Journal of Financial Economics* 46:321–355.

U.S. Department of Justice and Federal Trade Commission. 1997. *Horizontal Merger Guidelines.*

U.S. General Accounting Office. 2000. *Mutual Fund Fees: Additional Disclosure Could Encourage Price Competition.* Report to the Chairman, Subcommittee on Finance and Hazardous Materials; and the Ranking Member, Committee on Commerce, House of Representives, GAO/GGD-00-126.

U.S. General Accounting Office. 2003a. *Mutual Funds: Information on Trends in Fees and Their Related Disclosure.* Testimony Before the Subcommittee on Capital Markets, Insurance and Government Sponsored Enterprises, Committee on Financial Services, House of Representatives, Statement for the Record by Richard J. Hillman, Director, Financial Markets and Community Investment, GAO-03-551T.

U.S. General Accounting Office. 2003b. *Mutual Funds: Greater Transparency Needed in Disclosures to Investors.* Report to Congressional Requesters, GAO-03-763.

U.S. Securities and Exchange Commission. 1939. *Investment Trusts and Investment Companies: Part One.* House of Representatives, Docket no. 707, 75th Congress, 3d session.

U.S. Securities and Exchange Commission. 1939. *Investment Trusts and Investment Companies: Part Two.* House of Representatives, Docket no. 70, 76th Congress, 3d session.

U.S. Securities and Exchange Commission. 1940. *Investment Trusts and Investment Companies: Part Three.* House of Representatives, Docket no. 279, 76th Congress, 3d session.

U.S. Securities and Exchange Commission. 1941. *Investment Trusts and Investment Companies.* Parts Four and Five, House of Representatives, Docket no. 246, 77th Congress, 1st session.

U.S. Securities and Exchange Commission. 1966. *Report on the Public Policy Implications of Investment Company Growth.* House of Representatives, Report no. 2274, 89th Congress, 2d session.

U.S. Securities and Exchange Commission. 1992. *Staff Report, Protecting Investors: A Half-Century of Investment Company Regulation.* Chicago: Commerce Clearing House.

U.S. Securities and Exchange Commission. 2000. *Report on Mutual Funds Fees and Expenses,* http://www.sec.gov/news/studies/feestudy.htm.

U.S. Securities and Exchange Commission. 2004. *Investment Company Governance.* Proposed Rule, IC-26323, File no. S7-03-04, Federal Register 69:3472–3482.

Wahal, Sunil, and Yan Albert Wang. 2008. "Competition Among Mutual Funds." Working paper, Arizona State University.

Wallison, Peter J. and Robert E. Litan. 2007. *Competitive Equity: A Better Way to Organize Mutual Funds.* Washington, DC: AEI Press.

Walsh, Lori. 2004. "The Costs and Benefits to Fund Shareholders of 12b-1 Plans: An Examination of Fund Flows, Expenses and Returns." Working paper, U.S. Securities and Exchange Commission.

Wharton School of Finance and Commerce. 1962. *A Study of Mutual Funds.* Report of the Committee on Interstate and Foreign Commerce, 87th Congress, 2d session.

Yan, Xuemin (Sterling). 2006. "The Determinants and Implications of Mutual Fund Cash Holdings: Theory and Evidence." *Financial Management* 35:67–91.

Zhang, Andrew. 2007. "Mutual Fund Expense Ratios in Market Equilibrium." Working paper, University of Arizona.

Zhao, Xinge. 2005. "The Role of Brokers and Financial Advisors Behind Investments into Load Funds." Working paper, China Europe International Business School.

Zhao, Ying. 2006. "Price Dispersion in the Grocery Market." *Journal of Business* 79:1175–1192.

Legal Citations

Galfand v. Chestnut Corp., 545 F.2d 807 (2nd Cir. 1976).

Gertrude B. Schuyt v. Rowe Price Prime Reserve Fund et al., 663 F. Supp. 962 (1987).

In re Eaton Vance Mutual Funds Fee Litigation, 380 F. Supp. 2d 222 (S.D.N.Y. 2005).

Irving L. Gartenberg v. Merrill Lynch Asset Management et al., 528 F. Supp. 1038 (1981).

Irving L. Gartenberg v. Merrill Lynch Asset Management et al., 694 F.2d 923 (1982).
Irving L. Gartenberg v. Merrill Lynch Asset Management et al., 573 F. Supp. 1293 (1983).
Irving L. Gartenberg v. Merrill Lynch Asset Management et al., 740 F.2d 190 (2d Cir. 1984).
Jerry N. Jones et al. v. Harris Associates L.P., 527 F. 3d 627 (7th Cir. 2008).
John E. Gallus et al. v. American Express Financial Corporation, 370 F. Supp. 2d 862 (D. Minn. 2005).
John E. Gallus et al. v. Ameriprise Financial, Inc., 561 F.3d 816 (8th Cir. 2009).
Kathi Cooper et al. v. IBM Personal Pension Plan and IBM Corporation, 457 F.3d 636 7th Cir. (2006) and 274 F. Supp. 2d 1010 (S.D. Ill. 2003).
Krantz v. Prudential Investments Fund Management LLC et al., 77 F. Supp. 2d 559 (1999).
Krantz v. Prudential Investments Fund Management LLC et al., 305 F.3d 140 (2002).
Krinsk v. Fund Asset Management, Inc. et al., 875 F.2d 404 (2d Cir. 1989).
Pepper v. Litton, 208 U.S. 295 (1939).
Strigliabotti v. Franklin Resources, Inc., 2005 WL 645529 (N.D. Cal., March 7, 2005).
Yampolsky v. Morgan Stanley Investment Advisers Inc., 2004 WL 1065533 (S.D.N.Y. May 12, 2004).

Index